TO END ALL SEGREGATION

The Politics of the Passage of the Civil Rights Act of 1964

Robert D. Loevy
Colorado College

UNIVERSITY
PRESS OF
AMERICA

Lanham • New York • London

Copyright © 1990 by

University Press of America®, Inc.
4720 Boston Way
Lanham, Maryland 20706

3 Henrietta Street
London WC2E 8LU England

Library of Congress Cataloging-in-Publication Data

Loevy, Robert D., 1935–
To end all segregation : the politics of the passage of the
Civil Rights Act of 1964 / Robert D. Loevy.
p.   cm.
Includes bibliographical references.
1. Afro–Americans—Civil rights. 2. Civil rights movements—
United States—History—20th century. 3. United States—
Politics and government—1963–1969. 4. United States. Civil
Rights Act of 1964. I. Title.
E185.61.L687   1990   323.1'196073—dc20   89–29431 CIP

ISBN 0–8191–7688–5 (alk. paper)
ISBN 0–8191–7689–3 (pbk. : alk. paper)

"As far as the writ of Federal law will run,
we must abolish not some but all racial discrimination."

President Lyndon B. Johnson
State of the Union Address - 1964

The first time an American president called for
eliminating "all racial discrimination."

ACKNOWLEDGEMENTS

Major funding for this study of the Civil Rights Act of 1964 was provided by the Faculty Research and Development Board at Colorado College in Colorado Springs, Colorado. Additional funding was provided by the National Endowment for the Humanities. Transportation and lodging expenses to visit the Everett McKinley Dirksen Congressional Leadership Research Center in Pekin, Illinois, and other presidential and senatorial libraries, were partially funded by the Everett McKinley Dirksen Congressional Leadership Research Center.

TABLE OF CONTENTS

TABLE OF CONTENTS (CONTINUED)

CHAPTER 1

THE CIVIL RIGHTS ACT OF 1964

Prior to the passage of the Civil Rights Act of 1964, racial segregation was a definite aspect of American life, particularly in the South and the Border States. After the passage of this landmark legislation, the United States turned away from legal segregation and began a convincing and steady movement toward racial integration.

The Civil Rights Act of 1964 was hailed at the time of its passage as the most significant piece of civil rights legislation to be enacted by the United States Congress in almost 100 years. The bill produced the longest continuous debate ever held in the United States Senate, a record which still stood in the 1990s and did not appear likely to ever be equaled.

The reason the debate was so long was that the bill that later became the Civil Rights Act of 1964 was subjected to a filibuster by a determined group of Southern senators. Senate rules normally provide for unlimited debate, which means that a small group of senators can attempt to kill a bill by simply talking it to death and not letting it come up for a final vote. As a result of this Southern filibuster, the Civil Rights Act of 1964 was before the Senate for 83 consecutive legislative days -- from March 9 to June 17, 1964.

This record setting debate was ended by the first successful application of cloture to a civil rights bill. Cloture, a motion to close debate by a 2/3 vote of the Senate, previously had been used only when a small minority of senators, usually less than 10, were filibustering. Since 18 Southern senators were filibustering the civil rights bill in 1964, this cloture vote was the first important limitation of debate in the history of the United States Senate. This cloture vote gains even more significance when it is recognized that comprehensive civil rights legislation could not have passed without it.

The Civil Rights Act of 1964 altered the relationship between white and black Americans in United States society. Prior to its enactment, black Americans could be barred from entering and being served at such facilities as restaurants, soda fountains, taverns, motels, and swimming pools. This racial segregation of public accommodations was widely practiced in the American South, but it also could be found in the Northern United States, particularly in Border States such as Maryland, Kentucky, and Missouri.

The new law also banned discrimination against blacks and other minority groups in employment. It provided for the cutoff of United States Government funds to any business, educational institution, or state or local government that practiced racial discrimination. In a minor section that later became very important, the law banned employment discrimination against women. The law also provided for the United States Department of Justice and the Federal Bureau of Investigation (FBI) to intervene in certain situations in the American South where blacks were being denied their civil rights.

The Civil Rights Act of 1964 was a reflection of the great social and political changes that were taking place in the United States in the early 1960s. To some observers, its passage justified the nonviolent political techniques (sit-in demonstrations and protest marches) of Martin Luther King, Jr., and the Southern Christian Leadership Conference (SCLC), thereby making these techniques an acceptable method for attempting to precipitate major legal and social reform in American society. These forms of protest were subsequently copied by the women's movement, the anti-Vietnam War movement, and other groups seeking to effect social and political change in the United States.

The Civil Rights Act of 1964 represented one of the first times in American history that major national church organizations abandoned their previous policy of not getting involved in racial issues and came to Washington, D.C., to lobby directly for civil rights. The various religious and political groups supporting passage of the law organized behind one of the first and best examples of a single issue pressure group -- the Leadership Conference on Civil Rights.

While being debated in the Senate in 1964, the civil rights bill became the specific campaign target of a major Southern candidate for the Democratic nomination for president of the United States (Governor George Wallace of Alabama). The bill was guaranteed a successful cloture vote and final passage in the Senate only after Wallace had failed to win any Democratic presidential primaries in the North and the Border States.

The Civil Rights Act of 1964 set a precedent in the Senate for using a cloture vote to stop a Southern filibuster of a civil rights bill. Similar cloture votes were used in 1965 to pass a national law guaranteeing equal voting rights and again in 1968 to pass a national law guaranteeing equal housing.

CHAPTER 2

JOHN F. KENNEDY;
"THE FIRES OF DISCORD"

On February 28, 1963, President John Fitzgerald Kennedy sent the United States Congress a "Special Message on Civil Rights." A written statement rather than a public speech, the presidential message nonetheless contained strong words concerning the status of black citizens in American society:

> "Our Constitution is color blind," . . . but the practices of the country do not always conform to the principles of the Constitution. . . . Equality before the law has not always meant equal treatment and opportunity. And the harmful, wasteful and wrongful results of racial discrimination and segregation still appear in virtually every aspect of national life, in virtually every part of the Nation.

The presidential message went on to point out how great the differences were, in 1963, between the status of blacks and the status of whites in American society:

> The Negro baby born in America today -- regardless of the section or state in which he is born -- has about one half as much chance of completing high school as a white baby born in the same place on the same day -- one third as much chance of completing college -- one third as

5

much chance of becoming a professional man --
twice as much chance of becoming unemployed --
about one-seventh as much chance of earning [an
acceptable middle class income] -- a life
expectancy which is seven years less -- and the
prospects of earning only half as much.

No American who believes in the basic
truth that "all men are created equal, that they are
endowed by their Creator with certain inalienable
rights", can fully excuse, explain or defend the
picture these statistics portray.[1]

Along with the presidential message came a series of
specific legislative proposals to be addressed by Congress.
President Kennedy recommended some improvements in voting
rights laws and an extension of the Civil Rights Commission, a
government body which could study civil rights problems but had
no power to remedy them.[2]

President Kennedy was praised by civil rights supporters
for the strong words in his presidential message, but he was
criticized by these same civil rights advocates for the weakness
of his legislative proposals.[3] Joseph Rauh, Jr., a Washington
lawyer and a key lobbyist for civil rights causes, attributed
Kennedy's ambivalent behavior to wise political calculation:

President Kennedy was never one to demand Congressional action on need alone. His sense of
timing told him he could not overcome the
legislative roadblocks in the way of civil rights
legislation, and defeat, no matter how gallant, had
no appeal for him.[4]

The president was bowing to the generally accepted view
that a strong civil rights bill, one that would end racial segregation and racial oppression in the United States, was simply not
politically achievable, no matter how much a president might
throw his political will and his political strength into the battle.

6

THE SOUTHERN CIVIL RIGHTS "VETO"

The obstacles to passing a civil rights bill were formidable in early 1963. In the House of Representatives, regular legislative committees such as the House Judiciary Committee do not report bills directly to the House floor for a vote. Because debate is limited in the House of Representatives, committee bills first go to the House Rules Committee, where the length of time the bill will be debated and the manner in which the bill will be debated is decided. Many bills that make it through the regular committees, however, often are not reported out of the Rules Committee at all, and usually when this happens the particular bill is dead for the remainder of that session of Congress.

In 1963 the chairman of the House Rules Committee was Howard Smith, a conservative Southern Democrat from Virginia. Smith was ardently opposed to all civil rights legislation, and it was clear he would use his powers as chairman of the Rules Committee to delay any civil rights bill as long as possible. If Democratic President Kennedy wanted a strong civil rights bill, he would have to maneuver it past Democratic Rules Committee Chairman Smith.

Over in the Senate, the situation was even more difficult. The chairman of the Senate Judiciary Committee was James O. Eastland, a Democrat from Mississippi and, as one would expect, a staunch opponent of civil rights. Eastland had used his powers as Judiciary Committee Chairman to kill more than 100 proposed civil rights bills throughout the late 1950s and early 1960s. If Democrat Kennedy wanted a civil rights bill, he would have to find a way around Democrat Eastland and his Judiciary Committee.

A second obstacle in the Senate, and by far the largest obstacle of all, was the filibuster. Over the years Southern senators had made it their policy to filibuster all civil rights bills that came before the Senate, not stopping the debate until the bill was either withdrawn by its sponsors or else so badly weakened that it would not change things very much.

There was a way to stop a filibuster and force a vote on a bill, but this method had never been used successfully to stop a civil rights filibuster. Known as "cloture", this method required a 2/3 vote of the Senate (67 votes if all 100 senators were present and voting).[5] Most observers were predicting in early 1963 that it was highly unlikely that 67 senators could be found to vote cloture on a Southern civil rights filibuster.

CIVIL RIGHTS AND ECONOMICS

Another big problem President Kennedy had with civil rights was the continuing crucial role of the Southern Democrats in Congress. In 1963, the Democratic party was made up of an uneasy coalition of conservative Southern Democrats on the one hand and liberal Northern and Western Democrats on the other, exactly as it was in Franklin Delano Roosevelt's time. Kennedy had a wide assortment of programs other than civil rights that he wanted to get through the Congress, most of them economic programs such as a major tax cut bill, government aid to education, and raising the minimum wage. The only way Kennedy could get these liberal economic programs over the opposition votes of conservative Republicans in Congress was to keep the Southerners in the Democratic fold. Pushing hard for civil rights, however, would have antagonized the Southern Democrats, thereby jeopardizing the entire Kennedy economic program. Kennedy also was aware that many of the elements in his economic program, such as aid to education and raising the minimum wage, would be of direct benefit to blacks.

Clarence Mitchell, Jr., Washington director of the National Association for the Advancement of Colored People (NAACP), recalled that in 1953 Lyndon Johnson, then the Democratic leader in the Senate, gave him a good description of the effect of the civil rights issue on the Democratic party and its social programs: Mitchell said:

> He [Lyndon Johnson] said he believed in civil rights legislation, but he thought that it was unwise

to try to get it through Congress because it would split the Democratic party. He thought that most of the Democrats were poor people and they needed legislation in the social welfare field. He said, "If you could keep the Democrats working together for social welfare legislation then they wouldn't get into these bruising fights in Congress. And the poor people would benefit generally on civil rights." He said he thought it best to concentrate on court action and executive action [to advance civil rights], in order to avoid these party splitting fights in Congress.[6]

THE 1964 PRESIDENTIAL ELECTION

In addition, there was the political problem of keeping the support of Southern Democratic voters in the upcoming 1964 presidential election. Kennedy had defeated Richard Nixon in 1960 in one of the closest presidential races in American history. The electoral votes of several Southern states, particularly Vice-President Lyndon Johnson's home state of Texas, had been essential to Kennedy's victory. Kennedy was going to need that Southern Democratic support again in the 1964 presidential race. Similar to all Democratic presidents, Kennedy knew that, as of 1963, no Democrat had ever been elected president of the United States without carrying a substantial portion of the South. To antagonize the South with a strong push for civil rights could well be presidential political suicide.

CIVIL RIGHTS AND FOREIGN POLICY

The president also was aware that a civil rights battle could harm his foreign policy proposals and weaken his position in international affairs. Overseas problems such as the Soviet construction of the Berlin Wall and the Cuban Missile Crisis could be handled more successfully if public opinion in the United States was united behind the chief executive. Kennedy

9

was currently negotiating a nuclear test-ban treaty with the Soviet Union that would require a 2/3 vote of ratification in the Senate. The president knew that to provoke a national controversy over civil rights, a controversy that was likely to produce very little in the way of concrete progress, would divide the American public at a time when foreign policy initiatives called for national unity.

Thus, when dealing with civil rights, President Kennedy faced all the crippling constraints that so often hamper a president's ability to act. The Kennedy administration viewpoint was summed up by Theodore Sorensen, the president's speech writer. "There was no indifference to campaign pledges," Sorensen noted. "But success required selectivity. . . . He would take on civil rights at the right time on the right issue."[7] Kennedy himself told a news conference, "When I feel there is a necessity for congressional action, with a chance of getting that congressional action, then I will recommend it."[8]

THE LEADERSHIP CONFERENCE

Shortly after President Kennedy's recommended civil rights bill was released to the press and public in March of 1963, the leaders of more than 70 civil rights organizations, operating under the name of the Leadership Conference on Civil Rights, met to discuss the Kennedy proposal. According to Joseph Rauh, Jr., who served as a Washington lobbyist for the Leadership Conference, the group was greatly disappointed. Rauh explained:

> The consensus was clear: President Kennedy had yielded on civil rights legislation before the fight had even begun; the proposed bill was hardly worth fighting for. . . . [One] legislative representative . . . walked into the meeting with a sheaf of civil rights bills just then being introduced by liberal Republican senators and covering much of what the Democrats had [left out] . . . . But

10

there was not much solace in bills introduced by a handful of the Senate Republican minority, and the meeting broke up in disarray. Such comfort as there was came from the hope that [if Kennedy were reelected in 1964] the second Kennedy Administration would be different.[9]

BIRMINGHAM

Unexpected external events totally changed the picture and completely undid Kennedy's political strategy of delaying legislative action on civil rights. In April of 1963, demonstrations began in Birmingham, Alabama, under the direction of Martin Luther King, Jr. The purpose of the demonstrations was to protest and end the practice of segregation in almost every phase of community life, but the immediate target was the eating facilities in downtown Birmingham. In the traditional Southern manner, department stores that accepted black patronage in all other departments would not let blacks eat in the store restaurant or sit at the lunch counter.

WHY BIRMINGHAM?

Birmingham was known as one of the most segregated big cities in the South. From 1957 to 1963 there had been some 18 racial bombings, leading many civil rights supporters to call the city "Bombingham." More than 50 cross-burning incidents had taken place in an effort to scare and threaten blacks. Birmingham had disbanded its professional baseball team rather than let it play racially integrated teams from some of the other cities in the International League. City parks were closed rather than desegregate them as ordered by a U.S. Court. When the city refused to desegregate its municipal auditorium, the Metropolitan Opera Company was obliged to cancel its annual visits to Birmingham. Touring companies of Broadway plays and musicals had to cancel their scheduled programs in the city for the same reason.[10]

11

POLICE CLUBS, FIRE HOSES, POLICE DOGS, AND ELECTRIC CATTLE PRODS

By early May the intensity of the Birmingham demonstrations dramatically increased. Black school children marched into downtown Birmingham where they were met by clubs, fire hoses, and police dogs. Large numbers were arrested and hauled away for parading without a permit. In several instances, marching black school children were driven back by white policemen armed with electric cattle prods ordinarily used to drive reluctant cattle from the holding pen into the slaughter house.

The Birmingham police were under the direction of Police Commissioner T. Eugene (Bull) Connor, who also was the Democratic national committeeman from Alabama. As he ordered his police officers to arrest the demonstrators, Bull Connor gave interviews to the national news media that were filled with racial epithets and forceful arguments for white supremacy. As the demonstrations and arrests continued day after day without a settlement, Bull Connor came to symbolize unrelenting Southern white opposition to black demands for equal access to public accommodations.

No United States laws had been violated in Birmingham. There was no national law that guaranteed blacks the right to eat at Birmingham lunch counters or demonstrate in Birmingham streets in defiance of local ordinances. President Kennedy argued he was powerless to send any U.S. Government law enforcement officials to intervene in Birmingham because he had no authority to do so. What the president did do was send Assistant Attorney General Burke Marshall to mediate. To liberal supporters of civil rights, the entire situation illustrated, more than any other previous civil rights demonstration, the need for a national solution, backed up by national legislation passed by Congress, to the problem of Southern segregation.

Martin Luther King, Jr., was part of a task force of black civil rights leaders that had come to Birmingham to lead the drive for integration. They had intentionally picked Birmingham because of its reputation for dogged commitment to white supremacy. "If we can crack Birmingham, I am convinced we can crack the South," King argued. "Birmingham is a symbol of segregation for the entire South."[11]

"A LETTER FROM . . . JAIL"

When Bull Connor secured a state court injunction barring any further racial demonstrations in Birmingham, King defiantly led about 1,000 demonstrators on a march toward downtown. King and his chief aide, the Reverend Ralph Abernathy, were promptly jailed.

During the preparations for the demonstrations, a number of Birmingham white religious leaders -- Protestant, Catholic, and Jewish -- had issued a statement calling King's intervention in Birmingham "unwise and untimely." King wrote a lengthy reply to the clergymen from his jail cell. Entitled "A Letter From the Birmingham Jail," King's reply received extensive national attention. King wrote:

> Oppressed people cannot remain oppressed forever. The urge for freedom will eventually come. This is what has happened to the American Negro. Something within has reminded him of his birthright of freedom; something without has reminded him that he can gain it. . . . Recognizing this vital urge that has engulfed the Negro community, one should readily understand the public demonstrations.

King's letter to the white clergymen particularly emphasized the point that "the white power structure of this city left the Negro community with no other alternative" but to demonstrate. After serving five-day jail terms, King and Abernathy were released from prison and the demonstrations continued.

On 10 May 1963 an agreement was announced between

13

white and black negotiators endeavoring to solve the Birmingham crisis. Downtown eating places would be desegregated, and black demonstrators still in jail would be released. Tranquility began to return to Birmingham for the first time in more than a month, and it appeared that the crisis had been solved without the need for direct intervention from Washington.

VIOLENCE AND COUNTER-VIOLENCE

Two days later the Reverend A. D. King, Martin Luther King's younger brother and one of the local leaders of the Birmingham integration movement, was at home with his wife. Their five children were asleep. At 10:45 P.M. an automobile drove by and a dynamite bomb was thrown at the front of the house, blew up, and shook the entire building. King and his wife rushed the children to the back door, but as they were running to safety a second explosion, more violent that the first, furthered destroyed the home.

One hour later another dynamite bomb exploded, this one at the integration movement's headquarters at the Gaston Motel. Martin Luther King, Jr., was away from Birmingham at his home in Atlanta, but the bomb blew a hole in a downstairs motel room just below the one the national integration leader had previously occupied. Angry blacks gathered in the streets from nearby restaurants, pool halls, taverns, nightclubs, and small groceries. When police arrived, white officers were the targets of rocks, bricks, and bottles thrown by the black crowd. In this case the black response to racial oppression exceeded the limits of non-violence. Birmingham was having a violent black riot rather than a nonviolent civil rights demonstration.

Despite the efforts of A. D. King and the other nonviolent protest leaders to calm the black crowd, Birmingham had a four hour black riot in which more than 50 persons were injured. Two white owned grocery stores were set on fire, but the flames quickly spread to nearby black homes. Soon an entire block was ablaze. "Nearby, a telephone pole caught fire, giving the appearance of a flaming cross, symbol of the Ku Klux Klan."[12]

14

This time, however, it was blacks and not whites who had set the cross of violence ablaze.

TELEVISION AND BIRMINGHAM

Newspaper and television coverage of the civil rights demonstrations and riots in Birmingham was extensive. Television news film of nonviolent black demonstrators being abused, beaten, and arrested while they sat-in at Birmingham lunch counters was presented nightly in living rooms across the nation. As the intensity of the demonstrations increased, television cameras continued to bring Americans the sights and sounds of police arresting young black children and the segregationist rhetoric of Bull Connor. As a result of this media coverage, the average Northern and Western white became increasingly aware of the Southern black and his problems. A change in national public opinion began to take place as the nation watched an example of Southern white oppression of blacks first hand. Demands for legislative action began pouring into the White House and the Congress from across the country.

As the demonstrations and riots in Birmingham progressed, political commentator Eric Severeid wrote: "A newspaper or television picture of a snarling police dog set upon a human being is recorded in the permanent photo-electric file of every human brain."[13] "The cause of desegregation," wrote commentator Walter Lippmann, "must cease to be a Negro movement, blessed by white politicians from the Northern states. It must become a national movement to enforce national laws, led and directed by the national government."[14]

To policy makers both in the White House and on Capitol Hill, Birmingham was a crucial experience, the flash point that brought forth a large number of proposed civil rights bills. Two years later, a pro-civil rights congressional aide summed it up this way: "The key to the passage of the 1964 civil rights bill was Birmingham, which changed the entire emotional climate on the Hill."[15]

President Kennedy himself was well aware that

Birmingham was going to force a change in his civil rights policies. At a White House strategy meeting with civil rights leaders, one of those present referred in a hostile way to Bull Connor. Kennedy responded that "Bull Connor has done more for civil rights than anyone in this room."[16] Thereafter the president was often heard to say: "The civil rights movement should thank God for Bull Connor. He's helped it as much as Abraham Lincoln."[17]

"I SHALL ASK CONGRESS...TO ACT"

On 31 May 1963 President Kennedy made the decision that he would present a new, much strengthened civil rights bill to Congress. Although the details of that new bill were not yet decided upon, Kennedy elected to announce his decision to the American public immediately.

Governor George Wallace of Alabama provided the opportunity for Kennedy to announce his decision to introduce a new civil rights program. Wallace had pledged to "bar the school house door" rather than permit school integration in the state of Alabama. This pledge applied to the all white University of Alabama as well as the public elementary and high schools in the state. On 11 June 1963 Wallace was physically present at the University as two black students, Vivian Malone and James Hood, were escorted on to the campus by Justice Department officials and U.S. marshals. Because of the governor's threat to "bar the door," President Kennedy had "federalized" the Alabama National Guard and then had sent the commander of the Alabama National Guard to order Wallace out of the doorway. After reading a short speech condemning "the trend toward military dictatorship," Wallace "stood aside" and permitted the black students to register.

That evening President Kennedy gave a national television speech to explain the need for his actions at the University of Alabama. He used the occasion to announce that he was preparing a strengthened civil rights bill to go to Congress. His speech, partly extemporaneous and partly based on a draft by speech writer Ted Sorensen, is considered by many observers to be one of his most eloquent. Kennedy told the nation:

> We are confronted primarily with a moral issue. It is as old as the scriptures and is as clear as the American Constitution. . . . 100 years of delay have passed since President Lincoln freed the slaves, yet their heirs, their grandsons, are not fully free . . . and this nation, for all its hopes and all its boasts, will not be fully free until all its citizens are free.
> We preach freedom around the world, . . . but are we to say to the world . . . that this is the land of the free except for Negroes?

The president concluded:

> The fires of discord are burning in every city, North and South, where legal remedies are not at hand. . . .
> Next week I shall ask the Congress of the United States to act, to make a commitment it has not fully made in this century to the proposition that race has no place in American life or law.[18]

CHAPTER 3

WRITING THE ADMINISTRATION BILL

Once President Kennedy had decided to introduce a strengthened civil rights bill, there was no problem finding civil rights proposals or putting them into legal language. That job had already been done by the Civil Rights Commission. In a series of five reports issued in the fall of 1961, the commission had not only detailed the nature and extent of racial segregation and racial oppression in the United States but also made explicit legislative recommendations to remedy the situation.

THE CONTINUING ATTEMPT TO
NATIONALIZE THE CIVIL RIGHTS ISSUE

As the Civil Rights Commission was preparing to release its major report in 1961, one could look back over the past 100 years of race relations in the United States and detect a definite trend toward the progressive nationalization of the civil rights issue. Step-by-step, although very slowly at times, presidential orders and Supreme Court decisions had brought the power of the United States Government to bear on ending one or another aspect of racial segregation.

A major step occurred in 1863 when President Abraham Lincoln issued the Emancipation Proclamation freeing the slaves in those Southern states that had seceded from the Union during the Civil War. The three post-Civil War Amendments to the Constitution -- the 13th, 14th, and 15th Amendments -- abolished slavery, guaranteed the newly freed slaves equal protection of the

19

laws and other basic rights, and guaranteed all citizens the right to vote no matter what their race.

The reestablishment of white rule in the South following the removal of Union soldiers in 1877 essentially brought U.S. Government intervention into race relations in the South to a halt, and little further progress was made until the mid 20th Century. In 1941 President Franklin Delano Roosevelt banned racial discrimination in all factories making military weapons for the United States and appointed a Fair Employment Practices Committee to study racial discrimination in employment. In 1948 President Harry S. Truman issued an executive order racially integrating all of the armed forces of the United States.

BROWN V. BOARD OF EDUCATION

In May 1954 the Supreme Court ruled unanimously that segregation of school students into separate white and black school systems was unconstitutional. This landmark decision, Brown v. Board of Education of Topeka, Kansas, called for the "desegregation" of all public school systems in the nation "with all deliberate speed."

Instead of producing compliance on the part of local politicians and school officials, however, the Brown decision often produced "massive resistance," particularly in the South. White politicians and white government officials frequently maneuvered to delay the racial integration of local public school systems as long as possible. Rather than grudgingly accept the Supreme Court's decision, segregationist dominated Southern legislatures began passing laws providing for the denial of state school funds to any community that integrated its schools. State constitutions were amended to permit shutting down public schools rather than permit desegregation.

LITTLE ROCK

Delay of school integration by government officials in the South reached a peak in September 1957 when the local school

20

board in Little Rock, Arkansas, began to proceed with the integration of Little Rock's Central High School. On the pretext of preventing violence, Arkansas Governor Orval Faubus ordered the Arkansas National Guard to occupy Central High School and prevent the carrying out of court ordered integration.

The response of President Dwight D. Eisenhower to this direct attempt to nullify the integration decision was swift and powerful. Eisenhower "federalized" the Arkansas National Guard, thus taking it out from under the command of Governor Faubus and putting it under Eisenhower's control. The president then ordered the Arkansas National Guard out of Central High School and away from Little Rock. He then dispatched regular United States Army troops to occupy Central High School and the surrounding school grounds and to protect school officials and black students as they continued the process of court ordered school integration.

President Eisenhower's decisive actions at Little Rock had great symbolic significance. For the first time since Union troops were withdrawn from the South in 1877, United States soldiers had reentered a Southern city and state for the express purpose of imposing a national policy over the opposition of a state government official. For Southern blacks, the national intervention was a turning point. Until President Eisenhower acted so decisively at Little Rock there was no assurance that the power of the national government would be used to uphold the Supreme Court. After Little Rock, however, the precedent was set. From then on, blacks could always hope for United States Government intervention if local Southern school officials openly defied court orders integrating public schools. The result was to inspire black leaders and their white allies to press ever harder for an end to all forms of racial segregation.

THE MONTGOMERY BUS BOYCOTT

One year after the Supreme Court decision desegregating public schools, on 1 December 1955, a black seamstress, Mrs. Rosa Parks, was arrested in Montgomery, Alabama, when she refused to stand and give her seat on a city bus to a white man. At a subsequent meeting of black leaders in Montgomery, it was decided that blacks would boycott the segregated bus system in Montgomery until it was racially integrated. The Reverend Martin Luther King, Jr., was elected President of the Montgomery Improvement Association, an organization specially created to lead the bus boycott. For more than a year, more than 40,000 Montgomery blacks refused to ride the city's buses rather than be subjected to segregated seating. Car pools were formed to get bus boycotters to work and to school. Many Montgomery blacks simply walked wherever that had to go rather than ride a racially segregated bus.

The major accomplishment of the Montgomery bus boycott was that it turned a nonviolent demonstration for racial integration into a national news story. Because of the large number of boycotters involved, and because boycotters carpooling and walking made good television film, the national television networks covered the bus boycott extensively. When the white community in Montgomery reacted with random acts of violence (buildings bombed, buses fired upon, physical harm to boycotters, etc.), there was even more national coverage. It was this news attention that made Martin Luther King, Jr., a national symbol of the new black resistance to segregation and enabled him to present to the American people his ideas on the nonviolent demonstration as a means of producing political and social change.

The Montgomery bus boycott had two direct results. First, the transit system in Montgomery was integrated. The white leadership finally gave in to the demands of the black demonstrators. The success of the boycott revealed that the goal of racial integration could be achieved by the technique of the nonviolent demonstration.

The second result of the Montgomery bus boycott was that it made nonviolent forms of protest such as freedom rides and sit-ins big news items, both in the national and the local press. After Montgomery, no longer would demonstrators work in relative obscurity. Race relations, civil rights demonstrations, and violent white reactions to demonstrations henceforth were big news and played accordingly.

STUDENT SIT-IN DEMONSTRATIONS

On February 1, 1960, four black college students sat down at a lunch counter in Greensboro, North Carolina, and quietly waited to be served. Following extensive national new coverage of this "sit-in" demonstration, students at black colleges throughout the South, often joined by students from nearby white colleges, began similar sit-ins in an effort to racially integrate local restaurants and lunch counters. This wave of demonstrations, often involving high school students as well as college students, frequently provoked a violent response from the white community and thereby produced the desired coverage from the news media. By the spring of 1961 over 70,000 black and white youngsters had participated in the sit-ins, and a new civil rights organization, the Student Nonviolent Coordinating Committee (SNCC), had been created to recruit and train sit-in demonstrators throughout the nation.

FREEDOM RIDES

During this same period, civil rights groups organized "Freedom Rides" to test racial integration on interstate buses and in bus terminals in the South. Demonstrators would board the buses in the upper South and ride them into Alabama and Mississippi and other states in the deep South. One Freedom Ride ended with a Greyhound bus being stopped and burned by segregationists at Anniston, Alabama. Another ended in a riot in the bus station in Birmingham, Alabama, in which a white Freedom Rider was beaten so severely 53 stitches were required to close the wounds in his head.

THE CIVIL RIGHTS ACTS OF 1957 AND 1960

As a result of the increased attention which racial

23

problems received following the 1954 Supreme Court decision integrating public schools and the Montgomery bus boycott, Congress passed a civil rights bill in 1957 and again in 1960. Although both bills were subjected to Southern filibusters, the filibusters ended when House and Senate leaders removed from the bills those items that were objectionable to the Southerners. Civil rights supporters charged that the bills had been "gutted" of any meaningful civil rights reforms. The 1957 bill did provide, however, for the establishment of a Civil Rights Commission to study racial problems in the United States and make recommendations to Congress, and it was this commission which was issuing its major report to Congress in 1961, and whose findings served as the basis for the Kennedy Administration civil rights bill of June 1963.

VOTING RIGHTS

The first volume of the 1961 Civil Rights Commission report dealt with voting rights. The big problem, the report argued, was the arbitrary use by Southern election officials of "literacy tests" and "constitutional interpretation tests" to prevent blacks from registering to vote. These tests required prospective voters to be able to read and interpret the United States Constitution before being registered. In many instances, even blacks with college degrees were unable to read and interpret the Constitution to the satisfaction of local election officials. Such high standards usually were not set when white citizens endeavored to register to vote.

The Civil Rights Commission recommended that Congress enact a law making completion of six grades of school sufficient proof of literacy for voter qualification. This would give any black citizen who had completed elementary school (and who was not a convicted criminal or in a mental hospital) the automatic right to register and vote.[1]

EDUCATION

Reporting seven years after the Supreme Court's desegregation decision and four years after President Eisenhower's swift intervention at Little Rock, the Civil Rights Commission in 1961 found the nation's progress toward desegregating schools to be "slow indeed."[2] The commission therefore recommended a long series of legislative remedies to Congress. Local school boards should be required to file detailed plans for desegregating their schools, the commission said, and the attorney general of the United States should be given authority to see that those plans are carried out. In addition, Congress should provide financial aid to local school systems to encourage them to create special programs and hire specially trained employees to oversee and facilitate the desegregation process.

Perhaps the most interesting proposal by the Civil Rights Commission was the suggestion that Congress "cut off" up to 50 percent of the United States education funds going to any state that continued to practice school segregation. The amount of U.S. education funds cut off would be adjusted to the proportion of the state's public school districts that still had not been racially integrated. In the case of colleges and universities, however, the Commission went even further and recommended that all U.S. Government aid be cut off to those institutions of higher learning that discriminate on the basis of race, religion, or national origin.

EMPLOYMENT

In the field of employment, the 1961 Civil Rights Commission Report found black Americans caught in a vicious cycle of lacking the training for good jobs and, because of discrimination in hiring, never being able to get the training necessary to get the good jobs. The report explained:

> The vicious cycle of discrimination in employment
> opportunities is clear; the Negro is denied, or fails

25

to apply for, training for jobs in which employment opportunities have traditionally been denied him; when jobs do become available there are consequently few, if any, qualified Negroes available to fill them; and often, because of lack of knowledge of such newly opened opportunities, even the few who are qualified fail to apply.

If many blacks were weakly motivated to improve their educational and occupational status, the commission report concluded, it was because blacks were "the product of long-suffered discriminations."[3]

The Civil Rights Commission's major recommendation in the employment field was the creation by Congress of a Fair Employment Practices Commission (FEPC) to enforce a policy of equal employment opportunity in all U.S. Government agencies and also in private industry employment that was created or supported by U.S. Government contracts or U.S. Government aid programs. In the case of state employment offices, the commission again recommended a U.S. Government funds cutoff as the best way to achieve local compliance with national laws forbidding racial discrimination. The secretary of labor should be directed, the commission report said, to deny U.S. funds to state employment offices that operated on a discriminatory basis or which accepted and processed "whites only" or "colored only" job orders.

JUSTICE AND POLICE BRUTALITY

In its report on justice and law enforcement, the Civil Rights Commission concluded that, although there was much to admire in the American system of criminal justice, "police brutality is still a serious and continuing problem." The report went on to point out that "although whites are not immune, Negroes feel the brunt of official brutality, proportionately, more than any other group in American society."

Furthermore, the Civil Rights Commission charged, in

26

areas where local sentiment favored segregation, "some officers take it upon themselves to enforce segregation . . . [and] the Negro's subordinate status." This often took the form of police "connivance" in private violence, such as when "police are informed that violence will take place against blacks or white sympathizers and do nothing to prevent it."[4]

This problem of police connivance in private violence stemmed from a problem with the 14th Amendment to the United States Constitution. When that amendment had been proposed and adopted in the years immediately following the Civil War, its framers had mainly wanted to prevent state governments from denying civil rights to their newly emancipated black citizens. As a result, the prohibitions in the 14th Amendment all applied to the state governments and not to the individuals living in those states. The exact wording of the 14th Amendment was:

> No State shall make or enforce any law which shall abridge the privileges or immunities of citizens of the United States; nor shall any State deprive any person of life, liberty, or property, without the due process of law; nor deny to any person within its jurisdiction the equal protection of the laws.

Because of this "no state shall" form of wording, the 14th Amendment could not be used to protect black Americans from mistreatment by individuals. It could only be used to protect black Americans from official actions by the state governments. The result was a system of oppression, particularly practiced in the South, in which state officials would "not notice" or "wink" when private individuals discriminated against blacks or terrorized them. In certain localities, most of them in the American South, white citizens who beat, lynched, and murdered blacks could do so with almost complete confidence that state and local police, being committed themselves to the doctrine of white supremacy, would be less than zealous about investigating the crimes and catching the perpetrators.

Adding to the ability of Southern white individuals to discriminate against and terrorize blacks was "the free white jury that will never convict." Even in those cases where arrests were made and indictments sought, lynch mobs and race murderers could rely on the fact that a jury of their white neighbors and friends surely would acquit them.

The Civil Rights Commission Report of 1961 proposed several legislative remedies for the problem of police brutality. It recommended Congress pass a law spelling out in detail those acts that constitute police brutality and unlawful official violence. Such acts, even when committed by state and local government officials, would be national crimes and thus would be tried in United States courts. One of the forms of unlawful official violence that would be defined in the new law would be "refusal to protect any person from known private violence, or assisting private violence."[5]

The Civil Rights Commission also recommended that state and local government officials be made liable for damages when police officers under their control commit acts of brutality or unlawful official violence. In addition, the commission suggested that the Congress empower the attorney general of the United States to file suit against state or local court systems that permit the exclusion of citizens from juries because of their race or nationality. This last remedy was directly aimed at eliminating "the free white jury that will never convict."

PART III

Civil rights supporters had long argued that, as the Civil Rights Commission Report of 1961 pointed out, only intervention by the United States Government in Washington would end police brutality and unlawful official violence visited upon blacks in the South. To this end, the Eisenhower administration had proposed to Congress in 1957 that the attorney general of the United States be granted the power to secure court injunctions in civil rights cases and that such cases be removed from state courts to United States courts.

28

This provision soon became known on Capitol Hill as "Part III" because it was the third title of a proposed Eisenhower administration civil rights bill. Part III was an extremely important proposal to civil rights supporters. It would permit the U.S. attorney general to file civil rights suits, thus relieving the black individual in a hostile Southern community of the responsibility of filing such a suit. Many black individuals would not think of filing a civil rights suit, mainly because the threat of white retaliation, possibly in the form of a bombing or a lynching, was so great. The attorney general and the Civil Rights Division of the Justice Department would have no such fears, however, and could pursue civil rights cases in a vigorous and public way that would never occur if such cases were left to the individual initiative of isolated Southern black citizens.

Although the Eisenhower Part III was defeated in the Senate by a filibuster, almost all subsequent civil rights bill contained a provision similar to Part III that gave the attorney general the power to seek court injunctions to protect civil rights. The concept kept the nickname of Part III even when it was no longer the third part of the bill in question.

THE BATTLE OVER THE ADMINISTRATION BILL

Skillful lobby groups do not wait for presidential proposals to reach Capitol Hill before they begin their lobbying efforts. Pressure is applied both to the White House itself and, more importantly, to the particular bureaucrats who will be writing the exact legal language of the proposed legislation. In line with this strategy, civil rights groups began sending messages to President Kennedy and to the Justice Department (where the actual legislative proposal would be drawn) urging that the administration bill include the major legislative recommendations of the Civil Rights Commission Report of 1961.

There were still many voices of caution to be heard in the inner circles at the White House, however. Those concerned with the fate of the tax cut bill and the rest of the Kennedy economic program continued to see much to be lost and little to be gained from presenting a strong civil rights bill. Suddenly reports began spreading throughout Washington that something less than a really strong civil rights proposal would be forthcoming from the White House. The public accommodations section was going to be limited in scope, the rumors said, confined only to those restaurant and hotel facilities immediately engaged in interstate commerce. There would be a Part III, but the attorney general would be allowed to file suit only in school desegregation cases and not in all civil rights cases. There would be an Equal Employment Opportunity Commission (EEOC) to end job discrimination in U.S Government agencies and in private businesses operating under U.S. Government contracts, but there would be no Fair Employment Practices Commission (FEPC) with powers to end job discrimination in all private industry.[6]

On 19 June 1963 a weaker proposal than what was wanted by the civil rights forces went to Congress. "It was clear that the counsel of caution had, on the whole, prevailed."[7] One major concession was made to the pressure from the civil rights bloc. President Kennedy called for creation of a Fair Employment Practices Commission (with powers to end job discrimination in all private industry) in his civil rights legislative message. There was no FEPC language in his omnibus civil rights bill, however, only the EEOC limited to ending job discrimination in U.S. Government agencies and under U.S. Government contracts.

MAJOR PROVISIONS

The omnibus civil rights bill which the Kennedy administration sent to Capitol Hill contained seven major proposals. Title I concerned voting rights and provided that anyone who had a sixth grade education could not be required to take a literacy test in order to register to vote. Title II, the most important part of the proposed bill in view of the sit-in demonstrations in general and the Birmingham demonstrations in particular, outlawed racial discrimination in all places of public accommodation such as restaurants, snack bars, motels, hotels, swimming pools, etc.

Title III gave the attorney general of the United States the power to file suits to bring about the racial desegregation of public schools. It is interesting to note the impact of tradition here. Granting the attorney general the power to file suits in civil rights cases had always been known as Part III, and here it was placed as Title III of the Kennedy civil rights bill.

Title IV proposed the establishment of a Community Relations Service to assist state and local governments in resolving racial disputes. Title V extending the working life of the Civil Rights Commission for four more years (through November of 1967). Title VI provided for the cutoff of U.S. Government funds to any state or local government program that practiced racial discrimination. Because of the pressure it would put on Southern state and local governments to desegregate all government programs that were financed with U.S. Government aid, this was a very important part of the Kennedy bill, second in importance only to Title II and its guarantee of equal access to public accommodations.

Title VII created the Equal Employment Opportunity Commission (EEOC) with authority to limit job discrimination only in U.S. Government employment and work undertaken under U.S. Government contracts.

Compared to the relatively mild civil rights measure which President Kennedy had sent to Congress in March of 1963, his June of 1963 proposal appeared to many observers to be very strong. Strong as it was, however, it came under continuing criticism from civil rights groups, mainly for its lack of a Fair Employment Practices Commission (FEPC) to end job discrimination in all places of employment, private as well as public.

Worried by this continuing criticism of his civil rights legislative package, President Kennedy called the major civil rights leaders to a conference at the White House. He was determined to convince them that his proposed bill was the best that could be achieved under the circumstances. According to Joseph Rauh, Jr.:

> He [President Kennedy] said he realized that this
> fight might even endanger his reelection, but here
> was a moral issue and he was determined to wage
> the battle come what may. He stressed the need
> for an all-out effort by everybody in the room to
> mobilize the public behind his bill.[8]

President Kennedy left the meeting and was replaced by
Vice-President Lyndon Johnson. When asked what would happen
if the Leadership Conference on Civil Rights were to lobby
Congress hard to strengthen the Kennedy proposed bill, the Vice
President replied that there must be "flexibility" in a campaign of
this kind, and he saw no problems with the civil rights groups
going beyond the administration in their demands. According to
Joseph Rauh, Jr.: "This was the go-sign for the Leadership
Conference strategy from then on."[9] The civil rights movement
would give its wholehearted support to the Kennedy civil rights
bill, but it would demand more, and it would attempt to
strengthen the administration proposal at every opportunity.

A number of the civil rights leaders at the meeting were
not surprised that Vice-President Johnson took a stand in favor
of strengthening the administration civil rights bill. The major
black political leaders saw Vice-President Lyndon Johnson,
although a Southerner, as more in favor of civil rights than
Kennedy. Whitney Young, Jr., national director of the Urban
League, gave the following response to a question about
Vice-President Johnson's role in drafting the civil rights bill:

> He [Johnson] played a very key role and was
> actually more supportive of some of the measures
> than some of the administration, the other Kennedy
> people were. Initially we had seven or eight titles
> and there were any number of the members of the
> administration who were trying very hard to get us
> to cut down the number. . . . Mr. Johnson didn't
> feel that way.[10]

CONCLUSIONS

No legislation originates in a vacuum. Bills are introduced in the United States Congress because somewhere "out there" real people are upset with some aspect of the status quo and want to see things changed. The strengthened civil rights bill which President Kennedy sent to Congress in June 1963 originated, not in the White House or in the office of a particular senator or representative, but in the confrontational violence of the civil rights movement and the segregationist white response. Short of a declaration of war, few bills presented to Congress have had as violent and confrontational an origin as the strengthened Kennedy civil rights bill of June 1963.

As much as it originated in the streets, however, the Kennedy civil rights proposal of June 1963 originated in the television tube. The use of television news to dramatize racial repression in the South and to present the arguments of the civil rights demonstrators was crucial.

The racial demonstrations and their full coverage in the media forced President Kennedy to do something which he obviously had not wanted to do -- present a strong civil rights bill to the United States Congress. The record is clear that, until the Birmingham demonstrations and riots forced him to change his position, President Kennedy had no intention of sending a strong civil rights proposal up to Capitol Hill. A point to be noted here is that, despite all of their great constitutional and customary powers, presidents of the United States can often be forced by external events and external political actors to take steps that they otherwise might not take.

Adding to the excitement and tensions surrounding the presentation of the strengthened Kennedy civil rights bill to Congress were the formidable obstacles that the proposed legislation would face on Capitol Hill. The House Rules Committee would delay the bill as long as possible. Some way would have to be found to get the bill around the Southern controlled Senate Judiciary Committee. Most important of all, the bill would have to survive a determined Southern Democratic filibuster in the

Senate, something that had never been accomplished before with a strong civil rights bill. If civil rights supporters had the media impact of the civil rights demonstrations and confrontations working in their favor, the anti-civil rights forces had control over certain key points in the congressional law making process working for them. What was being set up was a classic confrontation between a media focused public demand for change and the procedural prerogatives and powers of certain key members of Congress.

It was clear in June 1963 that, as the civil rights struggle moved up to Capitol Hill, the Kennedy administration found itself caught in the middle between two strong and contending forces. The Southern Democrats in Congress were determined to either kill the strengthened Kennedy bill or else weaken it considerably. On the other hand, the civil rights forces (as represented by the Leadership Conference on Civil Rights) intended to strengthen the bill as much as possible. The job of successfully steering a middle course for the bill between these contending interests was the principal task facing Kennedy administration legislative strategists.

The argument can be made that few legislative proposals have ever arrived before the United States Congress with as much previous publicity and as much public awareness about their significance as did the Kennedy civil rights proposal of June 1963. Clearly the national spotlight on the civil rights issue was shifting to the United States Congress, and everyone involved knew that it was shifting there. This would be anything but the customary congressional battle, carried out quietly in the halls of Congress with little or no public attention and only the immediately affected government agencies and client groups involved. The civil rights movement leading up to June 1963 had been one of the most heavily publicized events in United States history. It set the stage for the strengthened Kennedy civil rights proposal to be one of the most extensively publicized congressional battles in United States history.

CHAPTER 4

SUBCOMMITTEE NO. 5;
"OUT OF CONTROL" FOR CIVIL RIGHTS

Prior to the Birmingham demonstrations and riots, the legislative course leading to the passage of the Civil Rights Act of 1964 was marked principally with partisan maneuvering rather than serious discussion of civil rights. Pro-civil rights members of both parties sought to portray themselves and their party as the great defender of civil rights while at the same time attempting to blame the opposition party for the lack of action on any major civil rights legislation.

On 12 March 1963, one month before Birmingham, a group of Democratic senators supporting civil rights met with Senate Democratic Whip Hubert H. Humphrey of Minnesota. In a memorandum reporting on the results of the meeting, Humphrey revealed that the spirit of the meeting was anything but bipartisan. Despite the fact that pro-civil rights Republican senators Jacob Javits and Kenneth Keating, both of New York, were "pressing hard" to cosponsor a civil rights bill with the Democrats, Humphrey and his colleagues decided that any Democratic civil rights bills would be sponsored only by Democrats. Humphrey made it clear that, with the Democrats so strongly in control in the Senate, only a Democratic sponsored bill would be reported out by a Senate committee.[1] By not allowing any Republican cosponsors, Humphrey implied, the Democrats would get all the credit for having introduced a strong civil rights bill in the Senate.[2]

Prior to Birmingham, the Republicans proved fully able to play the same game. On 28 March 1963, senators Javits and

Keating joined with six other liberal Republican senators to introduce a package of bills which would implement the Civil Rights Commission recommendations of 1961 which the Kennedy administration had so purposefully ignored. In a joint statement to the press, the eight liberal Republicans charged that the Kennedy civil rights program "fell far short" of the Civil Rights Commission recommendations and of both the Republican and Democratic 1960 party platforms. "If the president will not assume the leadership in getting through Congress urgently needed civil rights measures," the liberal G.O.P. Senators said, "then Congress must take the initiative."[3]

The liberal Republicans had everything to gain and nothing to lose by pressing the civil rights issue on the Democrats. Most of them were from large states like New York, California, Pennsylvania, and New Jersey. Along with large numbers of black voters, these states had even larger numbers of white voters that favored civil rights. Furthermore, these liberal Republican senators were well aware that Democratic power in the Congress and in presidential elections rested on maintaining a delicate balance between liberal Northern Democrats and conservative Southern Democrats. By pressing for strong civil rights legislation, the liberal Republicans were hoping to drive a wedge between the Northern and Southern wings of the Democratic Party. The major goal of these liberal Republican senators, therefore, was to place the blame for the lack of a civil rights bill on the Democrats and hope that the result would be black votes and liberal white votes for the Republicans in the North and the Border States. Senator Thomas H. Kuchel, a liberal Republican from California, had a legislative assistant who was a particularly strong advocate of Republicans using the civil rights issue in an attempt to divide the North-South Democratic coalition.[4]

Birmingham put a temporary hold on this form of partisan bickering and advantage grabbing. Everyone on Capitol Hill cognizant of the situation knew that, in order to overcome a Southern filibuster of a civil rights bill, Northern and Western Democrats would have to be joined by Northern and Western

Republicans in order to produce a 2/3 vote for cloture. Sixty-seven votes were required for cloture. The Democrats had 67 Senators in the 1963-1964 session of Congress, but 18 of them were from the South and could be expected to oppose any cloture motion on a civil rights bill. This meant a minimum of 18 Republican votes were required for a successful cloture vote, and more if certain Democratic senators from outside the South decided not to support cloture for philosophical reasons.

THE BIPARTISAN STRATEGY

On 3 June 1963, just four days after President Kennedy decided he would present a major civil rights bill to Congress, Assistant Attorney General Norbert A. Schlei met with Vice President Lyndon Johnson to discuss the proposed administration bill. According to Nicholas Katzenbach, a deputy attorney general under President Kennedy who specialized in civil rights issues, Vice-President Johnson was frequently consulted by the Kennedy administration on civil rights problems and strategies. Katzenbach recalled:

> [The civil rights bill] had been discussed in the White House with legislative leaders and very much with the then Vice-President Johnson, who had quite an input into the structure of that act. . . . I recollect that Vice-President Johnson was continuously present at meetings on this in the White House, and that President Kennedy was very much relying on his judgement on the legislative situation and what was possible and what wasn't possible to achieve in that legislation.[5]

In his meeting with Assistant Attorney General Schlei, Vice-President Johnson began by stating his complete loyalty to President Kennedy and his willingness to support whatever decisions the president might make. Johnson then proceeded to outline to Norbert Schlei an extensive plan for getting a major civil rights bill through both the House and the Senate. Item number one on Johnson's list was taking a bipartisan approach. Johnson told Schlei:

> [The president should] call in the Republican leaders, tell them about the plans and put them on the spot; make them give their promises in blood to support the legislation in an agreed form, indicating that credit would be shared with them for the success achieved and indicating that any failure on their part to agree and to deliver would be laid unmistakably at their doors.

Vice-President Johnson then proceeded to give Schlei the numerical reasons a bipartisan approach was absolutely essential:

> [The civil rights forces] would need 27 out of the 33 Republican votes in the Senate in order to obtain cloture, and as matters now stand we have no prospect at all of getting that many. We would be able to get that many only if we could enlist the full support of Senator Dirksen [the Republican leader in the Senate], among others.[6]

By mid June 1963 a bipartisan approach similar to the one suggested by Johnson was official administration strategy, and it was evident that Senator Everett Dirksen of Illinois would be viewed as the key to getting the bill through the Senate. A memorandum in the papers of Hubert Humphrey, dated 18 June 1963, revealed that the bipartisan approach would begin with the introduction of the bill in Congress. Senate Democratic Leader Mike Mansfield would introduce, with liberal Republican cosponsors, the full administration bill. Simultaneously, however, he would cosponsor with Senator Dirksen the same bill minus certain public accommodations sections to which the Senate Republican leader was opposed. The memorandum makes clear that senators Mansfield and Humphrey had carefully checked with Senator Dirksen to make sure that this method of introducing two forms of the administration bill had his complete support. The memorandum concluded with the following statements:

> The crucial factor [in the legislative agreement to introduce two different bills] was a common Mansfield-Dirksen front. It will be necessary at every step of the proceedings that this common approach be protected by complete communication between the two leaders.[7]

Introducing two bills in this manner, one cosponsored with liberal Republicans and the other cosponsored with Senator Dirksen, is a common practice in the Senate and the House of Representatives. Major legislation does not usually begin with only one bill being presented to Congress. Customary practice is for a wide variety of bills to be introduced on a given subject with a wide variety of cosponsors. It also is customary, as was done with the strengthened Kennedy civil rights bill of 1963, to introduce "simultaneous" bills, one in the House and one in the Senate. The congressional committees decide which of the many bills introduced will be selected for advancement.

By late June 1963 the Kennedy administration's bipartisan approach was being applied to Republicans in the House of Representatives as well as the Senate. In a memo to Attorney General Robert F. Kennedy, Deputy Attorney General Nicholas Katzenbach noted:

> We will probably need in the House around 65 Republican votes to pass this legislation. . . . I think we can get these votes only if we can get some support from [William] McCulloch [the highest ranking Republican on the House Judiciary Committee] and Gerry Ford [Gerald R. Ford of Michigan, the newly elected chairman of the House Republican Conference]. I assume we are not

39

likely to get support from Halleck [the House Republican leader], but McCulloch and Ford might be able to deliver the necessary votes despite Halleck. This is more than a question of Ford's support. He would have to work actively.[8]

At these early stages of work on the civil rights bill, Kennedy administration strategists were leery of the liberal Republicans in the House of Representatives, particularly John Lindsay of New York. The fear was that the liberal Republicans would press for a really strong civil rights bill and then blame the Democrats when the bill failed to get moderate support and thus was defeated. Katzenbach noted in his memo to Robert Kennedy:

> I do not think we can get [votes] from the liberal Republicans [i.e., John Lindsay], and working with them is likely to do nothing but build them up [and end] up in defeat for us.

It thus was clear that administration strategists would have a difficult time where Republicans in the House of Representatives were concerned. The civil rights bill would have to be strong enough to win the support of liberal Republicans like John Lindsay, but it would simultaneously have to be moderate enough to win the support of middle-of-the-road Republicans like William McCulloch and Gerald Ford. Deputy Attorney General Katzenbach later recalled:

> We, for example, refused to work with John Lindsay, which irritated Lindsay, but we refused to work with him because we felt the only way of getting the Republican support we needed in the committee, and more importantly in the House leadership, was through Bill McCulloch.[9]

This problem of differing Republican sentiments over civil

rights would have to be solved, however, because the bill would not pass the House of Representatives without strong Republican support. In the 1963-1964 session of the House of Representatives, the Democrats enjoyed a 256 to 178 (1 vacancy) majority over the Republicans. However, 101 of the Democrats were Southerners and could not be relied upon to vote for a strong civil rights bill. This left at best 155 Democrats to support the bill with 217 votes required for final passage (all members present and voting). Thus at least 62 Republican votes were needed to gain a majority in the House for the bill. Even more than 62 would be required because not all Northern and Western Democrats could be counted on to vote for a strong civil rights bill.

OVERALL LEGISLATIVE STRATEGY

Because of the ever present threat of the Senate filibuster, the strategy for getting the strengthened Kennedy civil rights bill through the House and the Senate required a great deal of careful strategy making. The essential problem was this. The bill had to be routed through the House and the Senate in such a way that the bill only went before the Senate once and thus was subject to only one Senate filibuster.

Under ordinary circumstances, a bill as important as the new administration civil rights bill would have been considered by the Senate twice. Major legislation traditionally is passed in differing versions in both houses of Congress and then a combined version of the two bills is produced by a House-Senate conference committee. The conference committee bill then returns to both the House and the Senate where it is debated and passed in each house a second time without amendment. The conference committee bill then goes to the White House for the president's signature.

If the strengthened Kennedy civil rights bill followed this traditional route to enactment, it would have been subject to a filibuster when it first came up for passage in the Senate. It would have been subjected to a second filibuster, however, when

41

the House-Senate conference committee bill came back to the Senate for final passage. In each case the filibuster would probably have had to be overcome with a 2/3 cloture vote. It was feared that there was neither adequate time nor sufficient support for a civil rights bill to survive two filibusters and two cloture votes. A strategy would have to be devised for seeing that the bill went before the Senate only one time and endured only one filibuster.

The strategy devised was this. The bill would be advanced first in the House of Representatives. There were two reasons for doing this. One reason was obvious. The House of Representatives rules provide for the limitation of debate, therefore there was no threat of a filibuster in the House. The second reason was less obvious but just as important. A civil rights bill in the House would automatically go to the House Judiciary Committee, where the chairman, Representative Emanuel Celler of New York, was a liberal Democrat and a strong supporter of civil rights. As committee chairman, Celler would see to it that the initial House of Representatives hearings on the civil rights bill were very favorable to the bill and would generate a great deal of favorable newspaper and television publicity for the bill.

Following passage on the floor of the House of Representatives, the civil rights bill would then go to the Senate. An overly optimistic strategy might call for having the Senate, following the inevitable Southern filibuster and a cloture vote, pass the House bill without amendment. With the same bill having passed both houses, the bill could then go directly to the president for his signature and final enactment into law.

The idea that the Senate might pass a House of Representatives civil rights bill without amendment was too much to expect. The two houses of Congress are too jealous of their various prerogatives for that to happen. A more realistic view would be that, following the filibuster and the cloture vote, the Senate would amend the bill passed by the House, probably weakening it in an effort to get those last few votes of Senate moderates to make the 2/3 vote for cloture. The amended Senate bill would then come back to the House.

At that point the final part of the strategy would be implemented. The House would have to repass the bill with the Senate amendments added. There could be no House amendments, because that would have the effect of sending the bill back to the Senate for another filibuster. But the House of Representatives is as jealous of it prerogatives as the Senate is. It would take delicate handling and skillful negotiating to prevail on a majority of the House to pass the Senate version of the bill without amendment. Probably the only way this could be done would be to clear all Senate amendments with key leaders in the House of Representatives, both Democrats and Republicans, before letting such amendments be added to the bill in the Senate.

Thus the strategy would be passage in the House, amendment in the Senate, and repassage with the Senate amendments in the House. The version of the Kennedy civil rights bill that was introduced in the House of Representatives was carefully routed to Emanuel Celler's Judiciary Committee. Celler began holding favorable hearings on the new administration civil rights bill almost at once.

POMP AND CIRCUMLOCUTION; THE SENATE JUDICIARY COMMITTEE

As action began on the House version of the strengthened Kennedy civil rights bill, action also began in the Senate. As noted previously, two versions of the Kennedy civil rights bill were introduced in the Senate, one the full administration bill and the other the Mansfield-Dirksen bill with certain public accommodations sections deleted at the request of Senator Dirksen. These bills were introduced mainly for publicity purposes and little more. Both bills were routed to the Senate Judiciary Committee, where it was assumed that Chairman James O. Eastland of Mississippi would hold perfunctory hearings and then quietly bury the two bills forever.

The Senate Judiciary Committee hearings began on 16

July 1963 with a strong statement of opposition to the bill by Senator Sam J. Ervin, Jr., a Democrat from North Carolina. An acknowledged expert on the United States Constitution, Ervin made it clear he was going to attack the bill "on the intellectual plane and not on the emotional plane." He argued that the bill was "condemned by its manifest unconstitutionality. Neither the commerce clause [of the Constitution] or the 14th Amendment can save it."[10]

The vast majority of the Senate Judiciary Committee hearings consisted of Senator Ervin asking nitpicking constitutional questions of the main administration witness, Attorney General Robert Kennedy. By late July the unceasing grilling of Robert Kennedy by Ervin inspired Republican Senator Kenneth Keating of New York to charge that the Judiciary Committee hearings were "rapidly approaching the appearance of a committee filibuster."[11]

On 23 August 1963 committee Chairman Eastland adjourned the Judiciary Committee hearings subject to the call of the chairman. The call of the chair never came, therefore consideration of the Civil Rights Act of 1964 by the Senate Judiciary Committee officially ended at that point. The assumption that Chairman Eastland would quietly bury the Senate version of the administration civil rights bill in the Judiciary Committee had been correct.

THE OPPOSITION ASSEMBLES

At the same time the Senate Judiciary Committee was holding its shortlived hearings on the Kennedy administration civil rights bill, the 18 United States Senators representing the Southern United States began holding strategy meetings to plan their opposition to the bill. The chairman of these sessions was Senator Richard Russell of Georgia. Russell was the acknowledged leader of the Southern Democrats and a veteran of many previous civil rights struggles in Congress.

Ten of the 18 Southern Democratic senators were chairmen of Senate committees. Along with Russell, they would use every legislative trick they knew to try to kill the administration civil rights bill. Their most important weapon -- the Senate filibuster -- would be turned full force on the civil rights bill the minute the bill came up for debate in the Senate.

Following one of these early Southern strategy sessions, Senator Russell described the Southern senators as "not without hope." He summed up the Southern mood as one of "grim optimism." A national magazine reviewed Russell's many legislative talents and concluded he was "the most formidable foe in the Senate."[12]

SAFETY BACKUP;
THE SENATE COMMERCE COMMITTEE

Although administration strategists were certain that President Kennedy's new civil rights proposal would receive favorable treatment before the House Judiciary Committee, they apparently were worried about what might happen to the bill after that. What if the House bill became hopelessly mired in the House Rules Committee? Suppose the House bill arrived in the Senate too late in the 1963-1964 session of Congress to permit a lengthy filibuster, cloture vote, and then a return to the House for acceptance of Senate amendments? To be absolutely safe, some sort of civil rights bill should be readied for presentation in the Senate in case the House version of the bill either did not make it to the Senate or arrived too late.

The result was the introduction in the Senate of a bill which incorporated only the public accommodations sections of the Kennedy civil rights proposal. Because the public accommodations sections were based on the interstate commerce clause of the Constitution, this particular bill could be routed to the Senate Commerce Committee rather than the Senate Judiciary Committee. The Commerce Committee chairman was Warren Magnuson, a Democrat from the state of Washington who was a loyal Kennedy man and a strong civil rights supporter. Administration influence over the Senate Commerce Committee was so great that Nicholas Katzenbach told Robert Kennedy:

> We have the votes to report out any bill we wish to in this committee. . . . The following are committed to support any bill: Democrats -- Magnuson, Pastore, Engle, Bartlett, Hartke, McGee, and Hart; Republicans -- Scott and Beall.[13]

The Kennedy strategists used their power on the Senate Commerce Committee to write a very strong public accommodations bill. If the House bill never made it to the Senate, the Commerce Committee bill could be presented for debate in the Senate in plenty of time to last out a filibuster and cloture vote. Once cloture had been obtained, this bill could then be amended on the floor of the Senate to include most of the other principal points in the Kennedy civil rights program. If all these Senate amendments were cleared beforehand with House Democratic and Republican leaders, the Commerce Committee bill could then be passed in the House without amendment and sent directly to the president for his signature.

The Senate Commerce Committee reported out its public accommodations bill on 8 October 1963. From that date forward, the bill could be brought up on the Senate floor at any point the Senate leadership felt it was necessary. The safety backup for the new Kennedy civil rights bill was firmly in place and, if ever needed, ready to go.

THE HOUSE JUDICIARY COMMITTEE

A popular saying around Capitol Hill is: "The committee system is not neutral."[14] What this concept means is that congressional committee chairmen can shape both committee hearings and committee bill writing sessions in order to favor one side or the other. Although committee hearings often have the appearance of a court trial, with witnesses being sworn to tell the truth and legislators questioning witnesses the way tough prosecuting attorneys cross-examine court defendants, there is no "judge" at a committee hearing to see that both sides of the issue get a fair chance or an equal say in the matter. By and large, committee chairmen will endeavor to use the committee hearings to build a strong public record either for or against the bill in question, depending on the political desires of the chairman.

As previously noted, Senator Eastland used the Senate Judiciary Committee hearings on the administration civil rights bill to produce testimony critical of the bill. The Senate hearings consisted almost exclusively of Senator Ervin reading into the record attacks on the bill. Chairman Eastland declined to call any witnesses that strongly favored the Kennedy civil rights bill other than Attorney General Robert Kennedy, and Robert Kennedy's every positive statement about the bill was promptly challenged on legal and constitutional grounds by Senator Ervin.

The "lack of neutrality" was going the other way in the House of Representatives, however. Chairman Celler of the House Judiciary Committee introduced the Kennedy legislative proposals on 20 June 1963, and the House clerk gave the bill the number H.R. 7152. When the bill arrived at the House Judiciary Committee, Chairman Celler immediately assigned the bill to Subcommittee No. 5. It was this subcommittee that held the first public hearings on the bill and then marked up its own version of the bill for later consideration by the full Judiciary Committee.

It would be hard to imagine a more favorable forum for a civil rights bill than Emanuel Celler's Subcommittee No. 5. For several years this subcommittee, which Celler chaired himself, had been carefully constructed to be strongly favorable to civil rights. Officially No. 5 was the antitrust subcommittee, but it was a measure of the arbitrary power of congressional committee chairmen in the 1960s that, when Celler sent the civil rights bill to the antitrust subcommittee, no one bothered to complain or question. Whenever a Democratic vacancy had occurred on the subcommittee, Celler had carefully filled it with a liberal supporter of civil rights. By 1963 none of the Judiciary Committee's senior Southerners were members of No. 5. The Democratic majority on the subcommittee consisted of Celler, five other Northerners, and a Texan favorable to civil rights.[15]

The hearings on the Kennedy civil rights proposal produced by this subcommittee were exactly what one would have expected -- a long string of favorable witnesses for the bill who, rather than being sharply questioned by Celler and the other subcommittee members, heard nothing but praise and support for their various statements. Attorney General Robert Kennedy was the first witness. He told the subcommittee:

> [The administration civil rights bill] will go a long way toward redeeming the pledges upon which this Republic was founded -- pledges that all are created equal, that they are endowed equally with inalienable rights, and are entitled to equal opportunity in the pursuit of their daily lives.[16]

The similarity between the attorney general's statement and the Declaration of Independence was unmistakable.

The parade of witnesses which followed Attorney General Kennedy was a veritable "who's who" of civil rights supporters. George Meany, president of the AFL-CIO, testified that civil rights "is not a matter for abstract debate but an immediate crisis." He argued the Kennedy administration proposals were "urgent, not because we say so, but because the course of history demands their enactment."[17]

Norman Thomas spoke in support of the bill for the U.S. Socialist Party, and the Reverend Walter E. Fauntroy testified on behalf of Martin Luther King, Jr., and the Southern Christian Leadership Conference. Other organizations sending representatives to endorse a strong bill included the Congress on Racial Equality (CORE), the Teamsters Union, the National Council of Churches, the National Lawyers Guild, the Medical Committee for Civil Rights, the National Students Association, Americans for Democratic Action, the United Automobile Workers, the American Veterans Committee, and the American Friends Service Committee.[18]

The most important sign that the Kennedy bill would experience smooth sailing before Subcommittee No. 5 was the strong support for civil rights legislation that had so frequently been expressed by Subcommittee Chairman Celler. At one point

Celler voiced his outrage over the white violence in Birmingham:

> Police clubs and bludgeons, firehoses and dogs
> have been used on defenseless schoolchildren who
> were marching and singing hymns.[19]

Equally important were the strong statements of moderate support from the ranking Republican on the Judiciary Committee, William McCulloch, who hopefully pointed out:

> Turmoil is a sign of birth, as well as decay, and, I am convinced that if the people of the country will continue to pursue a moderate but ever forward moving program for the insurance of individual equality, the day will soon come when we'll wonder why all the tumult and shouting had to happen.[20]

THE COMMERCE CLAUSE VS. THE 14th AMENDMENT

Although there was plenty of speechmaking during the subcommittee hearings, with the customary "pointing with pride" and "viewing with alarm," many important issues about the Kennedy civil rights bill were raised and seriously debated. A major issue concerned whether the public accommodations section of the proposed bill should be based on the commerce clause of the Constitution or upon the 14th Amendment. Attorney General Kennedy wanted to base equal access to public accommodations on the commerce clause because the Constitution clearly gave Congress the power to regulate interstate commerce and this would avoid a great deal of litigation. For reasons of party history, however, the pro-civil rights Republicans on the Judiciary Committee wanted equal access to public accommodations based on the 14th Amendment, the "Civil War" Amendment that had been passed by the Republican Party in 1868 and which guaranteed equal protection of the laws and other basic rights to all Americans.

Robert Kennedy went to great lengths to identify certain problems with the 14th Amendment. Because the amendment applied only to action by the states rather than individuals, Kennedy pointed out, Southern states would probably repeal all of their motel and restaurant licensing laws in order to leave individual motel and restaurant owners free to discriminate.[21]

Was perpetuation of racial segregation so important to Southern politicians and government officials that they would have their state legislatures repeal all motel and restaurant licensing laws in order to evade a national equal accommodations law? The Kennedy administration seemed to be committed to that idea. Assistant Attorney General for Civil Rights Burke Marshall claimed that there were places in the South where "feelings of racial supremacy are so ingrained that voluntary action is impossible."[22]

The Republicans argued, however, that the 14th Amendment's guarantee of equal treatment for all citizens would extend equal access to public accommodations to those smaller places of business that were not engaged in interstate commerce. The position was best summed up by Republican Senator John Sherman Cooper of Kentucky, a strong civil rights advocate:

> If there is a right to the equal use of accommodations held out to the public, it is a right of citizenship and a Constitutional right under the 14th Amendment. It has nothing to do with whether a business is in interstate commerce. . . . Rights under the Constitution go to the equality of all citizens, the integrity and dignity of the individual, and should not be placed on any lesser ground.[23]

As often happens in United States legislative politics, the dispute was settled with a "golden compromise," i.e., a brand new solution that leaves both sides satisfied. Republican Senator Kenneth Keating of New York proposed that equal access to public accommodations be based both on the commerce clause

50

and on the 14th Amendment. Such a combination, Keating suggested, would give the legislation the "broadest coverage consistent with the Constitution."[24] Keating's proposal was quickly endorsed by his fellow Republican Senator from New York, Jacob K. Javits, and the Justice Department quickly agreed and wrote the 14th Amendment as well as the interstate commerce clause into the official language of the administration bill.[25]

MRS. MURPHY'S BOARDING HOUSE

A second major issue which was hotly debated when the Kennedy civil rights bill was before Subcommittee No. 5 of the House Judiciary Committee was "Mrs. Murphy's boarding house." The hypothetical Mrs. Murphy was the invention of Republican Senator George D. Aiken of Vermont, who had created her when leaving a White House meeting of congressional leaders supporting civil rights. Some way had to be found, Aiken told the press, to distinguish between the types of accommodations which should be desegregated. He then said:

> Let them integrate the Waldorf and other large
> hotels, but permit the 'Mrs. Murphys,' who run
> small rooming houses all over the country, to rent
> their rooms to those they choose.[26]

The actual language of the civil rights bill was much too complex for the average person to understand, but everyone could identify with "Mrs. Murphy" and comprehend her problem. What Senator Aiken had done was to "sloganize" a complex concept into a simple, understandable idea. Such sloganizing is one of the major functions of congressional committee hearings. Senators and Representatives are always looking for simple and personal concepts, such as "Mrs. Murphy's boarding house," that will catch the public eye and make a complicated legal problem readily understandable. The news media are particularly adept at picking up slogans and simplified concepts when they are presented at committee hearings and other public forums.

Subcommittee No. 5 spent much of the summer of 1963 searching for a "Mrs. Murphy formula" which would exempt small rooming houses from the public accommodations section of the bill but would not prove to be a loophole for larger establishments that might wish to discriminate. By late summer agreement had been reached, however, that there would be a "Mrs. Murphy" exemption. In a 19 August 1963 memorandum to the attorney general, Deputy Attorney General Katzenbach put the idea directly. "[Assistant attorney general] Norb Schlei will do the following," Katzenbach wrote, and then in Schlei's list of duties for that week appeared the instruction, "Write a 'Mrs. Murphy' exemption."[27]

The exemption of "Mrs. Murphy" from coverage under the administration civil rights bill did not succeed in eliminating her from the public discussion of the bill. She had become too popular and too identifiable for that to happen. To the Southern Democrats opposing the civil rights bill, "Mrs. Murphy" became the "symbol of the average American whose rights were to be destroyed by the bill." To pro-civil rights Democrats and Republicans supporting the bill, however, she came to stand for "the absurd lengths to which the opponents of the bill would go in order to seek a basis for attacking the bill."[28]

Even Senate Democratic Whip Hubert Humphrey could not pass up the opportunity to get some personal publicity by referring to "Mrs. Murphy." In heavily Swedish and Norwegian Minnesota, Humphrey frequently quipped, it's known as "Mrs. Olsen's boarding house."[29]

FEPC

A third major point of discussion in Subcommittee No. 5 was the inclusion in the civil rights bill of a Fair Employment Practices Commission (FEPC). The Commission created by such a law would have the power to investigate racial discrimination in all employment, both public and private. If it found racial bias to exist, the FEPC could order business firms to hire more minority employees. This proposed provision was considered to be most controversial and politically dangerous because racial discrimination in employment was considered to be as big a problem in the North as it was in the South. President Kennedy's legislative strategists had left an FEPC provision out of the administration civil rights bill because they believed it had little chance of passing the House of Representatives and no chance at all of surviving "the fierce filibuster it would spark [in the Senate]."[30]

Chairman Celler soon found himself under intense pressure from certain directions to include FEPC as part of the subcommittee's recommended bill. A typical congressional power play to this end was attempted by Representative Adam Clayton Powell, a Democrat from New York City who was chairman of the House Education and Labor Committee and, at that time, the highest ranking black in the Congress. Representative Powell's committee had held hearings and reported out an FEPC bill which was currently waiting action (and would probably wait forever) in the House Rules Committee. Powell let it be known that he would try to bypass the House Rules Committee by bringing his FEPC bill to the House floor through the Calendar Wednesday procedure. Under this procedure, a committee chairman can bring a bill to the floor on a particular Wednesday without going through the House Rules Committee, but the bill must pass the House before adjournment that evening.

The Leadership Conference on Civil Rights was the first group to have a negative reaction to Powell's proposal. Joseph Rauh, Jr., of the Conference lobbying team, noted:

> The Calendar Wednesday strategy would have been a big show for Mr. Powell, but there was no chance of getting FEPC that way, and a defeat would have been a serious blow to the pending Kennedy civil rights bill.[31]

The Leadership Conference turned thumbs down, and Powell promptly announced that, since there were many more whites than blacks in the Leadership Conference, he was not bound by their decision.

Chairman Celler agreed with the Leadership Conference that "an early House floor vote on the FEPC bill alone -- when it might be defeated -- would be a major embarrassment for the administration and a psychological blow to the legislative drive for civil rights legislation." In a conciliatory move, Celler told Powell that he would try to incorporate provisions for a Fair Employment Practices Commission in the omnibus civil rights bill to be reported out by Subcommittee No. 5.[32] This was enough to get Representative Powell to drop the idea of trying the Calendar Wednesday procedure.

The flap over FEPC brought to the fore a difference of opinion on overall strategy for the bill. On one side was the Justice Department, the Kennedy Democrats on the subcommittee, and Republican Representative William McCulloch. They wanted to write a moderate bill that would have a chance of passing both the House and the Senate. On the other side were the strongly liberal Democrats and liberal Republicans on the subcommittee, who wanted to write a strong bill in the subcommittee for the express purpose of giving the Southerners something they could "cut out of the bill" when it got over to the Senate.

FEPC was seen as the most likely candidate to play this "give them something to cut out" role. According to Congressional Quarterly Weekly Report:

> Some civil rights strategists regard FEPC as something that could be traded off to break up a Southern filibuster and let the Southerners appear to have scored a victory while other key provisions of the administration civil rights bill are approved.[33]

Republican Representative Arch Moore of West Virginia said it was "vital" that a strong bill be sent to the Senate. "If we send them a water bill," Moore told the press, "we'll get back a water-water bill."[34] This problem of whether to pass a moderate bill or a strong bill in the House of Representatives continued to vex Kennedy legislative strategists throughout the summer and fall of 1963.

"AT THE COMMITTEE LEVEL"

"The real work of Congress takes place when the bill is at the committee level." This Capitol Hill saying refers to the fact that most of the legislation writing that takes place in the Congress occurs while bills are in committee rather than when bills are being amended and voted up or down on the floor of the Senate or the House of Representatives. A frequently heard rough estimate is that 90 percent of the nation's laws are written by the committees and subcommittees and only 10 percent are actually decided on the floor of either House.

Notice carefully, however, that the last four words of the Capitol Hill saying are "at the committee level." It does not say that the real work of Congress takes place during the committee hearings or in the "markup" session (where the committee writes the actual legal language it will "report" to the full House of Representatives or Senate). What the saying means is that the "real work of Congress" is the behind the scenes lobbying, compromises, and mutually beneficial deals that are made when the bill is "at the committee level." One view of committee hearings and committee markup sessions, in fact, is that they are simply "public confirmation of agreements reached in private." In other words, at the hearings and the markup sessions the committee members mainly read into the public record and write into legislation the closed door, private agreements that are made when the bill is "at the committee level."

Lobby groups are well aware of the fact that they must make their strongest pitch for their ideas and their interests when the bill is "at the committee level." The Leadership Conference on Civil Rights thus rapidly organized itself to put maximum pressure on Subcommittee No. 5 for a strong civil rights bill. Its efforts were a good example of what powerful lobby groups do when they wish to maximize their influence over pending legislation.

BUILDING A "SUPER LOBBY"

Shortly after President Kennedy introduced his omnibus civil rights package in mid June 1963, Walter Reuther of the United Automobile Workers called a meeting of the nation's most prominent civil rights leaders to discuss ways of mobilizing public support behind the bill. The Reverend Martin Luther King, Jr., talked of a gigantic March on Washington as the best means of dramatizing the need for the legislation. Roy Wilkins, who was chairman of the Leadership Conference as well as head of the NAACP, suggested enlarging the Leadership Conference to include all organizations favoring the legislation and "galvanizing them into [exerting] grass roots pressure for the bill."[35] Speedy action followed, both to organize the March on Washington and to enlarge the Leadership Conference.

On 2 July 1963, Roy Wilkins held a meeting at the Roosevelt Hotel in New York. Joseph Rauh, Jr., recalled:

> Not only were the 50 longtime civil rights organizations then in the Leadership Conference invited, but another 50 or so religious and other potentially helpful groups were asked to come. The mood was one of excitement that at long last there was a bill in the hopper worthy of a real struggle. The consensus was easily arrived at: The civil rights movement gave its wholehearted support to the administration bill -- but it demanded more -- an FEPC [that included private industry], Part III [permitting the United States attorney general to intervene in all civil rights cases], all public accommodations [not just interstate accommodations] covered. Not only were these additional provisions urgently needed,

but a good offense was obviously the best defense against weakening amendments.[36]

The members of the Leadership Conference, both new and old, were informed at the New York meeting of the monumental congressional roadblocks that would have to be overcome to pass the bill. The conservative character of the House Rules Committee; the fact that the Senate Judiciary Committee had never reported out a civil rights bill; the fact that conservative Republican votes would be required to vote cloture on a Senate filibuster -- these and other obstacles were identified and possible strategies for overcoming them weighed. At one point in the discussion Martin Luther King, Jr., whispered, "Mighty complicated, isn't it?" Despite the complications, the Leadership Conference was ready to go to work to eliminate the many legislative roadblocks ahead.[37]

As the New York meeting concluded, there was a general sense of urgency. To civil rights supporters, it seemed vital that the momentum created by President Kennedy's stirring speeches and his legislative proposals not be lost. At the same time, however, it was essential to begin to calm the stormy tensions which the continuing racial protests had produced across the country, both North and South. The civil rights movement was at an important watershed. The battle was going to move from the streets into the halls of Congress. The delicate process began of reducing the intensity of the civil rights demonstrations (so that they would not produce an adverse reaction in Congress) but at the same time maintaining the drive for civil rights which the racial demonstrations had created in the first place.

Up until this point in time, the Leadership Conference on Civil Rights had been headquartered in New York. With serious civil rights legislation in Congress, however, it was decided to open a branch office in Washington, D.C. Office space was provided by Walter Reuther of the United Automobile Workers, and Reuther and other civil rights supporters went to work raising the necessary funds to pay office rent and other lobbying expenses. A small paid staff, most of them with wide experience in the civil rights movement and neighborhood racial work, were hired to mobilize public support for the civil rights bill on a full-time basis. As events required, a "Memorandum" was mailed to each of the cooperating organizations in the Leadership Conference, informing them of the latest developments concerning the civil rights bill.[38]

Basically what the Leadership Conference had sought to create was a "super lobby," an alliance of powerful organizations supporting the bill. The United States is too large a nation and the Congress too vast an operation for a single organization to have much hope of pushing a major bill through to final passage. Individual organizations therefore have learned to combine with other organizations with similar interests and goals in order to get their pet bills enacted into law.

The super lobby which the Leadership Conference organized behind the Civil Rights Act of 1964 was probably one of the largest and most powerful lobbies ever organized in United States political history. It consisted of all the major labor unions, such as the AFL-CIO and the Teamsters Union. It included all the major church groups in the nation, such as the National Council of Churches, the National Catholic Welfare Conference, and the Synagogue Council of America. All the major civil rights groups were represented, such as the NAACP and CORE.

In the manner of powerful national interest groups, the Leadership Conference did much more than send a lobbyist or two up to Capitol Hill to talk with a few key senators and representatives. A constant barrage of press releases, fact sheets, and newsletters were sent to the member organizations, urging them, in turn, to acquaint their individual members with what was going on with the civil rights bill in Washington. At key points in the legislative process, members of the individual organizations were asked to write or telephone their senators or representatives, as the case might be, to urge them to move the bill along. High ranking officers of the various member groups periodically came to Washington to meet with their congressmen and urge them to support civil rights in general and the civil rights bill in particular. As the bill moved through the Congress, the religious groups in the Leadership Conference made a particular effort to have bishops, priests, and rabbis urge senators and representatives to support the bill for "moral" and "conscience" reasons.

Leadership Conference newsletters and mailings sought to equip its member organizations with information that would help identify those senators and representatives who might be influenced by lobbying from a particular Leadership Conference organization or individual. Thus senators and representatives were identified in terms of their religious affiliations, key financial contributors, and various organizations (such as veterans groups or service clubs) to which they belonged. The intention was to have senators and representatives lobbied by Leadership Conference representatives who were members of the same religion as the senator or representative, or who were large financial contributors, or who belonged to the same service clubs. For instance, if a Baptist church leader in the Leadership Conference saw that a particular senator was a Baptist, the church leader would call the senator and use their common religious affiliation to make the church leader's lobbying more effective.[39]

As a result of this extensive grass roots organizing and lobbying, the full-time professional lobbyists who represented the Leadership Conference on Capitol Hill were in an unusually strong position. The senators and representatives they spoke with were well aware of the large numbers of organizations and the millions of individual Americans on whose behalf the lobbyists were speaking. Members of Congress with large numbers of labor union members in their home states or home districts were particularly vulnerable to pressure from Leadership Conference representatives.

THE GOLD DUST TWINS

The Leadership Conference fielded an integrated lobbying team on Capitol Hill. The black member of the team was

Clarence Mitchell, Jr., director of the Washington office of the National Association for the Advancement of Colored People. The white member was Joseph Rauh, Jr., a prominent Washington lawyer and vice-chairman of Americans for Democratic Action, a national political lobbying organization that traditionally supported liberal causes. Because they had worked together lobbying for both the 1957 and the 1960 civil rights acts, Mitchell and Rauh were experienced and familiar faces in the halls, meeting rooms, and lounges of the Capitol building.

Typical of Washington lobbyists, both Mitchell and Rauh were somewhat older men with years of Washington experience behind them. Mitchell at one time had worked for the old Fair Employment Practices Committee which President Franklin D. Roosevelt had established in 1941. After Congress abolished the Fair Employment Practices Committee in 1946, Mitchell went to work as labor secretary for the NAACP, specializing in pressuring Congress for a fair employment law. It was perfectly understandable, therefore, that his voice would be one of the strongest in Washington clamoring for inclusion of an FEPC provision in President Kennedy's omnibus civil rights bill.[40]

Similar to Mitchell, Joseph Rauh, Jr., had worked for Franklin D. Roosevelt. It was Rauh, in fact, who wrote the presidential order setting up the 1941 Fair Employment Practices Committee. Rauh regarded Mitchell and himself as an ideal lobbying team. "We had," Rauh said, "a perfect relationship for grown men." Rauh always made it a point to let Mitchell speak first as the two of them went about the nation's capital lobbying for civil rights. "Clarence, after all, was the direct spokesman for the black people of America," Rauh noted, "and I always felt their views should be the first presented."[41]

Rauh pointed with pride as well as amusement to the fact that a segregationist Southern Democrat, Senator Harry Byrd of Virginia, had labeled Mitchell and Rauh "the Gold Dust Twins." The reference was to a picture of a white and a black child which had appeared on the label of cans of Old Dutch Cleanser, a cleaning and scouring powder widely in use in the United States in the early 20th Century.

60

"OUT OF CONTROL" FOR CIVIL RIGHTS

According to Joseph Rauh, Jr., the Gold Dust Twins spent the spring and summer of 1963 trying to convince the Kennedy administration to strongly support civil rights. Rauh recalled:

> Up until Birmingham, Clarence and I spent most of our time screaming at Kennedy. There is no question that King turned the tide. No Birmingham -- no bill. Then I spent the summer arguing with [Deputy Attorney General] Nick Katzenbach over putting FEPC in the bill. The Kennedy people kept telling us a strong bill could not pass, but Clarence and I knew better -- that a strong bill would pass.[42]

Similar to Rauh, Mitchell was "exasperated by the Kennedy administration and their downgrading of civil rights." President Kennedy himself had strong convictions for civil rights, Mitchell argued, but many of the people around him did not share those convictions. The problem, Mitchell believed, was that the Kennedy people were too "unoptimistic" about what Congress would pass in the way of a civil rights bill. "I could never convince them," Mitchell said, "that I could get large numbers of House and Senate Republicans to vote for a strong civil rights bill."[43]

Mitchell claimed that he learned the technique of getting exact counts on issues coming before Congress from Lyndon Johnson when Johnson was the Democratic leader in the Senate. The Kennedy Democrats, he argued, would estimate the possible Republican votes for civil rights rather than taking the trouble to do an exact count. Mitchell explained:

> I do know that nobody [in the Kennedy administration] thought that some of the things which we ultimately got into the law would be possible. I thought we'd get them mainly because I was applying the Johnson principle of vote counting. The Democrats were doing what

61

Democrats other than Mr. Johnson often did; that is, they were counting just the Democratic votes and estimating what they had among the Republicans. Usually much too low. I was counting both Republicans and Democrats and, as I said, I was just using the Johnson method. And I felt sure we could win . . . .[44]

THE MARCH ON WASHINGTON

In August 1963 Martin Luther King, Jr., successfully staged his "March on Washington for Jobs and Freedom." Patterned after the "Prayer Pilgrimage for Freedom" which had drawn 20,000 participants to the mall in May 1957, the 1963 March on Washington drew 200,000 people, the largest public demonstration held in Washington, D.C., up to that time.[45] Blacks and whites supporting civil rights legislation made a short and orderly march from the Washington Monument to the Lincoln Memorial, where a long series of speeches was climaxed by Martin Luther King, Jr., and his integrationist appeal, "I have a dream."

President Kennedy did not attend the March on Washington but did meet with the leaders of the various civil rights groups supporting the march at the White House. Although the Kennedy administration was not enthusiastic about the March on Washington at the time it took place, within seven months White House staff came to view the March on Washington as having directed the energies of black Americans away from more violent forms of racial protest. A recommendation was made to institute a similar type of event or events for the summer of 1964. A White House memo in March 1964 detailed this line of thinking:

One of the key reasons that we got through last summer [1963] without serious violence, death, injury, and destruction was the fact that the August 28 March on Washington provided an outlet for

the energies, emotions, and time of the Negro
community. I believe some thought should be
given to providing similar constructive channels to
those energies for the summer of 1964.[46]

Once again, television coverage was a critical factor in a
civil rights demonstration. Live broadcasts of the march were
featured on afternoon television followed by prime time news
reports in the evening and special summary reports following the
late news. Thus millions of Americans witnessed the March on
Washington in their own homes. Political writers commented
extensively on King's speech, and several predicted that its effect
would be lasting.[47]

BIRMINGHAM AGAIN

Shortly after the March on Washington, and just at the
moment when Mitchell and Rauh were putting the maximum
amount of pressure on Subcommittee No. 5 to report a strong
civil rights bill, Southern white violence against blacks once
again came to dominate the national news media. Four black
girls attending Sunday school in Birmingham, Alabama, were
killed when a bomb was thrown into their church. The building
bombed was the 16th Street Baptist Church, a central point for
civil rights strategy making during the Birmingham
demonstrations the previous spring. It was the 21st time in eight
years that blacks had been victims of bombings in Birmingham.
None of the 21 bombings had ever been solved.[48]

As the pictures of the four slain girls appeared on the
front pages of newspapers throughout the country, civil rights
leaders pointed out that the time for action on civil rights was at
hand. Martin Luther King, Jr., said:

Unless some immediate steps are taken by the
U.S. Government to restore a sense of confidence
in the protection of life, limb and property, my
pleas [for nonviolence] will fall on deaf ears and

we shall see in Birmingham and Alabama the worst racial holocaust the nation has ever seen.

King then pointed out that the deaths of the four little girls showed the desperate need for Part III, "legislation empowering the attorney general to file suit on behalf of citizens whose civil rights had been violated."[49] The fact that Martin Luther King, Jr., was now publicly telling President Kennedy the exact language needed in the civil rights bill dramatized the extent to which civil rights leaders were using every possible means of communication to press Subcommittee No. 5 for a stronger bill.

King also sent a telegram to Alabama Governor George Wallace charging that Wallace's segregationist rhetoric contributed to the bombing. "The blood of our little children is on your hands," King wired. Senate Democratic Whip Hubert H. Humphrey asked President Kennedy to "set aside next Sunday as a day of national mourning for the victims of last Sunday's bombing." James Reston, editorializing in the New York Times, labeled the central black neighborhood in Birmingham "Dynamite Hill" because of all the bombing attacks that had occurred there.[50] Throughout the nation, both North and South, memorial services and memorial marches were held for the four black girls killed in "the Sunday school bombing."

Roy Wilkins, executive secretary of the NAACP, related the Birmingham church bombing directly to the pending civil rights bill. In an obvious reference to the provision of the bill which called for the cutoff of U.S. Government funds to states and cities that discriminate, Wilkins urged President Kennedy to cutoff "every nickel" of U.S. funds going to Alabama, and suggested that as a first step the president close Maxwell Air Force Base near Montgomery. Wilkins also "urged the president to push for legislation empowering the attorney general to initiate suits in cases of violations of civil rights and to push for a Fair Employment Practices law."[51]

"OUT OF CONTROL" FOR CIVIL RIGHTS

The combination of the heavy pressure from the Leadership Conference and the public reaction to the Sunday school bombing in Birmingham was too much for the more liberal members of Subcommittee No. 5. As the subcommittee began marking up the Kennedy omnibus civil rights proposal, the liberal majority on the subcommittee began voting into the bill everything the Leadership Conference had asked for. From the Kennedy administration's point of view, the subcommittee was completely out of control. It approved a complete Part III and, most controversial of all, a Fair Employment Practices section ending job discrimination in private industry. Chairman Emanuel Celler himself, who ordinarily was loyal to the Kennedy people, had been unable to resist the blandishments of lobbyists Mitchell and Rauh and joined the subcommittee majority in supporting FEPC.

Deputy Attorney General Nicholas Katzenbach gave the following evaluation of the tendency of liberal supporters of civil rights to always support as strong a civil rights position as possible:

> You get as much trouble from the liberals as you do from the conservatives. . . . [They are always] wanting to go further than it is possible to go. At the drop of a hat, they want troops sent in. This was my constant battle . . . .[52]

STAYING BACK FOR THE TAX CUT

Emanuel Celler knew that the announcement of the subcommittee version of the bill would produce shock waves in the Congress and the nation. The day of the subcommittee's tentative approval of the strong bill, the House of Representatives was voting on one of the major bills in President Kennedy's economic program -- a major cut in both personal and corporate income taxes. The president was pushing the tax cut measure in hopes it would put more spending money in the pockets of American consumers and businesses and thereby stimulate an economic recovery. In fact, Kennedy administration spokesmen were touting the tax cut and the civil rights bill as the "big two" pieces of legislation that the President wanted enacted into law during the 1963-1964 session of Congress.

Celler very carefully waited until after the House of Representatives had approved the tax cut bill before announcing the subcommittee civil rights proposal. Celler and administration legislative strategists feared that many Southern Democrats would have joined with conservative Republicans in voting against the president's tax cut if they had known how comprehensive the proposed civil rights bill was going to be.

"No legislation goes through Congress in a vacuum," is the way oldtimers on Capitol Hill express the idea that seemingly unrelated bills can have a big effect on each other.[53] At first glance one would not think there was any relationship whatsoever between the tax cut bill and the civil rights bill. This was not the case, however. The Kennedy administration wanted the tax cut enacted into law first, and whenever necessary the Kennedy forces were willing to slow down the civil rights bill in order to make way for the tax cut bill. There also was the perpetual fear that the Republicans might make a deal with the Southern Democrats on both bills. The Republicans would vote against the civil rights bill in return for the Southern Democrats helping to vote down the tax cut. Thus the two bills were definitely related to each other, and strategy making on one of the bills had a definite effect on strategy making for the other bill.

THE REVOLT OF THE MODERATE

The press conference at which Emanuel Celler announced the subcommittee's strong civil rights bill was a happy moment for the Leadership Conference on Civil Rights. Clarence Mitchell, Jr., and Joseph Rauh, Jr., immediately called upon the full House Judiciary Committee to approve the subcommittee bill "without dilution or delay."[54]

Suddenly, major problems began to develop for the subcommittee bill. Conservative politicians and conservative newspaper columnists began to label the subcommittee bill "extreme." William McCulloch, the ranking Republican on the Judiciary Committee, expressed great concern over the far-reaching effects of the bill, particularly the FEPC section.[55] McCulloch's wavering support was of great concern to the Kennedy people. Administration strategists had considered McCulloch's wholehearted support to be essential. They were counting on McCulloch to round up the moderate Republican votes needed to get the bill passed on the floor of the House of Representatives. Justice Department lawyers had spent hours negotiating with McCulloch in an effort to write a bill to his liking. When Celler and the subcommittee majority abandoned the moderate bill that had been agreed to by McCulloch and reported a strong civil rights bill, the Kennedy people saw defeat on the floor of the House of Representatives as a certainty.

Deputy Attorney General Nicholas Katzenbach recalled that Representative McCulloch was emphatic that the same bill that passed in the House would have to be the one that passed in the Senate. Katzenbach said:

> The only Republican man I could work with was McCulloch. . . . McCulloch at the outset insisted that he would support us, . . . but not if we were bargaining the House against the Senate. And I had to make a commitment to McCulloch that we would do everything possible in the Senate to get the same bill the House passed through the Senate and that the administration would not remove any title of that bill as a deal in the Senate. . . . McCulloch said that the House would not stand for that, and he wanted my personal word and that of President Kennedy that this would not be done.[56]

STRENGTHEN IT TO DEFEAT IT

The Southern Democrats on the full Judiciary Committee agreed with the administration view that a strong bill would be easily defeated. In fact, the segregation supporters on the full committee made known their intention to vote for the subcommittee bill when it came up for final approval by the Judiciary Committee. They knew that marginal support would be scared off by a strong bill.[57] One of the oldest of legislative strategies is to strengthen a bill you dislike in committee on the assumption that such a strong bill will have no chance of final passage by the entire legislative body. With the votes of the Southern Democrats on the Judiciary Committee added to the liberal Democrats and liberal Republicans who wanted a strong bill, there were more than enough votes in the full committee to adopt the subcommittee bill. If the Kennedy administration strategists were going to tone the bill down, they would have to act quickly.

"A BILL, NOT AN ISSUE"

In mid October Attorney General Robert Kennedy asked to speak to an executive session of the full House Judiciary Committee. "What I want is a bill, not an issue," the attorney general said. He then recommended that the full committee trim some portions of the subcommittee bill which he considered legally unwise or so sweeping that they would provoke unnecessary opposition to the bill. The attorney general was particularly concerned about FEPC for private industry, which he said the administration supported but which he felt might mire the civil rights bill forever in the House Rules Committee. He suggested an alternative strategy of deleting FEPC from the committee bill, letting the milder bill sneak past the House Rules Committee, and then adding FEPC as an amendment when the civil rights bill was safely up for debate on the House floor.[58]

Representative McCulloch went out of his way to strongly endorse Robert Kennedy's testimony before the full Judiciary

Committee. Kennedy had made some "very useful, very constructive suggestions," McCulloch told the press, "some that I would make and have been making."[59] Clearly the Democratic attorney general and the Republican representative from Ohio were working together to keep the liberal Democrats and liberal Republicans on the Committee from passing too strong a bill.

Clarence Mitchell, Jr., and Joseph L. Rauh, Jr., refused to go along with the Kennedy administration view that a strong bill could not pass the House of Representatives. The Leadership Conference on Civil Rights sent Emanuel Celler a three page letter urging him to stand by the stiffer provisions written by Subcommittee No. 5.[60] According to Rauh, he and Mitchell did everything in their power "to get the liberal representatives to hold out for the stronger bill."[61] The day after Robert Kennedy's testimony before the Judiciary Committee, Mitchell fired a public broadside at the Kennedy administration. He told the media:

> There is no reason for this kind of sellout. The administration should be in there fighting for the subcommittee bill. . . . Everybody in there [in the closed Judiciary Committee session] is a white man, and what they are doing affects [the] 10 percent of the population that is black. I don't know if the Negroes are being protected.[62]

But even as Mitchell was making this strong statement, House Judiciary Chairman Celler began to retreat from the strong subcommittee bill. Clearly feeling the pressure from both Robert Kennedy and McCulloch, Celler announced that he would "put aside my own feelings" and support a more moderate version in order to win congressional approval of the bill. The coalition of strong civil rights liberals on the committee was unmoved by Celler's action, however. Now led by Republican Arch Moore of West Virginia and Democrat Robert W. Kastenmeier of Wisconsin, they remained adamant in opposing any modification of the subcommittee bill.[63]

It was in this highly charged atmosphere of pressure and

counterpressure that the House Judiciary Committee met on 22 October 1963 to begin voting on the final version of the bill to be recommended to the House of Representatives. A motion by the Southern Democrats to return the bill to the subcommittee (in effect to kill it) was easily defeated. Republican Arch Moore then moved that the Judiciary Committee report the subcommittee bill. Ironically, the subcommittee bill was now opposed by the subcommittee's own chairman, Emanuel Celler, who spoke strongly against it. Celler soon realized, however, that the votes were still there to easily pass the subcommittee bill. Exercising his prerogatives as chairman of the House Judiciary Committee, Celler adjourned the meeting and then abruptly cancelled another meeting scheduled for the next day. In the manner of powerful congressional committee chairmen in the 1960s, Celler was not going to let the Judiciary Committee meet if the committee was not going to do what he wanted it to do.

PRESIDENTIAL INTERVENTION

At this moment John F. Kennedy stepped personally into the fray. The president called a late night secret strategy conference in his office at the White House. Attending this meeting were Emanuel Celler and William McCulloch of the House Judiciary Committee. Also present, however, were the speaker of the House of Representatives, Democrat John W. McCormack of Massachusetts, and the House Republican leader, Charles Halleck of Indiana. The president asked the House legislative leaders to explore possibilities for a compromise bill that could win majority approval in the House Judiciary Committee while at the same time retaining sufficient Republican support to get out of the House Rules Committee and also pass on the House floor.

The first indication that the president's efforts were going to bear fruit came the following day when House Republican Leader Halleck said he would help the Kennedy administration block Judiciary Committee approval of the sweeping subcommittee bill. In the five days of intense negotiations that

70

followed, the Democratic and Republican leadership of the House of Representatives, with the aide of Justice Department lawyers, began to formulate a new version of the bill. Suddenly Subcommittee No. 5 and its strong version of the bill were being superseded by the president and the House leadership of both political parties.

President Kennedy found the biggest problem to be the mutual distrust between the liberal Democrats and the moderate Republicans on the House Judiciary Committee. The liberal Democrats were fearful that the Republicans would outmaneuver them by voting for the more liberal subcommittee bill and thereby make the liberal Democrats who supported the presidential compromise appear to be "soft on civil rights." The moderate Republicans, on the other hand, feared that they would be tricked into "walking the plank," i.e. they would take all the risks of supporting a Democratic president's civil rights bill and then, when the bill reached the Senate, would see the bill "gutted" to end a Southern Democratic filibuster. A second late night meeting at the White House was required to get the two sides to begin trusting each other and to agree to support the bipartisan compromise all the way from the House Judiciary Committee to the House Rules Committee to the House floor.[64]

By 29 October 1963 negotiations on the bipartisan compromise were completed. On that day Chairman Celler called the House Judiciary Committee into session and voting on the civil rights bill resumed. The broad version of the bill written by Subcommittee No. 5 was rejected by a vote of 15 For and 19 Against. The new bipartisan compromise was then presented and adopted by a vote of 20 For and 14 Against. The Judiciary Committee then ordered the compromise bill reported to the House of Representatives by a vote of 23 For and 11 Against.[65]

Deputy Attorney General Nicholas Katzenbach recalled how narrow the victory was for the Kennedy administration in the House Judiciary Committee:

We very nearly failed because of a liberal-conservative coalition in the House Judiciary Committee, when the Southerners agreed to vote out the bill the liberals wanted. And they obviously agreed to it because they knew that when it got on the floor it would be recommitted, and there would be no civil rights bill. By working with the moderate and liberal Republicans and then getting enough of our Democratic liberals, we were able to defeat that . . . .[66]

THE FURLED UMBRELLA

House Republican Leader Charles Halleck was forced to "pay the price" for supporting the president's bipartisan compromise and successfully pushing it through the House Judiciary Committee. Charging that Halleck had "appeased" the Democratic enemy, a group of conservative Republicans placed a furled umbrella on his desk and then carefully pointed out to the news media that the furled umbrella was symbolic of former British Prime Minister Neville Chamberlain, who carried such an umbrella, and of Chamberlain's "appeasement" of Adolph Hitler prior to the start of World War Two.

The Kennedy administration and the House leadership launched a media blitz supporting the bipartisan bill. According to Attorney General Robert Kennedy, the compromise bill was a "better bill than the administration's in dealing with the problems facing the nation." He later added, "In my judgment, if it had not been for their (Halleck's and McCulloch's) support and effort, the possibility of civil rights legislation in Congress would have been remote."[67]

Halleck himself publicly praised the bipartisan bill. "I've always been for a good effective bill. This was a determination of what we ought to do -- not as a political question, but as a matter of what's right." Halleck was joined by McCulloch in lauding the compromise effort. McCulloch particularly praised Republican Representative John Lindsay of New York for convincing a significant number of liberal Republicans on the

Judiciary Committee to abandon their preference for the broad subcommittee measure and support the bipartisan bill.[68]

Republican Arch Moore of West Virginia stayed with the subcommittee bill to the very end, however. In an unusually bitter and scathing attack, he later described the compromise bill as "sprung upon the committee from out of the night." It was, he charged, "conceived in segregation, born in intolerance, and nurtured in discrimination."[69]

Although not using as sharp words as Moore's, civil rights groups were publicly critical of the compromise. James Farmer, executive director of CORE, found the bipartisan bill "not acceptable." Roy Wilkins, executive secretary of the NAACP, said: "Today's events are no cause for rejoicing but are a challenge to work to strengthen the bill." His remarks were seconded by Clarence Mitchell, Jr., speaking on behalf of both the NAACP and the Leadership Conference on Civil Rights, who charged that the Judiciary Committee's performance had been "shabby" and that the Kennedy administration had been arrogant.[70]

PUBLIC VS. PRIVATE VIEWS

There appears to have been something of a gap between what civil rights leaders were saying about the bipartisan compromise and how they really felt about it. According to Joseph Rauh, Jr., the compromise version of the bill was not all that watered down when compared with the subcommittee version. The Fair Employment Practices Commission (FEPC) for private industry was still in the bill, even if it was to be called the Equal Employment Opportunity Commission (EEOC) and have its rulings enforced by the courts rather than by government administrators. Part III remained in the bill, even though the attorney general could not intervene in civil rights cases on his own volition but would have to wait until a private citizen first filed a suit. The cutoff of U.S. Government funds to states and cities that discriminate had not been watered down at all, and the part of the bill granting equal access to public accommodations had been limited only by the exemption for "Mrs. Murphy's Boarding House."

In fact, Rauh argued, "the Leadership Conference was well satisfied. . . . [Its] efforts had strengthened the bill and the Republican leadership, including McCulloch and [Republican] leader Halleck, were now tied to the bill." Rauh then cited a New York Post editorial as a perfect statement of why the Leadership Conference publicly criticized the bipartisan bill as too weak but, in private, was delighted with it. The New York Post editorial, printed 31 October 1963, said:

> The civil rights bill voted by the [House] Judiciary Committee is an improvement over the administration's original proposal. It vindicates the fight waged by the Democratic and Republican liberals for a stronger measure. . . . The lesson of this episode so far is that faint heart rarely prevails on Capitol Hill.[71]

As was to be expected, the Southern Democrats in the House of Representatives were highly critical of the civil rights bill that had been approved by the House Judiciary Committee. Representative Watkins M. Abbitt of Virginia described the new version of the bill as the "most iniquitous, dangerous, liberty-destroying proposal that has ever been reported to Congress."[72]

Six Southern Democrats in the House of Representatives issued a statement criticizing the committee bill. They described the bill as "the most radical proposal in the field of civil rights ever recommended by any committee of the House or Senate. . . . [It] constitutes the greatest grasp for executive power conceived in the 20th Century . . . ." If the bill became law, the Southern representatives concluded, "the basic and fundamental power of the states and the power of our local governments to regulate business and govern the relation of individuals to each other will have been preempted."[73]

Although the House Judiciary Committee approved the bipartisan compromise bill on 29 October 1963, the Southern

Democrats on the committee stalled the writing of the official report of the bill until 20 November 1963.[74] On the day the report of the bill was officially filed, House Judiciary Chairman Emanuel Celler asked House Rules Committee Chairman Howard Smith for an early hearing on a rule for floor debate. Southern Democrat Smith, of course, was not expected to expedite the process, and, when asked about the bill, simply said no hearings were planned.[75]

As the nation's capital prepared itself for the inevitable House Rules Committee fight over the administration's civil rights bill, President John F. Kennedy boarded Air Force One to fly to Dallas, Texas. It was to be the first step in the president's campaign for reelection. It was symptomatic of the problems of Democratic presidents that Kennedy was taking his reelection bid first to Texas, the key southern state that had to be kept in the Democratic party if the Democrats were to retain the White House in 1964.

An assassin's bullets ended President Kennedy's life while he was in Dallas. Vice-President Lyndon Johnson succeeded Kennedy as president of the United States.

CONCLUSIONS

The exact role of President Kennedy in the great civil rights struggle of the early 1960s is hotly debated. Although not as much as civil rights leaders wanted, the civil rights bill which he presented in June 1963 was "still by far the boldest and most comprehensive ever proposed by any president to advance the cause of civil rights."[76] On the other hand, as a pro-civil rights legislative aide in the United States Senate later put it, "The bill [the Kennedy civil rights bill] would not have passed if Kennedy had still been president."[77]

The criticism of Kennedy on civil rights was prevalent enough that all of his biographers made an elaborate effort to defend his record on the subject. Theodore Sorensen's main argument was that there was more than ample proof in 1961, 1962, and early 1963 that the votes simply were not there to get a major civil rights bill around the filibuster in the Senate. Until the white violence and black counter violence at Birmingham changed everything, Sorensen's view was that Kennedy was absolutely correct in his political judgement that pressing for civil rights legislation would be doomed to failure.

In 1963, Sorensen argued, Kennedy "was deeply and fervently committed to the cause of human rights as a moral necessity," but Sorensen carefully pointed out that the moral necessity was "inconsistent with his political instincts."[78] Kennedy himself put it very concisely in a private talk with Sorensen:

> If we drive Sparkman, Hill and other moderate Southerners to the wall with a lot of civil rights demands that can't pass anyway, then what happens to the Negro on minimum wages, housing and the rest?[79]

President Kennedy thus did everything for blacks and the cause of civil rights except press hard for congressional legislation. He forced the integration of the Washington Redskins professional football team over the heated opposition of the team's owner. He had the son of a black member of the White House staff attend his children's White House nursery school. It can be argued that Kennedy used the executive powers of the presidency so thoroughly on behalf of blacks that he felt no need to make a suicidal attempt at making legislative advances as well. In fact, Kennedy used the executive power so thoroughly for civil rights that, when Lyndon Johnson became president following Kennedy's assassination, only the legislative arena remained as a place where Johnson could build his own record with black Americans.

A careful reading of John F. Kennedy's speeches and press conferences reveals that he repeatedly called for mediation and negotiation between whites and blacks in the South as the best solution to the civil rights crisis. It was clearly his hope that Southern attitudes might change, the various civil rights

76

crises would be solved by local settlements and agreements, and there would be no need for congressional action.

Kennedy also appears to have hoped that the attitude of Southern Democrats in the Senate might change and that a civil rights bill might then have a chance of getting through the Senate without a filibuster. Theodore Sorensen, President Kennedy's speechwriter, later wrote:

> The president hoped -- but never with much confidence -- that a "Vandenberg" would emerge among the Southern senators, a statesman willing to break with the past and place national interests first. Despite idle speculation that Arkansas' Fulbright might play such a role, no Southern solon came forward to place the judgement of history ahead of his continued career.[80]

Kennedy's speech to the nation the night of the standoff with Governor Wallace at the University of Alabama was the high point of his civil rights fight in the public sphere. In announcing he would send a major civil rights bill to Congress, Kennedy was doing what no American president had done in almost a century. With his dramatic speech and his civil rights bill, Kennedy had taken the crucial "first step" in getting Congress to consider major civil rights legislation.

Consideration of the Kennedy civil rights bill by Subcommittee No. 5 and the full House Judiciary Committee illustrates the extent to which the Kennedy administration was the main source of pressure behind the bill. The language of the original bill introduced in the House of Representatives was written by a team of lawyers from the Civil Rights Division at the Kennedy Justice Department. As the bill proceeded through the subcommittee hearings, these same Kennedy administration lawyers continued to maintain a high degree of control over the bill. As new ideas were presented at the subcommittee level, it was the Justice Department lawyers who would write them into the official legislative language of the bill. Justice Department lawyers were present at all subcommittee hearings and were available if wanted at all the mark up sessions. It is important to note that the Justice Department was not only handling the official language of the bill but was also helping to make the strategy for getting the bill passed.

One need only read Nicholas Katzenbach's periodic memoranda concerning the Kennedy civil rights bill to realize how completely the administration was involved in the day-to-day details of House consideration of the legislation. His memos repeatedly ordered Justice Department attorneys to do those things which, at least in theory, might have been done by individual members of the House of Representatives or congressional staff. "Write a [small boarding house] exemption!" "Clear our redraft of Title VI [the funds cut off provision] with Celler, McCulloch, and Lindsay!" "Form a drafting team . . . . This drafting team will meet each day at 2:00 P.M. to review what has gone on within the committees and to prepare suitable language to meet committee objections."[81]

Katzenbach also had the Justice Department negotiate with the key lobby groups supporting the bill. He told Attorney General Robert Kennedy: "Last week I met with Joe Rauh's group . . . . This group continues to be insistent that FEPC be included in the omnibus bill, and there will be some problem heading them off."[82] The Justice Department's efforts even extended to trying to tone down the activity of civil rights leaders contemplating further racial demonstrations in cities far away from Washington. "I think Burke Marshall," Katzenbach wrote Robert Kennedy, "should keep in close touch with Negro groups in an effort to channel and control their activities."[83]

Katzenbach and his team of Justice Department lawyers took it upon themselves to help maintain relations between the Senate and the House of Representatives. Katzenbach assigned himself the task of clearing redrafts of key titles of the bill with Mansfield, Dirksen, and other Senators, even though the bill was at the subcommittee level in the House of Representatives and would not be over to the Senate until several months later.

The extent of executive branch control over the bill was

best illustrated, however, when President Kennedy held his two secret, late night meetings at the White House and arranged for Justice Department officials and the House Democratic and Republican leaders to write a completely new version of the House bill. As a result, the legislation reported to the House floor was not written by Subcommittee No. 5 or, for that matter, the House Judiciary Committee. It was written at the White House, at the call of the president, with legal experts from the Justice Department penning the exact legal language. The legislative product of a subcommittee of the House of Representatives -- Judiciary Subcommittee No. 5 -- received major modification upon the application of stiff presidential pressure.

Later on in the passage of the Civil Rights Act of 1964, the Justice Department and others supporting the bill had to develop legislative techniques for "bypassing" the House Rules Committee and the Senate Judiciary Committee because they were dominated by Southern Democrats who were anti-civil rights. It is interesting to note that President Kennedy and the Justice Department found it equally necessary to "bypass" Subcommittee No. 5, only in this instance it was because the subcommittee was excessively pro-civil rights rather than anti-civil rights.

As the Kennedy civil rights bill moved through the subcommittee and full committee process in the House of Representatives, William McCulloch of Ohio slowly began to emerge as the "unsung hero" behind successful House consideration of the bill. At the time when both the liberal Democrats and the liberal Republicans were throwing in behind the strong subcommittee bill, Representative McCulloch stood by the Kennedy administration and continued to work for a moderate, compromise, bipartisan bill that, in his view, could have a chance of passing both the House and the Senate. As a result, McCulloch earned respect from those who agreed that only a moderate bill could get passed. McCulloch also earned himself a great deal of influence over the final form of the bill as it continued to make its way through the House of

Representatives and then the Senate.

It is the conclusion of this author that President Kennedy deserved more praise from civil rights leaders than he received as the compromise bipartisan bill emerged from the House Judiciary Committee and made its way to the House Rules Committee. As Theodore Sorensen, Kennedy's speechwriter, pointed out, Celler and most of the other liberals pushing for a strong civil rights bill took the "easy course" and supported the broad subcommittee bill. President Kennedy resisted taking the "easy course" and did not support the subcommittee bill. He would have been praised by the civil rights lobby, and the "death" of "his bill" on the floor of the House of Representatives would have been blamed on the House of Representatives, not on the President. But Kennedy did not take the "easy course."[84] He chose instead to call the secret meetings at the White House, put his executive prestige behind a compromise bipartisan bill, and come up with legislation that could be passed. It was the high point of his civil rights fight in the private sphere. In this author's opinion, it was also one of the high points of Kennedy's career as president of the United States.

If President Kennedy is a "hero" of civil rights, why did the sophisticated leaders of the civil rights movement not see him as a hero. The answer was the legislative strategy adopted by the Leadership Conference on Civil Rights. Since the Leadership Conference decided it would press for "the strongest bill possible" and would criticize strongly any attempt at compromise, it was inevitable that President Kennedy would come to have a negative image where civil rights was concerned. No matter how strong for civil rights a Kennedy compromise bill might have been, the Leadership Conference still would have criticized the bill and lambasted the president. It was a "no win" situation for the president. By taking a "no compromise" position the Leadership Conference was pursuing good legislative strategy, but the image seeped into the minds of strong civil rights supporters that President Kennedy was not strong for civil rights. From the president's point of view, however, he was doing exactly what was required to get the bill enacted into law.

Although their legislative strategy weakened the national image of President Kennedy as a strong supporter of civil rights, Mitchell and Rauh cannot be faulted for that strategy. By taking a strong pro-civil rights position, they did force the Kennedy administration to back a stronger bill than that administration originally had wanted to support. It is only coincidental that, in pressing John F. Kennedy to take a stronger stand on civil rights, Mitchell and Rauh possibly gave an incorrect historical view of the extent of President Kennedy's civil rights efforts.

It is often said that President Kennedy was considered a civil rights hero by the average black person in America but was not considered a civil rights hero by the more sophisticated black leaders who knew his true record. It is this author's opinion that the sophisticated black leaders were too much under the influence of the negative publicity given Kennedy, as a matter of legislative strategy, by the Leadership Conference on Civil Rights. In seeing Kennedy as a hero of civil rights, it is this author's opinion that the average black person in America was exactly right.

CHAPTER 5

LYNDON B. JOHNSON;
"TO WRITE IT IN THE BOOKS OF LAW"

The assassin's bullets that killed President Kennedy in Dallas changed many things, but nothing quite so much as the political situation concerning civil rights. Kennedy's successor, Vice-President Lyndon Johnson, was a Democrat from the Southern state of Texas. At first civil rights supporters believed this would doom the civil rights bill, but actually the reverse situation was the case. As a Southerner, Lyndon Johnson was mainly concerned with winning political support in the North. Similar to Kennedy, he would have to run for reelection in 1964, and he had less than a year to convince skeptical Northern and Western liberals that a Southerner was an acceptable leader for the national Democratic party.

Clarence Mitchell, Jr., Washington Director of the NAACP, recalled the great contrast between what certain newspaper columnists were predicting about Lyndon Johnson and civil rights and what the new president was actually doing:

> Bill White . . . used to work for the New York Times as a columnist. He was very close to . . . Johnson in the Senate. And most people assumed that when Bill said something in his column, that this was really coming [from Johnson] . . . . Shortly after President Johnson took office, Bill wrote a column in which he said that, "You can expect the shift away from the Kennedy provisions, which probably means that the civil

rights bill will be shelved . . . ." Well, under
normal circumstances, you could have assumed that
this really was what President Johnson was
thinking. But almost at the same time his column
was coming out, the president was calling people
in to tell them how he had to get on the ball on
civil rights.[1]

The idea that a Southern president would work extra hard
to prove he was not racist also was explained by Louis Martin,
deputy chairman of the Democratic National Committee under
President Johnson:

Now my feeling about Johnson, and this is what
I used to tell many Negroes in the newspaper
business and others -- is that since Johnson was a
Southerner, he would normally, being a good
politician, lean over backwards to prove that he
was not a racist. Further, there's something in the
folklore of Negro life that a reconstructed
Southerner is really far more liberal than a liberal
Yankee. And I exploited this part of the folklore.[2]

Nicholas Katzenbach, a deputy attorney general at the
time of President Kennedy's assassination, took the position that
President Johnson was under much greater pressure than
President Kennedy to be a strong supporter of the civil rights
bill:

Both President Kennedy and President Johnson
made very clear their views on civil rights. In a
way President Johnson, I think to establish his own
credentials, since he came from a Southwestern
state, wanted to make very clear what his views on
this were and to be very vigorous in the
enforcement of it. I do not say this to take away
from President Kennedy, but I think that President

84

Johnson wanted to make absolutely clear to the Negro community and to others that there was going to be no letup in this. . . . [President Johnson] wanted to make it very clear -- and did -- right at the outset of his administration that this [civil rights] was something he was going to move forward in every possible way and with much more than deliberate speed.[3]

President Johnson seized on the civil rights bill as the perfect instrument for establishing his credentials with Northern and Western liberals. Five days after Kennedy's assassination, the new president told a joint session of the House and Senate, "We have talked long enough in this country about equal rights... It is time now to write the next chapter -- and to write it in the books of law."[4]   Johnson asked the Congress to adopt the civil rights bill in memory of his slain predecessor, John F. Kennedy.

REACHING OUT TO BLACK POLITICAL LEADERS

Back on 4 June 1963, when Assistant Attorney General Norbert A. Schlei interviewed then Vice-President Johnson about strategies for getting a civil rights bill passed, Johnson outlined to Schlei exactly how he would attempt to get support and loyalty from black political leaders. Schlei reported:

[Johnson] said he would call in all of the Negro leaders of importance in the country and would tell them that the administration was unreservedly on their side in the battle for the objectives they have been seeking. He would tell them that the administration intended to seek civil rights legislation . . . before the end of the session; that the bill would be introduced and considered as soon as the president's tax [cut] program was enacted or defeated, one way or the other, and that Congress would stay in Washington until hell freezes over if necessary in order to get the [civil rights] legislation passed. . . . He would tell the Negro leaders that their help would be absolutely essential in getting the civil rights bill enacted. He would tell them that we need . . . Republican votes in the Senate and ask them to get busy on the task of obtaining them. He said he thought what the Negro leaders wanted was an absolute assurance that we were with them and that we meant business . . . .[5]

Now president himself, Johnson's first move was to implement the strategy he had outlined to Schlei. He called black leaders and civil rights leaders to well publicized meetings in the Oval Office at the White House. As Johnson himself told it:

I spoke with black groups and with individual leaders of the black community and told them that John Kennedy's dream of equality had not died with him. I assured them that I was going to press for the civil rights bill with every ounce of energy I possessed.[6]

It is important to note that, at these White House meetings with black leaders and civil rights leaders, President Johnson was asking for support as well as promising it. Whitney Young, Jr., executive director of the National Urban League, recalled:

He [Johnson] was not, at that point, trying to get unity as much as he was saying, 'I need your help.' And he was giving full recognition to the shock of the country [over the assassination] and the possible anxiety people might have about a Southerner being president. He wanted very much to convey that not only did we not have to worry, but he wanted to do far more than any other president.[7]

Roy Wilkins, of the NAACP, saw Johnson's pro-civil rights views as having become visible long before the new president called the White House meetings with civil rights leaders:

> Mr. Johnson began to emerge during the Kennedy administration wholly unexpectedly and to the delight of the civil rights forces in areas that we didn't expect him to be active [in] as Vice-President. For example, he took a very personal concern on the fair employment business. He . . . called all manner of people -- unions and employers [--] all over the country on the matter of increasing their employment of Negroes. Now, for a Vice-President of the United States to do this, and especially a man who knew his way around . . . Washington, this was very effective."[8]

Clarence Mitchell, Jr., Washington director of the NAACP, confirmed this view that black leaders and civil rights leaders were favorably disposed toward Johnson long before they met with him at the post assassination meetings at the White House. Mitchell was receptive to Johnson because, in the past, Johnson had been friendly to him when other Southerners had been unfriendly:

> It might be a little difficult for some people who were living in that period to understand this, but the Southern contingent in Congress was so hostile that when someone [Lyndon Johnson] came in [from the South] who was not hostile, you immediately felt that here was somebody you could respect and would like to work with, and would like to maintain their friendship.[9]

In addition to reassuring black leaders of his support for the civil rights bill, Lyndon Johnson was urged by White House staff to use the White House meetings with civil rights leaders to press for a reduction in racial protests and demonstrations. "Although a moratorium on demonstrations is probably not possible," one White House staff member wrote, "whatever the [black] leadership can do to restrain physical activities or channel energies and interest into such positive programs as educational and vocational training should be encouraged."[10] Another White House memorandum noted that President Johnson was "making a personal plea" to CORE, the Congress of Racial Equality, a civil rights group, to "work with the other groups . . . and try to coordinate . . . activities through the White House . . . ."[11]

NO COMPROMISES

If John F. Kennedy's early behavior on civil rights was a case study in a president trying to avoid a divisive domestic issue that could not be avoided, Johnson's behavior was a case study in what a president can do when he throws himself and the vast powers of his office totally into the fight. Johnson spoke out in favor of the civil rights bill at every suitable occasion -- press conferences, public speeches, messages to Congress, etc. In a memorandum summarizing civil rights activities during President Johnson's first 100 days in office, a White House staff member noted the "urgency and importance that have been given to civil rights." Under the topic of General Attitude, the memorandum emphasized that "numerous presidential speeches and informal statements have made crystal clear the president's commitment to equal treatment and opportunity for all Americans . . ."[12]

Knowing that civil rights advocates feared the civil rights bill would be compromised and watered down the way all the previous civil rights bills had, Johnson took the position that he and his administration would not compromise with the segregationist Southern Democrats in any way. "So far as this administration is concerned," Johnson told a press conference, "its position is firm."[13]   There would be no room for bargaining. Johnson would win his spurs as a pro-civil rights president by getting the Kennedy civil rights bill past the House Rules Committee, the House, the Senate Judiciary Committee, and the Senate filibuster.   Furthermore, he would get the bill through substantially intact.

Clarence Mitchell, Jr., Washington director of the NAACP, noted that President Johnson went out of his way to assure black political leaders that there would be no compromises on the civil rights bill:

> He [Johnson] was in Texas and we [civil rights leaders] were up in the White House meeting . . . on strategy in the House [of Representatives] . . . . Somebody came on the air [radio news], I think it was Roger Mudd [then with <u>CBS</u> News] or somebody.   I got the program as I was leaving the White House and turned on my car radio. This person, whoever it was, said, "Well, the president has already reached an agreement with Senator Russell that he'll get the civil rights bill through, but <u>not</u> with fair employment in it."   And I was incensed because I knew that wasn't true on the basis of the conversations we were having.   I called Roy Wilkins [of the NAACP] in New York to suggest to him that I didn't believe it was true and he said, "Well, the president just called me from Texas and said that it wasn't true."   I cite that because it shows his [Johnson's] sensitiveness and his determination at all points along the way to give reassurances on things.[14]

It was President Kennedy who had put Johnson in a position to say "no compromises" and mean it.   As previously described, one of Kennedy's final acts prior to his assassination had been to negotiate the key compromise with House Republican Leader Charles Halleck that would provide

89

Republican support for the civil rights bill in the House of Representatives. Few observers stopped to realize that Johnson was taking a "no compromises" position on a bill that had already been "compromised" for him by his predecessor.[15]

Apparently Johnson, as vice-president, knew about the compromise that Kennedy had made with the House Republican leadership and was present when one of the Republican leaders made his commitment to President Kennedy. In off the record remarks to the nation's governors meeting with Johnson at the White House immediately following the assassination, Johnson said: "A Republican leader told President Kennedy in my presence that he would help him get it [the civil rights bill] reported and help get it passed, . . ."[16]

THE DISCHARGE PETITION

Civil rights supporters had good reason to think that the administration civil rights bill would experience long delay and possibly a slow death while before the House Rules Committee. Committee Chairman Howard Smith had a way of vanishing from Washington for days on end when a bill he did not like was before the Rules Committee. In 1957 Smith disappeared to his Virginia farm because, according to him, his dairy barn had burned down. He absented himself again in 1959, claiming that his dairy cattle were sick and required his full attention. On both occasions liberals were awaiting a rule on a bill that Smith strongly opposed.[17]

On 3 December 1963 President Johnson told Democratic congressional leaders he would give full support to a discharge petition to dislodge the civil rights bill from the Rules Committee.[18] If a majority of the members of the House signed the discharge petition, the bill would move directly from the Rules Committee to the House floor.

Apparently President Johnson believed that Rules Committee action and House of Representatives action on the civil rights bill could be completed before Christmas. Immediately following the assassination of President Kennedy, he told an off the record gathering of the nation's governors: "We are hoping that we can get a rule on that bill [the civil rights bill] and get it passed [in] the House and as far along in the Senate as we can this session, and then come back in the early part of the next session and finish that."[19]

There was a strong precedent for using the discharge petition in an effort to get Chairman Smith to act. A discharge petition had been instrumental in forcing the Rules Committee to send the bill that became the Civil Rights Act of 1960 to the House floor. The petition came within 10 names of the 218 required signatures when, two days later, the Rules Committee granted a rule for debate on the bill.[20] Apparently only the "threat" of a successful discharge petition was enough to shake the bill free.

On 9 December 1963 House Judiciary Chairman Emanuel Celler officially filed a discharge petition on HR 7152, the bipartisan civil rights bill. Now that the discharge petition actually existed and could formally be signed by members of the House, President Johnson's support could be more than just verbal. Each day the new president was briefed on who had signed the petition, and "holdouts" would get a personal telephone call directly from the president himself.[21] The White House was so committed to the discharge petition that plans were made to get the assistance of prominent businessmen to lobby representatives who had not signed the petition.[22]

More than 100 representatives signed the discharge petition the first day it was available, but a considerable number resisted signing, mainly because most members of Congress believe in the committee system of reviewing legislation and are hesitant to ever bypass a committee or its chairman. There also was the problem that, upon hearing that President Johnson was going to back a discharge petition, Chairman Smith had announced that he would hold Rules Committee hearings on the civil rights bill "reasonably soon in January."[23]

Sometime in January was not good enough for the Leadership Conference on Civil Rights. According to Joseph Rauh, Jr.: "The target was the required 218 signatures [a majority of the House] by December 13th, so that the civil rights bill could be called up in the House on December 23rd and passed before year's end."[24] Rauh and Clarence Mitchell, Jr., began to put heavy pressure on various representatives to sign the discharge petition in order to get the bill on the House floor in December and not wait for Chairman Smith's "January hearings."

PARTISANSHIP AGAIN

The biggest problem with the discharge petition, however, was that it was opposed by the House Republican leadership. Halleck and McCulloch, citing their meetings at the White House with President Kennedy, argued that they had an agreement with the Democratic leadership to furnish Republican votes to clear the bill through the Rules Committee. The only reason the liberal Democrats were circulating the discharge petition, the Republicans charged, was so that they could get all the credit for getting the civil rights bill out of the Rules Committee. The Democrats, the Republicans said, wanted to prevent civil rights supporters throughout the nation from seeing that there was strong Republican support for the civil rights bill on the Rules Committee.[25]

Apparently the Republican opposition to the discharge petition came as a surprise to the Johnson White House. In a memorandum to President Johnson dated 29 November 1963, Lawrence F. O'Brien, special assistant to the president for congressional relations, suggested that the White House actively seek Republican signatures for the discharge petition. O'Brien wrote:

> [In] order to have the civil rights bill enacted, we must have . . . sixty to seventy House Republicans on the discharge petition. . . . The immediate signal is to push House Republicans generally to sign the discharge petition . . . ."[26]

Five days later, at his first congressional leadership

breakfast at the White House, President Johnson was proposing that the Republicans be asked to sign the discharge petition one-for-one with the Democrats. The president said: "Does everybody agree that you get as many signatures as you can? Then tell the Republicans they must match us man for man." Later in the breakfast, Johnson stated traditional objections to signing a discharge petition but noted the unusualness of the current situation:

> I was always reluctant to sign a discharge petition, but you have a great moral issue. People have been denied a right they should have -- a discussion in [the House of Representatives].[27]

When the Leadership Conference continued to push for signatures on the discharge petition, the Republicans struck back with a Calendar Wednesday ploy. Pointing out that the bill could be brought to the House floor and enacted in one day under the Calendar Wednesday rule, the Republicans challenged the Democrats to do just that on Wednesday, 11 December 1963. Knowing what was about to happen, the Democratic leadership moved to dispense with Calendar Wednesday on that particular day. A lively and bitter partisan debate ensued.

Republican Representative John Lindsay of New York charged that the Democrats had failed to consult "the Republicans who developed this civil rights bill" when they started circulating the discharge petition, thus endangering the "delicate bipartisan coalition" needed to get the bill passed. Democratic Representative Richard Bolling of Missouri countercharged that "Calendar Wednesday is an impractical, if not impossible way to consider the civil rights bill." Republican representatives Frank J. Becker of New York and Thomas M. Pelly of Washington then said that the Democratic leadership's insistence on a discharge petition, while opposing Calendar Wednesday, was "political demagoguery at its lowest level."[28]

Rather than let the Republicans continue to push for

bringing the bill up under the Calendar Wednesday rule, the Democrats made a motion for immediate adjournment. The motion passed by an almost straight party line vote of 214 to 166. The Republicans had achieved their goal, however. The liberal Democrats had been forced to cast a record vote against "immediate" consideration of the civil rights bill in the House of Representatives. When in the future Democrats charged that certain Republican representatives were not "really for civil rights" because they would not sign the discharge petition, the Republicans could answer back that the Democrats were not "really for civil rights" because they voted against trying Calendar Wednesday.

Clearly there was plenty of partisan politics left to be played with the "bipartisan" civil rights bill. The Calendar Wednesday fireworks in the House of Representatives were a reminder that politics is a continuing game of credit taking for your side and blame placing on the other side. If the liberal Democrats were going to try to get "one up" on the Republicans with the discharge petition, the Republicans were going to "retaliate" with Calendar Wednesday. When the debating and the voting finally ended on Wednesday, 11 December 1963, William McCulloch said, perhaps more hopefully than knowledgeably, that he "did not think the partisan sparring would endanger the bill's bipartisan support."[29]

The Leadership Conference's hopes of getting the civil rights bill on the House floor by late December were thoroughly dashed, however. By 13 December 1963 only 150 of the needed 218 signatures had been obtained, and conspicuously absent from the discharge petition were the names of such key Democrats as House Speaker John W. McCormack of Massachusetts and House Democratic Leader Carl Albert of Oklahoma. The next day, the national board of Americans for Democratic Action (ADA) lambasted the Democratic House leaders for failing to sign the discharge petition. They had, the ADA charged, "shown a callous disregard for the urgency of civil rights legislation" and "betrayed the memory of President Kennedy." The statement concluded with backhanded praise for the Republicans.

94

"Republican leadership in the House", the ADA said, "has, at least, been more candid in its admitted opposition to the discharge petition."[30]

The top Democratic House leaders had a good reason for not signing the discharge petition. They had an agreement with the Republican House leaders to vote the bill out of the Rules Committee at the appropriate time, and they were most anxious to in no way disturb that bipartisan agreement. Apparently President Johnson agreed with this strategy because the White House pressure to sign the discharge petition ceased. The House of Representatives went home for Christmas with the administration civil rights bill still firmly in the grasp of Chairman Smith and the House Rules Committee.

"ABOLISH . . . ALL RACIAL DISCRIMINATION"

The second session of the 1963-1964 Congress convened at noon on Tuesday, 7 January 1964. Both the House and the Senate met briefly on procedural matters and then adjourned to await President Johnson's State of the Union message the following evening. With its pomp and ceremony and live coverage by all three major television networks, the State of the Union address offered Lyndon Johnson an opportunity to restate to the American people his commitment to the cause of civil rights:

> Let this session of Congress be known as the session that did more for civil rights than the last hundred sessions combined. . . . As far as the writ of Federal law will run, we must abolish not some but all racial discrimination. For this is not merely an economic issue -- or a social, political or international issue. It is a moral issue -- and it must be met by the passage this session of the bill now pending in the House.

Johnson's statement was forceful. It was the first time an

95

American president had ever called for eliminating "all racial discrimination." It was also the first presidential request that it be done "as far as the writ of Federal law will run." Johnson concluded the civil rights portion of his State of the Union address with a patriotic reference to the increasing role that blacks were playing in the American military:

> Today Americans of all races stand side by side in
> Berlin and in Vietnam. They died side by side in
> Korea. Surely they can work and eat and travel
> side by side in their own country.[31]

DRESS REHEARSAL

Exactly as he promised he would, Howard Smith began Rules Committee hearings on the administration civil rights bill on 9 January 1964. It soon became clear, however, that Smith's agreement to hold hearings in no way represented a capitulation on his part where opposition to civil rights was concerned. It represented little more than a shift in tactics. Smith's intention was to make sure that the hearings dragged on for weeks and perhaps months, thus stopping House action on the civil rights bill as effectively as if hearings were not held at all.

For a while Smith's new strategy appeared to be working. A long list of Southern Democrats opposed to the bill lined up to testify against it. Although civil rights strategists endeavored to speed the hearings along by having only a few of the bill's supporters testify, Celler and McCulloch had to present the bill on behalf of the House Judiciary Committee, and this provided Smith and his fellow Southerners the opportunity to ask endless technical and constitutional questions. After seven days of these desultory hearings, only ten representatives had testified, three in favor and seven against.

The Rules Committee hearings, it soon turned out, were providing an excellent opportunity for Southern congressmen to try out their various arguments against the civil rights bill. In the same way, Celler and McCulloch presented at the committee

96

hearings the arguments which liberal supporters of the bill would use when the bill came up for formal debate on the House floor. The Rules Committee hearings thus became a "dress rehearsal" for the ideas, speeches, and ploys that would be used later when the "main performance" was presented on the floor of the House of Representatives.[32]

In presenting the administration civil rights bill to the Rules Committee, Judiciary Chairman Emanuel Celler hammered away on a theme that would be repeated over and over again on the House floor -- that the black campaign for equal rights could not be halted. "You can no more stop it than you can stop the tide," Celler said. The black American, he argued, "still wears some of the badges of slavery. . . . It is small wonder that Negro patience is at an end." Celler said he understood that the bill would be painful medicine for the white South to have to swallow. "It means changing patterns of life that have existed for a century or more. I wish it could be otherwise, but it cannot. The die is cast, the movement cannot be stayed."[33]

The major Southern Democratic arguments against the bill were "previewed" by Chairman Smith and Representative Edwin E. Willis of Louisiana. Smith charged that Celler had "railroaded" the bill through the Judiciary Committee with no opportunity for individual committee members to offer amendments. "This nefarious bill," Smith said, "is as full of booby traps as a dog is of fleas." He particularly attacked the public accommodations provisions, saying they stretched the commerce clause beyond all intention of the Constitution.

Representative Willis strongly supported Smith on the idea that the bill was unconstitutional. The civil rights bill, he said, was "the most drastic and far-reaching proposal and grab for power ever to be reported out of a committee of the Congress in the history of our Republic." Willis said the voting section of the bill was unconstitutional because it would regulate the qualifications of voters, which the Constitution leaves to the state legislatures. He argued the public accommodations section would shift the 14th Amendment of the Constitution to areas of individual discrimination, a misuse of the Amendment since it was designed to restrict only state action and not individual "custom or usage."

The Judiciary Committee's ranking Republican, William McCulloch, used the Rules Committee hearings to restate his firm conviction that House members would not be forced to cast unpopular votes to pass a strong civil rights bill and then see the bill watered down in the Senate to escape a filibuster. "I would never be a party to such a proposal," McCulloch said. "My head is still bloody from 1957 (when a House-passed Part III provision was stripped off the bill in the Senate). I feel very strongly about this."

THREE SOURCES OF PRESSURE

On 23 January 1964 House Democratic Leader Carl Albert of Oklahoma announced that the bipartisan civil rights bill would be reported out of the House Rules Committee on January 30, and that floor debate in the House of Representatives would begin the next day. When asked by news reporters about this somewhat surprising announcement, Rules Committee Chairman Howard Smith confirmed that he had reached an agreement with the House leadership to continue the Rules Committee hearings until January 30 and then to allow a vote that day to clear the bill for House action.[34]

There were many opinions as to why Chairman Smith agreed to release the bill. Joseph Rauh, Jr., of the Leadership Conference on Civil Rights, argued that the situation changed because of what happened over the Christmas recess. "Congressmen had found real support for the bill in their districts at Christmas time," Rauh stated. "Additional signatures on the discharge petition were virtually certain."[35]

A second view holds that a bipartisan group on the Rules Committee itself was ready to take an extreme course of action and hold a vote on the bill without Chairman Smith's approval. Under the committee's own rules, three members of the committee could formally request a vote on the bill and, if Chairman Smith denied the request, a majority of the committee

could meet and vote the bill out themselves. If the bipartisan group on the committee did what they said and applied this rarely used committee rule, Chairman Smith would have suffered the embarrassment of publicly losing control of his committee.[36]

A third reason cited for the release of the bill was increasing pressure placed on Chairman Smith by his longtime friend on the Rules Committee, Republican Clarence Brown of Ohio. Brown repeatedly pointed out to Smith that the Republican votes were there to vote the civil rights bill out of the Rules Committee over Smith's objections. Brown supposedly personally asked Smith to end his obstructionism.[37]

Probably for all three reasons, Smith surrendered and made his agreement with the House leadership to release the bill. His one sour comment was, "I know the facts of life around here!"[38] No one questioned that the bill would be brought to a Rules Committee vote on the date that Smith had specified. "Politicians may violate pledges made to their constituents, but they seldom break promises to one another."[39] Smith let the committee vote on 30 January 1963 and the bipartisan civil rights bill was sent to the House floor by a vote of 11 to 4.[40] All five Republicans on the Rules Committee had voted in the affirmative. John F. Kennedy's late night bipartisan agreement had, as it was designed to do, moved the civil rights bill through the Rules Committee.

RULES COMMITTEE AUTHORIZED AMENDMENTS

Before the civil rights bill finally left the Rules Committee, however, two interesting things occurred. At the same time it puts a rule on a bill governing the way it will be debated, the House Rules Committee can also authorize that certain amendments be officially offered to the bill on the House floor. By a wide margin, the Rules Committee voted down an amendment that would have created a U.S. Government resettlement commission to move blacks out of the South and find new homes for them in the North. Offered by Democratic Representative George W. Andrews of Alabama, the amendment

was an obvious attempt to make the point that most blacks lived in the South and therefore the bill would really effect only the Southern states.[41]

Of more importance, however, was a proposed amendment which failed to clear the Rules Committee by only one vote. It would have barred discrimination by sex as well as by race, color, or religion. The presentation of this amendment was truly a "dress rehearsal." The so-called "sex amendment" would make a dramatic reentrance when the civil rights bill reached the House floor.[42]

Time Magazine took a humorous approach to this early discussion of having the civil rights bill apply to sex as well as race:

> Then, taking a new tack, [Rules Committee Chairman] Smith complained that while the bill guarantees against discrimination on grounds of race, it does not forbid discrimination on grounds of sex. . . . [Judiciary Committee Chairman] Celler vowed he could not recall that sex had ever before been an issue in the civil rights bill. Remarked New York's Republican Representative Katharine St. George, the reason might be that sex was "just a dim memory" for the 75-year-old Celler.[43]

As the bipartisan bill finally left the Rules Committee, approximately 60 Southern Democratic members of the House of Representatives attended a closed-door caucus to develop an opposition strategy to the bill. Representative William M. Colmer of Mississippi was the chairman of this informal opposition group. After the meeting he told the news media that the Southerners had decided to concentrate their attack on three principal parts of the bill -- public accommodations, the Equal Employment Opportunity Commission (EEOC), and the U.S. Government funds cutoff. Colmer said the Southerners decided against delaying tactics, preferring instead to avoid

antagonizing middle-of-the-road members of the House whose support possibly could be won for key weakening amendments.[44]

CONCLUSIONS

Who won the House Rules Committee fight over the bipartisan civil rights bill? In one sense, Chairman Smith won, because the delay of the bill while it was before the Rules Committee was considerable. The bipartisan bill was reported out of the House Judiciary Committee on 20 November 1963 and did not clear the Rules Committee until 30 January 1964, exactly two months and ten days later. The unusually lengthy Rules Committee hearings orchestrated by Chairman Smith also gave the Southern Democrats a well publicized national platform on which to practice their constitutional arguments against the civil rights bill.

Was the delay before the Rules Committee really damaging to the Johnson administration and the bipartisan coalition supporting the bill? A look at the "total legislative picture" would suggest that this was not the case. It had been constantly stated that the tax cut bill should be enacted prior to the civil rights bill. All during the time the civil rights bill was tied up in the House Rules Committee, the tax cut bill was gaining final approval in the House, undergoing committee hearings and markup in the Senate, and coming up for debate, amendment, and final passage on the Senate floor. As a result, there was no particular rush about getting the civil rights bill out of the House Rules Committee and over to the Senate. Once in the Senate, it would have just had to wait for the tax cut bill.

Also, by letting Chairman Smith take his time and hold hearings on the civil rights bill, the administration and the bipartisan House leaders were protecting themselves from possible criticism for "rushing the bill through" and "cutting off the opposition before it had a chance to speak." Furthermore, the bill had cleared the Rules Committee in the appropriate manner -- it had been voted out by a majority of the committee members. By not using the discharge petition, Calendar

Wednesday, or any of the other exotic methods proposed for "blasting" the bill out of the Rules Committee, the bipartisan House leaders protected themselves from Southern charges of "ramming the bill through" in "procedurally high-handed style."

More important was the fact that the heavy vote for the bill in the Rules Committee demonstrated that the bipartisan coalition behind the bill really did exist and really could deliver the votes. The fact that every Republican on the House Rules Committee voted for the bill was impressive. Since Halleck and McCulloch had shown they could deliver the necessary Republican votes for the civil rights bill in the House Rules Committee, there now was good reason to think they could deliver the necessary Republican votes for the bill on the House floor.

CHAPTER 6

"VULTURES" IN THE GALLERIES; "MIRACLES" ON THE FLOOR

Lyndon Johnson continued to take every conceivable opportunity to increase the public awareness of civil rights. The president repeatedly linked the bipartisan civil rights bill to Abraham Lincoln and the fact that the nation had recently celebrated, in July 1963, the 100th anniversary of the Emancipation Proclamation. In response to a reporter's question about the civil rights bill at a White House press conference, Johnson said:

> I hope it is acted upon in the House before the members leave to attend Lincoln Day birthday meetings throughout the nation, because it would be a great tribute to President Lincoln to have that bill finally acted upon in the House before we go out to celebrate his birthday."[1]

At that same press conference, again in response to a reporter's question, Johnson gave what looked like a "go ahead" for some sort of women's rights amendment to be added to the bipartisan civil rights bill. The transcript of the question and answer read like this:

> REPORTER: Mr. President, Thursday in the [House] Rules Committee an amendment was offered to include women in the ban on discrimination in the civil rights bill. . . . That

was defeated by one vote and will be brought up again on the floor of the House.

In the Democratic platform it says -- and if I may read you just a few words -- "We support legislation which will guarantee to women equality of rights under the law."

Would you support an amendment to include women in the civil rights bill?

PRESIDENT JOHNSON: I supported that platform and embraced that platform, and stated that view in 43 states in the Union. I realize there has been discrimination in the employment of women, and I am doing my best to do something about it. I am hopeful that in the next month we will have made substantial advances in that field.[2]

Although the president did not say specifically that he wanted a women's rights amendment added to the civil rights bill, his answer clarified that he was a supporter of the principle of equal rights for women, particularly where equal employment opportunity was concerned. He thus left the option open for the civil rights bill to be amended to ban discrimination on the basis of sex.

STRENGTHENING AMENDMENTS?

The Leadership Conference on Civil Rights faced a tactical problem as the bipartisan civil rights bill moved to the House floor -- whether to seek strengthening amendments. Up to this point the Leadership Conference's guiding strategy had been that the best defense is a good offense, and there were plenty of strengthening amendments for which to press. The "Mrs. Murphy" loophole could be removed from the public accommodations section. Part III could be amended to permit the attorney general to initiate, not just intervene in, civil rights suits. The EEOC provision could be strengthened by permitting administrative rather than judicial enforcement of fair labor practices.

At the time the Leadership Conference was considering strengthening amendments, however, there were increasing numbers of news reports and editorial speculations that the bill was going to be dramatically weakened on the House floor, and that EEOC might be amended out of the bill entirely. At a White House meeting on 21 January 1964 President Johnson personally informed Clarence Mitchell, Jr., and Joseph Rauh, Jr., that he opposed any change in the bill, either making it stronger or making it weaker. Rauh described the effect of this meeting with President Johnson on Leadership Conference strategy:

> Recognizing the unlikelihood of strengthening amendments and the danger in adopting a different strategy on the House floor from that of the administration, the Leadership Conference modified its position to one of opposition to all weakening amendments and reserving decision on strengthening amendments."[3]

THE HOUSE DEBATE

General debate on the civil rights bill began on 31 January 1964 and provided the customary opportunities for "flowery" opening remarks. Emanuel Celler offered the following opinion about the prospective enactment of the civil rights bill:

> [It] will shine in our history. . . . It will bring happiness to 20 million of our people. . . . Civil rights must no longer be merely a beautiful conversation of sweet phrases and pretty sentiments. Civil rights must be the woof and the warp of the life of the nation.[4]

William McCulloch quickly joined Celler in giving his views on the need for the bill:

Not force or fear, . . . but the belief in the inherent equality of man induces me to support this legislation. . . . No one would suggest that the Negro receives equality of treatment and opportunity in many fields of activity today. . . . Hundreds of thousands of citizens are denied the basic right to vote. Thousands of school districts remain segregated. Decent hotel and eating accommodations frequently lie hundreds of miles apart for the Negro traveler. . . . These and many more such conditions point the way toward the need for additional legislation."

McCulloch went on to answer what he believed would be the main Southern charge against the civil rights bill -- that it went too far in terms of interfering in the daily lives of the people. "This bill is comprehensive in scope," he pointed out, "yet moderate in application. It is hedged about with effective administrative and legal safeguards."

Clarence Brown, the senior Republican on the House Rules Committee, called on his fellow representatives to avoid bitterness and acrimony as they debated the bill. He appealed to House members to "conduct this debate on so high a plane that we can at least say to our children and grandchildren, we participated in one of the great debates of modern American history and we did it as statesmen and not as quarreling individuals."

Exactly as Cellar and McCulloch were doing, the Southerners used the same arguments that had been practiced and perfected during the hearings before the House Rules Committee. Rules Committee Chairman Howard Smith once again pointed out that the bill reported out by the House Judiciary Committee had been written at the Kennedy White House and was not the bill that had been debated and amended by Judiciary Subcommittee No. 5. He said:

The only hearings that were ever held on this bill

were held, over the protest of a great many people, before the Committee on Rules. Apparently, nobody who favored this bill wanted the people to know what was in it, . . . [or what it] proposed to do for 90 percent of the people of this country whose liberties are being infringed upon. . . . What we are considering now is a . . . monstrosity of unknown origin and unknown parentage . . . .

Representative William Colmer of Mississippi attacked the great extent to which the funds cutoff provision of the bill would effect life in local communities throughout the nation. He urged House conservatives, "particularly some of my Republican brethren," to recognize this flaw in the bill:

Power would be given not only to the president and the attorney general, but more than that, given to every bureaucrat in the executive department to cut off all federal aid from your hometown, from your county, and from your state.

Later in the debate, Emanuel Celler responded to Colmer with a firm defense of the funds cutoff provision:

As a matter of simple justice, federal funds, to which taxpayers contribute, ought not to be expended to support or foster discriminatory practices. . . . The toll of the "separate but equal" principle begins at birth. In the segregated hospital, built with federal funds, the chances of survival of a Negro infant or of a Negro mother giving birth in the limited and inadequate facilities provided to their race, are significantly lower than for whites.[5]

When the Southern Democrats were not attacking the civil rights bill itself, they turned their attention to the bipartisan coalition supporting the bill. Representative Jamie L. Whitten of Mississippi noted:

> It is unfortunate that we see an agreement between the Republican leadership over here and the Democratic leadership over there to pass through this House every last bad provision that is in this bill, of which there are hundreds."[6]

Edwin Willis of Louisiana used almost unchanged the material he had presented before the House Rules Committee. Those who had been present at the Rules Committee hearings heard a second time that the bill was "the most drastic and far-reaching proposal and grab for power ever to be reported out of a committee of the Congress."[7]

THE COMMITTEE OF THE WHOLE

In accordance with normal practice in the House of Representatives, the bipartisan civil rights bill was first considered in the Committee of the Whole. This meant that the entire membership of the House sat as a committee to debate the bill and to amend it. Only two visible changes occur when the House meets as the Committee of the Whole. The mace (the medieval club, topped by an ornamental metal head, used since the Middle Ages to symbolize parliaments, universities, and city governments) is taken down from its mounting, and the speaker of the house is replaced as presiding officer by a member of his choosing.

In the early 1960s approximately 90 percent of the business of the House of Representatives was conducted in the Committee of the Whole. One reason for this was that there was a very lenient quorum rule. Instead of a majority of the House (218 members) constituting a quorum, only 100 members needed to be present at the Committee of the Whole. More importantly, however, there were no roll call votes. There were only teller votes where the representatives walked down the aisle past a

108

teller to be counted for or against an amendment to the bill. When the Committee of the Whole finished its work, the House of Representatives itself reconvened and then merely decided whether to accept or reject the bill that the Committee of the Whole had produced.

It was frequently charged that the Committee of the Whole provided members of the House of Representatives with unusual opportunities for deception. Since there were no roll call votes in the Committee of the Whole, a member could vote anonymously for amendments that greatly weakened the bill under consideration. Then, when the House reconvened, the member could cast a recorded vote for the now weakened bill and pass himself or herself off to his or her constituents as a strong supporter of the legislation in question.

THE DEMOCRATIC WHIP SYSTEM

When the House was meeting in the Committee of the Whole, some semblance of order was maintained by the Democratic and Republican party whip systems. Party whips and their assistants spread the word to party members on the floor about how the party leadership wanted them to vote. Whips and their assistants also noted which members were present for votes on key amendments and kept track of who voted for or against the party position. As the bipartisan civil rights bill was taken up in the Committee of the Whole, a serious problem developed with the normal party whip system. The Democratic whip in the House, Representative Hale Boggs of Louisiana, would have received quick retribution at the polls if he had taken any public actions in support of the bill. The result was that the regular Democratic whip system did not function during the debate on the bill. Once again, Southern Democratic power at a key point in the legislative process had to be evaded by the civil rights forces by extraordinary means.

THE DEMOCRATIC STUDY GROUP

Civil rights supporters replaced the normal Democratic whip system with an ad hoc whip system manned by the Democratic Study Group, an informal organization of activist Democratic Representatives that had been formed for the purpose of pressing for liberal legislation. The Democratic Study Group (DSG) had been organized in September 1959 in an attempt to counter the awesome power of conservative Southern Democrats in the House of Representatives. It was the logical group to take over when the Southern dominated regular Democratic whip system failed to operate on behalf of the civil rights bill. Representative Frank Thompson of New Jersey and 20 other DSG members set up and operated the ad hoc whip system.

The Leadership Conference on Civil Rights was particularly concerned about keeping control in the Committee of the Whole. According to Joseph Rauh, Jr., over 220 representatives had committed themselves to the bill "without dilution," but these commitments were of little value unless the representatives were on the floor and voting correctly.[8]

Clarence Mitchell, Jr., noted that, while the civil rights bill was being considered in the Committee of the Whole, the civil rights forces were worried about losing the votes on key amendments of both Republicans and liberal Democrats:

> It is true on the basis of our assessments that the votes were there, but you can have the votes and still not win if you don't handle it correctly. I feel there were many times -- in fact I know there were many times when we could have lost on the House floor. . . . Now you see, actually there are those who say, "Well, in the House Judiciary Committee a compromise had been worked out," which is true, and that leading Republicans, Halleck and McCulloch and the rest of them were for it, but there were many times on that floor when even Halleck, in spite of his commitment,

110

would vote for crippling amendments. . . . Now one of the things that was in jeopardy of course was the fair employment title. . . . The other was [the funds cut off]. And the trouble there was that many of the liberal Democrats were ready to sacrifice that. They were ready to sacrifice it because they felt it was better, or at least they said they felt it was better, to have government money going into things like education and public improvement, even if it is used for segregation, that to cut if off because this would mean you wouldn't have some of the things that this money permits. And we could easily have lost . . . ."[9]

Another problem when the House of Representatives was working as the Committee of the Whole was the fact that no writing or note taking was permitted in the House visitor galleries. Ushers would request anyone seen writing or note taking to either stop or else leave the gallery. If the Leadership Conference was going to keep track of the presence and the votes of the bill's supporters, it would all have to be done by memorization.

GALLERY WATCHERS-OFFICE VISITORS

The Leadership Conference worked out an elaborate system for keeping tabs on representatives supporting civil rights. As the visitor galleries opened before each session of the Committee of the Whole on the civil rights bill, numerous members of the various Leadership Conference organizations would enter and get good gallery seats. These activist organization members had been called to Washington specifically to monitor the civil rights debate in the House. Each one had a specific responsibility -- to watch a small number of representatives (4 or 5), observe their attendance, and memorize their votes on all proposed amendments. Under this system, suggested by Clarence Mitchell, Jr., of the NAACP, an effort was made to pair each "watcher" with a representative he knew personally, so that he could also call him off the floor to ask for support on important votes. Frequently, however, the gallery watchers had not previously met the representatives they were to cover.[10]

When a watcher saw that one of the representatives he was to watch was away from the floor too long, a telephone call would be placed to the Leadership Conference offices in the nearby Congressional Hotel. At the hotel, a master chart of office locations in the various House office buildings was maintained. The civil rights groups had sought out a friendly representative on each floor and arranged to have two of their members stationed at a telephone in his office. Whenever the absence from the floor of a pro-civil rights representative was reported, a telephone call would go to the civil rights workers on his office floor. Immediately, an "office visitor" would go to the office of the "truant" to urge him to be present in the House chamber.

The Leadership Conference made an extraordinary effort to fit the office visitor to the particular representative being visited. House members who had received labor union support in previous election campaigns were buttonholed by union officials. Labor lobbyists steered clear, however, of the offices of Republicans or Democrats they had opposed in past elections. In these instances the office visitor usually was from a church group or a civil rights organization. Due to the general lack of affinity between labor unions and the Republican party, most of the calling on Republicans was done by religious organizations.

Clarence Mitchell, Jr., gave the following description of the care with which the gallery watcher-office visitor system was operated:

> We had brought into Washington from the NAACP persons from all of the key states. We had asked that these NAACP people [be] individuals who were active in politics in their own party, and who knew personally the congressman . . . they would

112

talk with. We also tried to make certain that they would not be the victims of any kind of evasion. We pretty carefully schooled them in what to expect in the way of evasive answers. We had the very good fortune of getting in people who were really top-notch operators in the Republican Party. The reason I say it that way is, it's no secret that the majority of Negroes in this country are Democrats and most of the really skillful, intelligent Negroes are Democrats. So that often when you have a meeting of this kind in Washington, you get a lot of skilled Democratic operators, but no skilled Republican operators.[11]

Mitchell went on to describe the efforts of one of his Republican operators, and concluded that the civil rights forces were able to keep track of how Republicans were going to vote with "99 percent accuracy."

According to Joseph Rauh, Jr., this system of gallery watchers and office visitors began working very effectively. Full galleries let the representatives know that, though there was no record voting in the Committee of the Whole, there would be one in the minds of the watchers.[12] About halfway through the debate, some House members began to express resentment over the close control of representatives by congressional outsiders and the wholesale violation of the idea that voting in the Committee of the Whole would be anonymous.

According to Clarence Mitchell, Jr., representatives supporting the civil rights bill eventually came to the Leadership Conference and asked them to drop the gallery watcher-office visitor system. "In return for our turning off the pressure," Mitchell said, "Frank Thompson and the Democratic Study Group made a firm commitment that they, alone, would see that supporters were present and voted right."[13]

Over the course of the ten day debate on the bill, therefore, attendance and voting in the Committee of the Whole were at unusually high levels. This was particularly true of East

Coast representatives who lived close enough to Washington to go home to their districts every weekend. Known as Tuesday to Thursday congressmen," suddenly these representatives were present for Monday, Friday, and even Saturday sessions. As Joseph Rauh, Jr., put it: "When the Tuesday to Thursday eastern congressmen, even including Congressman Buckley of New York, answered present to a quorum call on a Saturday, old-timers began talking about miracles."[14]

A different view of Mitchell's gallery watcher-office visitor system came from a Southern Democrat, Representative James A. Haley of Florida. This "monstrous bill," Haley said, could not have passed without the "vultures" in the galleries.[15]

JUSTICE DEPARTMENT ROLE

Similar to when the civil rights bill was before Subcommittee No. 5 and the House Judiciary Committee, the Justice Department was close by to analyze amendments and write new legal language when needed. Deputy Attorney General Nicholas Katzenbach and Burke Marshall, head of the Civil Rights Division at the Justice Department, were in the House gallery during the debate and served as key Johnson administration contacts with the representatives backing the bill on the floor. If a crisis arose over an amendment during the debate, a signal would be made from one of the bill's managers to Katzenbach and Marshall. The Justice Department leaders, often joined by Clarence Mitchell, Jr., and Joseph Rauh, Jr., would then come down for a strategy session off the floor. At times these strategy conferences were held in the office of the speaker of the house.[16]

Meetings, meetings, and more meetings were the order of the day as debate proceeded in the House. Each day before the House convened, a basic strategy session was held in the office of Democratic Study Group leader Frank Thompson of New Jersey. Lawrence O'Brien, the president's special assistant on congressional relations, often attended these strategy meetings, as did Mitchell and Rauh. Republican members of the House

114

were specifically not included in these meetings, the liberal Democrats preferring to keep legislative strategy making completely under their control. Church group representatives also were not allowed at these meetings, but they were included in daily meetings earlier in the morning which were open to members of any group within the Leadership Conference on Civil Rights.

The Republican forces supporting the bill were led by William McCulloch of Ohio. As had been the case at the subcommittee and the committee level, McCulloch conferred mainly with Justice Department officials. According to Congressional Quarterly Weekly Report, his relationship with labor groups and civil rights groups backing the bill was "at arm's length." When the Leadership Conference needed to deal with the Republicans, they generally went to a dedicated liberal Republican like John Lindsay of New York rather than speak with McCulloch.[17]

McCulloch's most important function was to keep his close associate, House Republican Leader Charles Halleck, informed on what was happening to the bill on the House floor. Living up to the terms of the agreement struck at the Kennedy White House when the bipartisan version of the bill was first negotiated, Halleck gave his general support to McCulloch and the bill's backers. Halleck was present for very little of the debate, however, and participated in few of the teller votes.

Deputy Attorney General Nicholas Katzenbach later gave a possible explanation as to why House Republican Leader Charles Halleck absented himself from the civil rights bill debate and voting. Several times Representative Halleck had stated his firm opposition to the equal employment opportunity provisions of the civil rights bill, but somehow Katzenbach got the mistaken impression that Halleck was "on board" on the employment provisions, and Katzenbach "misled two presidents" (Kennedy and Johnson) by repeatedly assuring them that Halleck supported the bill with the equal employment opportunity provisions included. A year later Katzenbach looked at his notes and was shocked to find they said, "Halleck not on board on [employment] provision." Katzenbach concluded it was "a case of being lucky" that Halleck had continued to support the bill (albeit quietly) despite the fact that no one in either the Kennedy or the Johnson administrations had responded to his opposition to the employment opportunity section.[18]

WEAKENING AMENDMENTS

With the Leadership Conference watching so carefully from the galleries and a bipartisan agreement to support the bill in effect on the floor, the 10 days of House debate on the civil rights bill consisted mainly of weakening Southern amendments being voted down by substantial majorities. Amendment after amendment was offered. If the amendment was a weakening one, Representative Celler or Representative McCulloch would speak against it. This usually was all that was required for the supporters of the bill to know to vote the amendment down.

Occasionally Southern Democratic amendments proposed to the bill were serious in nature and, as a result, received honest consideration by the civil rights forces in control on the House floor. Representative Willis of Louisiana introduced an amendment to the provision of the bill which would cutoff U.S. Government funds to state and local government programs that practice racial discrimination. The amendment required that a government agency report to the appropriate congressional committees the intent to cut off funds at least 30 days before such a cutoff was to take place. An exchange of comments between Emanuel Celler and William McCulloch served as a cue to rank and file supporters of the civil rights bill that the amendment had the approval of the bipartisan leadership:

> MR. CELLER: Mr. Chairman, will the gentleman yield?
> MR. WILLIS: I yield to the gentleman from New York.
> MR. CELLER: The amendment is acceptable to myself and most members of the

116

Committee on the Judiciary.

MR. MCCULLOCH: Mr. Chairman, will the gentleman yield?

MR. WILLIS: I yield to the gentleman from Ohio.

MR. MCCULLOCH: I am pleased to say that the amendment is an improving amendment to this title, and I hope it will be agreed to.

The signal had been given. The debate was over. Representative Willis's amendment passed with only 21 negative votes.[19]

The Committee of the Whole proceeded through the bill title by title. First the voting rights section was approved, then public accommodations, then desegregation of public facilities, and then school desegregation. The tone of the debate was noteworthy for its respectability, politeness, and moderation. In the opinion of Joseph Rauh, Jr., of the Leadership Conference on Civil Rights, only Howard Smith of Virginia overstepped the bounds of propriety. Commenting on the fact that a chiropodist (foot doctor) in a hotel would be covered by the public accommodations section, Smith stated: "If I were cutting corns I would want to know whose feet I would have to be monkeying around with. I would want to know whether they smelled good or bad."[20]

THE BOGGS INCIDENT

Throughout the debate, there was only one incident that seriously threatened the bipartisan coalition backing the bill. On 7 February 1964 Representative Oren Harris, a Democrat from Arkansas, offered an amendment that would have seriously weakened the funds cutoff provision. The amendment would have given U.S. Government bureaucrats wide latitude in deciding whether or not to cutoff U.S. funds to specific agencies and programs practicing discrimination.

The liberal and moderate Republicans backing the bill

117

became seriously alarmed when House Democratic Whip Hale Boggs rose to support the Harris amendment. Boggs, from New Orleans, Louisiana, was simultaneously a Southerner and, as Democratic whip, a key member of the House leadership. As Boggs began lavishing extensive praise on Harris's amendment to make the funds cutoff discretionary, wary House Republicans began to suspect a Democratic plot. No Republicans had been informed that Oren Harris would offer his weakening amendment or that Democratic Whip Boggs would support it.

The situation appeared particularly sinister because most of the House Republican leaders were off the floor in a strategy session when Boggs spoke on behalf of the Harris amendment. New York Republican John Lindsay was present, however, and he quickly rose to the attack. Lindsay charged the Harris amendment would "gut" the funds cutoff provision and thus was "the biggest mousetrap that has been offered since the debate on this bill began." Lindsay added: "I am appalled that this is being supported in the well of the House by the majority whip [Boggs]. . . . Does this mean there is a cave-in on this important title."[21]

Representative McCulloch returned hastily from the Republican leadership meeting and conferred hurriedly with Emanuel Celler. He then grabbed a microphone and announced that, if the Harris amendment passed, "my individual support of this legislation will come to an end."[22] Celler quickly joined McCulloch in opposing the amendment, and it was easily rejected on a teller vote.

Later in the day Hale Boggs denied that he had been speaking for anyone but himself when he gave his strong speech in support of the Harris amendment. The House Republicans continued to voice suspicions to the press, however. They publicly theorized that this public attempt by a member of the House Democratic leadership to "gut" a key provision "might have been the first in a possible series of maneuvers to weaken the bill so that it could escape an all-out Southern filibuster in the Senate."[23]

Whatever his intentions, Boggs had given McCulloch a

golden opportunity to sternly repeat his now familiar main theme -- House Republicans would not be tricked into "walking the plank" by voting for highly controversial civil rights provisions in the House and then see these provisions "traded away" in a Northern Democratic-Southern Democratic deal in the Senate. If the Senate deleted controversial titles from the bill, McCulloch had made it crystal clear that he and other influential House Republicans would probably withdraw their support from the bill, thus jeopardizing final passage when it came back to the House for approval of Senate amendments.

EQUAL EMPLOYMENT OPPORTUNITY FOR WOMEN

The Southern Democrats opposed to civil rights mainly introduced two types of amendments during House consideration of the bill. One type of amendment, very straightforward in nature and intent, would eliminate provisions and thus substantially weaken the legislation. The second type of amendment was somewhat more subtle. At first glance, these amendments would appear to strengthen the bill by expanding its provisions. The real goal, however, was to so broaden the bill as to make effective enforcement impossible. In some cases these broadening amendments sought to destroy the bill by making it patently unconstitutional.

In line with the logic of this second type of Southern amendment, Representative John Dowdy of Texas had been offering a series of amendments which would have prohibited sex discrimination at every point where the bill prohibited race discrimination. Women's rights were not a particularly important issue in the early 1960s. The women's liberation movement would not occur in great strength until the early 1970s. Dowdy's strategy here was pure legislative politics. If he could get the word "sex" added everywhere the words "race, religion, and color" appeared, he might steal away from the bill the votes of those civil rights supporters who were opposed to equality of the sexes.

Dowdy's amendments were routinely defeated. Even

119

those civil rights loyalists who supported women's rights saw through the subterfuge and urged their colleagues to not complicate the issue of racial discrimination with the separate and different issue of sex discrimination.

On 8 February 1964 Representative Howard Smith of Virginia offered an amendment to prohibit discrimination in employment due to sex. The amendment was somewhat similar to the one which had failed by only one vote when the civil rights bill was before Smith's House Rules Committee. Chairman Smith even gave a high spirited speech in support of his amendment: "It is indisputable fact that all throughout industry women are discriminated against and that just generally speaking they do not get as high compensation for their work as do the majority sex." Smith also made a comment that suggested his feelings about both the bill and his amendment. "This bill is so imperfect, what harm will this little amendment do?"[24]

To Smith's amazement and the total surprise of Celler and McCulloch, Smith's amendment was suddenly receiving strong support from the female members of the House. Democrat Martha W. Griffiths of Michigan pointed out that black women would be protected under the employment provisions of the act but that white women would have no protection at all:

> White women will be last at the hiring gate. . . . You are going . . . to have white men in one bracket, you are going to take colored men and colored women and give them equal employment rights, and down at the bottom of the list is going to be a white woman with no rights at all. . . . A vote against this amendment today by a white man is a vote against his wife, or his widow, or his daughter, or his sister.[25]

New York Republican Katharine St. George suggested that the amendment was "simply correcting something that goes back, frankly, to the dark ages. . . . The addition of that little, terrifying word 's-e-x' will not hurt this legislation in any way." Speaking directly to her male colleagues, Representative St. George noted: "We outlast you -- we outlive you -- we nag you to death. We are entitled to this little crumb of equality."[26]

Only one woman member of the House opposed the amendment. Edith Green, a Democrat from Oregon, was a staunch civil rights supporter who did not want to take any action that might jeopardize final passage of the bill. "At the risk of being called an Aunt Jane, if not an Uncle Tom," she said, "let us not add any amendment that would get in the way of our primary objective." She added: "I do not believe this is the time or the place for this amendment."[27]

Celler, McCulloch, and even John Lindsay of New York joined Representative Green in calling the women's employment rights amendment inopportune. They were unable to offer any substantive arguments against the amendment, however, and it was subsequently approved by a standing vote of 168 to 133. A woman in the gallery jumped to her feet and shouted: "We made it! We made it! God bless America!" She was promptly ejected from the gallery by the Capitol police.[28]

Celler and McCulloch took their defeat at the hands of Representative Smith and the women of the House of Representatives with good grace. Representative Celler even added a bit of levity, pointing out that it was a bit ludicrous that two men the age of himself and Representative Smith would be arguing about sex. Celler went on to note that at home he always had the last words: "Yes, dear."[29]

Several years after enactment of the Civil Rights Act of 1964, Representative Martha Griffiths, by then one of the leading women members of the House, told an interviewer she had originally intended to sponsor the equal employment for women amendment but held off when she learned of Howard Smith's intention to introduce it. Griffiths knew that if she let Smith introduce the amendment, he would bring about 100 Southern Democratic votes with him, votes that Griffiths needed to get the amendment passed since dedicated civil rights supporters like Celler, McCulloch, and Edith Green were opposing it. Because of all the sex related jokes and the surprise when the amendment passed, the event went down in congressional history as "Ladies Day in the House."[30]

EEOC

With the equal employment for women amendment safely approved, the Committee of the Whole moved on to final approval of the entire Equal Employment Opportunity section of the bill. This was the section that the editorial writers, political columnists, and pundits had been so certain would never survive in the House of Representatives. Little damage was done, however. The House did spontaneously approve an amendment denying atheists the right to protection under EEOC, but liberals immediately marked this anti-atheism amendment for removal when the bill got over to the Senate. When the debate and voting were finally over for the day, the EEOC, the one provision that had been so strongly supported by the Leadership Conference and organized labor, was in the bill.

COMMUNITY RELATIONS SERVICE

Shortly before the final House vote was taken on the civil rights bill, Democratic Representative Robert T. Ashmore of South Carolina offered an amendment creating a Community Relations Service to help mediate racial disputes in cities and towns throughout the United States. The idea for a U.S. Government agency to mediate between black protesters and local government officials had originated with Lyndon Johnson when he was vice-president.

Apparently the Birmingham demonstrations gave several persons the idea for a Community Relations Service similar to the one which Johnson had been proposing ever since the late 1950s. A memorandum from Vice-Presidential Assistant George E. Reedy to then Vice-President Lyndon Johnson on 7 June 1963 illustrated this point:

Ramsey Clark has . . . proposals. [One is a] community relations service similar to the one that you have proposed. The amazing part of this to me is that Ramsey, on the basis of one trip to Birmingham, returned thinking precisely along the same lines that you have been thinking for a number of years -- that conciliators could perform a world of good in this situation.[31]

Representative Ashmore's amendment establishing a Community Relations Service was greeted by the now familiar Celler and McCulloch statements of acceptance and passed without significant debate.

FINAL PASSAGE IN THE HOUSE

On Monday night, 10 February 1964, the House of Representatives passed the civil rights bill by a vote of 290 to 130. The Leadership Conference on Civil Rights was elated with the results. Joseph Rauh, Jr., noted that "a bipartisan coalition [in the House] had succeeded in [passing] a far better bill than the one President Kennedy had sent to Congress eight months earlier."[32] From the Leadership Conference point of view, crippling amendment after crippling amendment had been defeated while only comparatively negligible amendments were adopted. Just as it was designed to do, the bipartisan agreement that President Kennedy had negotiated at the White House back in October of 1963 had carried the civil rights bill through both the House Rules Committee and the House of Representatives itself. Congressional Quarterly Weekly Report described the House bill as "the most sweeping civil rights measure to clear either house of Congress in the 20th Century."[33]

The Southern Democrats were disappointed by the large size of the final House vote in favor of the civil rights bill. Only 22 Republicans and 4 Democrats from outside the South joined the Southerners in voting against the bill. The South had not even been able to keep its own coalition completely together;

123

11 Southern Democrats, 4 of them from President Lyndon Johnson's home state of Texas, voted for the bill.[34]

CONCLUSIONS

Is it possible for a lobby group to be overorganized in its efforts to get legislation enacted? One could almost say that was true of the Leadership Conference on Civil Rights as it worked to get the administration civil rights bill through the House of Representatives. Not content with the idea that a bipartisan agreement among the House leadership was all that was required to get the bill enacted, Joseph Rauh, Jr., and Clarence Mitchell, Jr., added their gallery watcher-office visitor technique.

This form of personal pressure proved so intense that it eventually had to be turned off, and the Southerners began using the heavy pressure of the civil rights lobby as an argument against the bill. The "most intensive, extensive, and effective lobby assembled in Washington in many years," a Southern senator later ruefully called it.[35] The Southern Democrats were particularly angered by the large number of church men and women who participated in the lobbying effort. There was much grumbling about the "cardinals, bishops, elders, stated clerks, common preachers, priests, and rabbis [who had] come to Washington to press for passage of the bill."[36]

In contrast, there were few lobbyists of any kind on the anti-civil rights side. Virtually no clergymen came to Washington to lobby against the bill, not even Southern fundamentalist preachers who often do lobby for conservative causes. There was only one official organization working against the bill, the Coordinating Committee for Fundamental American Freedoms, a group that was specifically created by the state government of Mississippi to oppose civil rights and was financed in large measure by the Mississippi state treasury. A national newspaper advertisement taken out by the Coordinating Committee for Fundamental American Freedoms was taken seriously enough by the Johnson administration that the Department of Justice issued a charge by charge refutation.[37]

124

"VULTURES" IN THE GALLERIES

One of the most interesting things that happened during House consideration of the civil rights bill was the way in which equal employment opportunity for women was added to the bill. Rather than introduce this amendment themselves, the women in the House of Representatives shrewdly decided to support the amendment once it was presented as a weakening amendment by Howard Smith. That probably was the greatest irony of all. Rules Committee Chairman Smith, a diehard conservative opponent of civil rights, went down in history as the author of the first major provision ever passed by Congress granting equal employment opportunity to women. It is fair to speculate that, if Smith had even remotely suspected that the women members of the House would take his amendment seriously and add it to the bill, he would not have introduced it.

Even after it was adopted, the members of the House of Representatives, men and women alike, did not appear to have realized the significance of what they had done. All the mighty protections in the bill, particularly the funds cutoff provision, could now be used against employers who discriminated against women job applicants. If finally enacted into law, the EEOC provision would provide equal employment opportunity protection to approximately 20 million American blacks, but with the women's amendment added it would provide equal employment opportunity protection to over 100 million American women. Katharine St. George had labeled it "this crumb of equality." As it turned out, the amendment was anything but a "crumb."

William McCulloch of Ohio and the House Republicans emerged from the House civil rights fight in unusually strong shape for a minority party. McCulloch repeated the point over and over again that all future Senate amendments would have to be cleared with his critical band of House Republicans if the bill was to make it back through the House for final passage. McCulloch's reasoning was that the Johnson administration could not take the political risk of having no civil rights bill at all be passed, therefore the Johnson people would take McCulloch's threat seriously and would use all the influence they could muster to prevent any major weakening of the bill in the

125

Senate.[38]

The Republicans also made much of the fact that a higher percentage of Republicans than Democrats had voted for the bill at final passage. Everywhere they went, House Republicans would repeat the partisan statement: "80 percent of House Republicans voted for the civil rights bill, but only 60 percent of House Democrats supported it."[39]

The news media gave much of the credit for getting the civil rights bill through the House to President Lyndon Johnson, although Time Magazine was careful to point out that "President Kennedy had already laid the groundwork for congressional action."[40] Burke Marshall, assistant attorney general for civil rights under President Kennedy and then under President Johnson, was emphatic in his recollection that the meetings at the White House between President Kennedy and the House Republicans had guaranteed passage of the bill:

> I was sure. I had been sure even since October that it was going to go through the House, because I was just sure we had -- once we got it through in Judiciary Committee, and McCulloch and Ford and all those Republicans -- what's his name from [Indiana], Charlie Halleck -- all of these people were committed to it to President Kennedy, and I just didn't see that they could go back on it because he was dead. In fact, they'd be less apt to. And if the Republicans were that committed to it, I didn't see -- I was just sure it would go through the House as it came out of the [Judiciary] Committee, and it did.[41]

President Johnson's heavy involvement in the day-to-day efforts to get the civil rights bill through the House of Representatives actually worried some of his close advisers at the White House. The president's aides, in fact, were warning him that he might be dissipating his considerable influence over Congress with too many phone calls and elbow squeezings. "We don't want him to be one of the boys," said one aide.   "We only want to use these calls where they will have maximum impact."[42]

Ordinarily the hardworking lobbyists for the Leadership Conference on Civil Rights might have expected to have a moment of rest once the civil rights bill had been passed by the House.   Both Clarence Mitchell, Jr., and Joseph Rauh, Jr., recalled, however, that there was no rest, especially with Lyndon Johnson so intimately involved in the day-to-day work on the legislation.   The bill had just passed the House when a message came to Mitchell and Rauh to call the president.   "What are you fellows doing about the Senate," the commander in chief had said to them over the telephone.   "We've got it through the House, and now we've got the big job of getting it through the Senate!"[43]

CHAPTER 7

MIKE MANSFIELD AND HUBERT HUMPHREY; "CONDITIONING FOR THE LONG ORDEAL"

"The big job of getting it through the Senate," President Lyndon Johnson had called it. To those faced with the direct responsibility of getting the civil rights bill through the Senate, the phrase "big job" must have appeared to be an understatement. First civil rights supporters would have to bypass the Senate Judiciary Committee, which previously had refused to report out 121 consecutive civil rights bills. Then they would have to overcome the filibuster, that firmly established Senate practice that had successfully defeated or weakened those few civil rights bills that had ever made it to the Senate floor.

THE FILIBUSTER

The filibuster is a well-known activity of the United States Senate, but few average citizens of the United States understand how the filibuster actually works. To many the word filibuster symbolizes bombastic Southern senators giving never ending speeches on irrelevant subjects. Filibustering senators are often portrayed in a comic manner, held up for ridicule as they read from the Bible, or the morning newspaper, or tell long stories that, they argue, relate in some way to the bill being debated.

By the early 1960s this type of "comic" filibuster no longer occurred in the Senate. By that time senators participating in a filibuster tended to stay on the subject and only introduce materials that were directly relevant to the debate. To do otherwise would result in extensive criticism in the press for

129

wasting time and unnecessarily slowing the legislative process.

One major misconception about the filibuster is the idea that one senator alone can conduct an extended filibuster. The image here is of the lone individual staging a marathon oratorical effort day and night on the Senate floor. Seemingly unaffected by either exhaustion or the need to visit the rest room, this legendary lone filibusterer reputedly speaks in the Senate for as much as 24 hours at a time.

In reality, the lone filibusterer presents no long-term problem to the Senate. Since no one individual can remain awake and talk without relief for much more than 24 hours, the Senate membership need only wait a day or two for the single senator filibuster to come to an end.

The single senator filibuster can be effectively used, however, to dramatize an issue and get the particular senator's point of view covered in the newspapers and on television. There is also the situation that, late in the congressional session and with a majority of senators anxious to adjourn, a single senator filibuster can pose the threat of a day or two delay at a time when there is not a day or two to spare. Under such end of session conditions, a single senator filibuster can kill, delay, or significantly modify an important bill.[1]

There are two claimants to the honor of having delivered the longest Senate speech of all time. Senator Strom Thurmond, a Democrat from South Carolina, gave a 24 hour speech against the Civil Rights Act of 1957. That was the longest speech in Senate history, but Thurmond's fellow Southerners helped him by requesting quorum calls every few hours, thus permitting him to leave the Senate chamber briefly. Senator Wayne Morse, a Democrat from Oregon, gave a 23 hour speech against an offshore oil drilling bill and never once left his desk on the Senate floor, thus illustrating that he had somehow solved the major problem connected with an uninterrupted single senator filibuster.[2]

The type of filibuster that presents a major problem to the Senate occurs when a sizable group of senators unite to continuously debate a bill until it is either withdrawn or seriously weakened by amendments. By dividing up into teams, and by holding "debates" with each other which in effect are no more difficult to carry on than a pleasant conversation, they can hold the floor indefinitely. Knowing that the legislation they oppose will be enacted if it ever comes to a vote, they talk on endlessly and thereby prevent other senators from taking action on other bills until they finally give up and capitulate to the filibusterers.

The filibuster exists because of Senate Rule 19. This rule provides simply that "no senator shall interrupt another Senator in debate without his consent." That rule exists in the United States Senate because, completely separate from the issue of civil rights, a majority of senators have believed in it.

THE SENATE AS A UNIQUE INSTITUTION

Carved in marble on the west side of the New Senate Office Building are the words: "The Senate Is The Living Symbol Of Our Union Of States." This slogan, emblazoned in letters more than one foot high and stretching for over 1/2 block long, attempts to sum up the unique role which the United States Senate plays in the American democracy. The Senate was not intended by the Founding Fathers to be a popular body, subject to the will of whatever temporary majority won the last general election. The Founding Fathers, working through the instrument of the United States Constitution, insulated the Senate from the popular will in several ways.

In the first place, representation in the Senate is not based on population but is distributed equally among the several states. The major historical role of the Senate, therefore, was to protect the smaller states from being dominated by the larger states. The filibuster fits perfectly with this historical role. By banding together and filibustering a bill they oppose, small state senators have an additional weapon with which to protect their constituents from oppressive legislation favored by large states.

The Senate was further removed from the will of the popular majority by having senators serve 6 year terms of office and by having only 1/3 of the Senate elected every 2 years. The result is that the Senate is a "continuing body" that cannot be completely changed by the results of just one election. In every 2 year cycle, 1 out of every 3 senators is up for reelection, but 2 out of every 3 senators are held over without having to face the wrath of the voters. The result is a unique legislative body designed to respond mainly to long-term changes in United States politics and somewhat insulated from temporary or short-term political changes.

Senators as a group are very proud and very protective of their unique institutional role as the defenders of the interests of the small states and the legislative body most removed from the "mad passions" of the most recent congressional elections. In such an atmosphere, the filibuster does not appear to be an unusual or oppressive institution at all, but more a logical extension of the Senate's special position as the most "deliberative" of the two houses of Congress. As Professor Lindsay Rogers of Columbia University put it: "The filibuster is a weapon that the constitutional framers who constructed the Senate failed to anticipate but one that they would view with favor."[3]

The irony of the filibuster was that it was rarely used in the Senate to protect the interests of the smaller states. It was mainly used by Southern senators to prevent Northern and Western senators from passing national laws that would protect the basic civil rights of Southern blacks. Thus the filibuster, proclaimed as an instrument for the protection of minority rights, was mainly used to oppress a minority rather than protect it.

THE FILIBUSTER AT FULL FORCE AND FURY

By the early 1960s the Southern Democrats in the Senate had perfected the filibuster into a formidable instrument. Under the skillful tutelage of Georgia Senator Richard Russell, the post World War Two leader of the Southern Democrats, the 18 hard core filibusterers divided into 3 teams of 6 senators each and assigned each team to cover the Senate floor for one day. This provided each Southern senator at least 2 days rest between assignments, plus additional rest on the weekends. Even when it was a filibusterer's day on the Senate floor, the work was not very hard. Only 3 of the 6 senators had to be on the floor at any particular time, therefore each member of the team had half the day off. When on the floor itself, only 1 of the 3 senators had to be speaking, and he was helped out by the other two senators. They would periodically interrupt him with lengthy, complex questions or spontaneous thoughts that had popped into their minds as the first senator was talking.

The filibustering senators thus had a very easy time of it, a complete contrast to the popular image of the leather-lunged, near exhaustion filibusterer making an all-night stand on the Senate floor. In reality, the situation was much tougher physically on those trying to defeat the filibuster, and again the problem was a Senate rule. In order to be officially in session, the Senate must have a quorum of 51 senators present. Every 2 hours, just like clockwork, the filibustering Southerners would suggest the absence of a quorum, thereby requiring the civil rights forces to round up and rush to the floor a minimum of 51 senators.

Whereas the Southern Democrats conducting the filibuster only had to work one 1/2 day every 3rd day, the civil rights forces had to come up with a quorum of 51 senators every 2 hours. Anytime a senator opposing the filibuster wanted to go back to his home state to campaign or leave Washington to give a speech, he would have to make sure that at least 51 senators opposing the filibuster were remaining in Washington. This regimen of having to stay on Capitol Hill every day and answer a quorum call every 2 hours soon became both physically and emotionally wearing on the senators opposing the filibuster. As the weeks would go by and the filibuster did not end, the Southerners would become ever more chipper and relaxed, the anti-filibuster forces ever more harried and pale looking.

Of course nothing suited the filibustering Southerners better than for the pro-civil rights forces not to be able to make a quorum of 51 senators. Debate on the Senate floor would immediately come to an end, and the speeches the Southerners had prepared to give that day could be put away and saved for another day. Even more importantly, when the Senate fails to make a quorum, it <u>adjourns</u> rather than <u>recesses</u> until the next day. This really suited the interests of the filibusterers because, when the Senate reconvenes after an adjournment, several time-consuming formalities must take place. The <u>Congressional Record</u> for the proceeding day must be read, and the Senate must hold a "morning hour" during which senators may introduce bills and insert items of interest, such as newspaper articles from their hometown newspapers, in the <u>Congressional Record</u>. If there was a morning hour during a filibuster, the Southern Democrats always found plenty of bills to introduce and many newspaper articles to place in the <u>Congressional Record</u>, thus eating up ever more time.

A skillful team of filibustering senators will disrupt the Senate's normal routine in as many ways as possible. Procedural shortcuts in the consideration of legislation, made possible by unanimous consent of all the senators present, will be eliminated because one of the filibustering senators will automatically object. Under this situation, minor Senate business that is usually dispatched instantly, such as reading bills and bringing bills up for consideration, can take hours. Filibusterers will not permit committees to meet while the Senate is in session, with the result that legislation starts to back up on the various committee calendars. Under such hostile working conditions, the tempers of those trying to defeat the filibuster are apt to fray and their emotions start to rise. Clearly the filibuster exacts a much greater toll from those trying to break the filibuster than from those working to continue it.

During the late 1950s and the 1960s, when the Democrats had solid control of both houses of Congress, the senator most harmed by a civil rights filibuster was the Senate Democratic leader. His ability to schedule and control the conduct of the Senate disappeared. Suddenly it was the filibustering senators who were in control of what was happening on the Senate floor. Furthermore, a civil rights filibuster made it virtually impossible for the Democratic leader to avoid fragmentation of his party in the Senate. Once a civil rights filibuster began, differences between the Northern and Southern wings of the Democratic party in the Senate became more difficult to resolve. "Senators tend to assume public positions that cannot be compromised easily. Some senators simply get mad at each other. But the fact that a filibuster takes place on the Senate floor, the Democratic leader's domain, means it will be largely his responsibility to somehow bring the Senate through its time of trouble."[4]

In 1964 the Senate Democratic Leader was Mike Mansfield of Montana. There was going to be a major filibuster of the House passed bipartisan civil rights bill, and it was going to be Mansfield's problem to end the filibuster, one way or another.

ANTIDOTES FOR THE FILIBUSTER

A party leader faced with a filibuster has three alternatives if he desires further action on the bill in question: (1) concede to the substantive demands of the opponents so the filibuster stops voluntarily, (2) break the filibuster by exhausting the filibusterers, or (3) produce a 2/3 majority to apply cloture and thereby limit the debate and produce a final vote on the bill.[5]

As noted previously, option (1), conceding to the demands of the filibusterers, had been the traditional way to end a civil rights filibuster in the Senate. In both 1957 and 1960, the Democratic and Republican leaders in the Senate had removed most of the "objectionable" provisions from the two civil rights bills in order to get the Southern Democrats to stop talking. The result, of course, was laws that barely affected the institution of racial segregation in the American South.

Also as previously noted, it is a myth that option (2), exhausting the filibusterers, can be used. The filibuster exhausts those who must meet the periodic quorum calls, not those who are filibustering. "Hold their feet to the fire," shout strong proponents of the bill being filibustered as they demand round-the-clock sessions, but in reality it is their feet that will be held to the fire, and the Southerner's toes will stay "as cool as a cucumber."

Then Senate Democratic Leader Lyndon Johnson had tried round-the-clock sessions to end the 1960 civil rights bill filibuster. He succeeded only in demonstrating that a team of filibustering senators cannot be exhausted. Although Johnson had provided civil rights supporters with a wide choice of "uncomfortable places in which to nap," such as army cots, office couches, and even rundown tables in the Old Senate Office Building, the round-the-clock sessions turned out to be a comedy rather than a way to end a filibuster. The entire situation hit bottom when Republican Senator Clifford Case of New Jersey roused himself from a deep sleep in his office chair and dashed into the Senate chamber to answer a quorum call that he had only dreamed about.[6]

Option (3) for ending a filibuster, producing a 2/3 vote for cloture, presented many problems to the Democratic leadership in 1964. "The infrequency of cloture being applied on any bill, much less a civil rights bill, suggests the difficulty of this approach."[7] From 1927 to 1964 the Senate successfully invoked cloture on a filibuster only once, and that was in 1962 on a communications satellite bill that only a small number of senators were filibustering. The historical record therefore suggested that a cloture vote would not be a likely outcome of the Southern filibuster of the 1964 bipartisan civil rights bill.

If party leaders in the Senate decide to "go for cloture," they must give special attention to the group of 8 to 15 Senators who represent the difference between a simple majority for the bill and the two-thirds majority needed for cloture. Although cloture is strictly a procedural device, these 8 to 15 senators usually will demand substantive changes in the legislation as their price for votes for cloture. Notice here the direct effect which a procedural rule, cloture, comes to have on a policy outcome, civil rights. Since the filibuster cannot be stopped by cloture without the votes of this final group of senators, their bargaining leverage with the party leaders in the Senate is greatly enhanced. "A major effect, then, of any filibuster is to involve the Senate

Democratic leader far more deeply than usual in questions of substance as he struggles to accumulate the 2/3 majority required [for cloture]."[8]

The filibuster rule, therefore, puts the Senate Democratic leader in a position where he must negotiate with someone and make substantive changes in the bill to get that someone's support. If a civil rights filibuster is to end voluntarily, the Democratic leader must negotiate with the Southerners and weaken the bill to virtual impotence. If the filibuster is to end with a cloture vote, the Democratic leader must negotiate with the group of senators who will produce those 8 to 15 final votes for cloture, meeting their demands for amendments, whatever those demands may be. In 1964, as the Senate debate on the bipartisan civil rights bill began, it was clear to all concerned that the critical 8 to 15 senators were a band of conservative Republican senators, mainly from the Midwest and the Rocky Mountain West. It also was generally agreed that their leader was Everett M. Dirksen of Illinois, the Republican leader in the Senate.

As the bipartisan civil rights bill entered the Senate, strong civil rights supporters had no idea which way Democratic Leader Mansfield would choose to go. Would he negotiate a settlement with the Southern Democrats? After all, they were his fellow Democrats, and he would need their votes in the future to pass other Johnson administration bills. But the price would be very high. Reportedly equal accommodations, the funds cutoff, and equal employment opportunity would have to be stripped from the bill in order to get the Southerners to stop talking voluntarily.

Or would Mansfield choose instead to negotiate with Dirksen and his band of conservative Republicans? This meant cooperating with the opposition party, which coincidentally meant giving the opposition much of the credit for getting the civil rights bill enacted. And what sort of substantive concessions would the Republicans demand? The entire EEOC section of the bill appeared to be the most likely candidate here, but it also had to be kept in mind that Senator Dirksen said he had strong objections to the equal accommodations section, to most

137

observers the most important part of the bill.

One simple fact was clear. Senate Democratic Leader Mansfield, sooner or later, was going to have to negotiate with someone to end the filibuster. As the debate began, no one in the nation's capital could be absolutely certain of which of the two "someones", the Southerners or Dirksen, that was going to be.

MANSFIELD'S STRATEGY

As the House of Representatives was completing action on the bipartisan civil rights bill in early February 1964, two factors were pressing Senate Democratic Leader Mansfield to think in terms of cloture rather than compromise with the Southern Democrats, at least at the start. One factor was the tough line being taken by William McCulloch and the House Republicans that they would not accept major dilution of the bill in the Senate. The second factor was that President Lyndon Johnson had given a blanket endorsement to the House passed bill, repeatedly calling for the bill's adoption, without any amendments whatsoever, in the Senate.

With these two factors firmly in mind, Mansfield developed, in conjunction with President Johnson and Democratic and Republican civil rights supporters in the Senate, an elaborate strategy for surviving an extended filibuster and, if necessary, eventually achieving a 2/3 vote for cloture.

STAYING ABOVE THE FIGHT

One of the first things Mansfield decided to do was to not become overly involved in the floor debate in the Senate on the civil rights bill. Although Mansfield would officially be working for passage of the bill, he would make an effort to "stay out of the trenches" where day-to-day debate on the bill was concerned. The main reason to stay somewhat aloof from the debate was so that Mansfield would be available for negotiations. These negotiations probably would be with Senator Dirksen and the

138

conservative Republicans, but, who knew, perhaps they would be with the Southern Democrats. By staying out of heated, vituperative, pro-civil rights debates on the Senate floor, Mansfield could negotiate with either Dirksen or the Southerners without losing face or giving the appearance of abandoning strongly held positions.

If Mansfield was not going to fight for the bill on the Senate floor, who was?

NO REGULAR FLOOR MANAGER

Ordinarily a bill before the Senate or the House of Representatives has as its floor manager the chairman of the committee that considered the legislation and marked up a committee version of the bill for consideration on the Senate or House floor. Thus, when the bipartisan civil rights bill was before the House of Representatives, its floor manager was Emanuel Celler, chairman of the House Judiciary Committee.

Under regular conditions, therefore, the bipartisan civil rights bill should have been reported to the Senate floor by the Senate Judiciary Committee and the committee chairman, James Eastland of Mississippi, should have served as floor manager. As previously noted, however, it was obvious to all concerned that Eastland would neither allow the Judiciary Committee to report the bill or himself to be designated as floor manager. "The aversion of . . . Eastland . . . to assuming the job of floor manager was exceeded only by the administration's determination to keep the bill out of his hands."[9]

Senator Eastland's refusal to serve as floor manager for the civil rights bill gave Mansfield a power the Democratic leader in the Senate usually does not possess -- the power to appoint a floor manager for a critical piece of legislation coming before the Senate. Ordinarily the Democratic leader has to accept as floor manager for key administration bills whoever is chairman of the appropriate committee, and often that chairman is not very enthusiastic about the bill in question. From this perspective, Eastland's renowned negativism toward civil rights actually

139

worked to Mansfield's advantage and gave him more control over the civil rights bill than he otherwise would have enjoyed.

HUBERT HUMPHREY AS FLOOR MANAGER

Mansfield selected his Democratic Whip, Senator Hubert H. Humphrey of Minnesota, to be floor manager of the bipartisan administration civil rights bill. For many reasons, Humphrey appeared to civil rights supporters to be an excellent choice. He was a longtime and clearly identified champion of civil rights. Humphrey first come to national attention as a civil rights supporter in 1948 when he presented a strong civil rights plank at the Democratic National Convention and succeeded in getting it adopted as part of the official Democratic party platform. As a result of this and his reflex action cosponsorship of virtually every civil rights bill that had ever been presented in the Senate, Humphrey's credentials with civil rights lobby groups were impeccable.

In addition to being a well-known supporter of civil rights, Humphrey was also a well informed and realistic legislator. Since becoming Democratic whip in January 1961, Humphrey had proven very adept at floor leadership, doing well at such tasks as nose counting, stalling for time, timing amendments, switching votes, etc. If Mike Mansfield was the perfect senator to remain "above the fray" and "out of the trenches," Hubert Humphrey was the perfect senator to "jump in the trenches" and "gut fight" it out with the Southerners on a day-by-day, point by point basis.

In a memorandum which he dictated concerning his role in Senate consideration of the Civil Rights Act of 1964, Humphrey pointed out that he had been part of administration planning for the civil rights bill from the very beginning: "I recall that after the troubles in Birmingham, the president [John Kennedy] had the attorney general [Robert Kennedy] discuss with Senator Mansfield and myself, along with a few others in the Senate, the possibility of some legislation in the civil rights field."[10]

Humphrey went on to note that, from that point on, "there

were innumerable meetings. Some at the majority leader's [Mansfield's] office, some at the White House, some at the Department of Justice." At all of these meetings, and also at the regular Tuesday morning White House breakfasts which the president holds with his party leaders in Congress, Humphrey said he "fought hard . . . for a broad program of civil rights and for a strong message on the part of the president. I urged the president to take command, to be the moral leader, and recall time after time urging that his message go all the way . . . ." Humphrey one time bluntly told President Kennedy: "The leadership for civil rights has to either take place in the White House or it is going to take place on the streets."[11]

"CONDITIONING FOR THE LONG ORDEAL"

Humphrey had desperately wanted the job of floor leader for the bipartisan civil rights bill, but at the same time he recognized that taking direct responsibility for beating a Southern Democratic filibuster was an awesome task. He recalled:

> This assignment was one that I appreciated, and yet one that I realized would test me in every way. I had to make up my mind as to my mental attitude and how I would conduct myself. I can recall literally talking to myself, conditioning myself for the long ordeal. I truly did think through what I wanted to do and how I wanted to act.[12]

REPUBLICAN FLOOR LEADERSHIP

The Republican leadership in the Senate organized itself in exactly the same way the Democrats did. Everett Dirksen, the Republican leader, elected to hold himself aloof from the day-to-day floor fight with the Southern Democrats, preferring to make himself available, as Mansfield had done, for critical negotiations and compromise. Just as Mansfield had named

Democratic Whip Hubert Humphrey to floor manage the civil rights bill for the Democrats, Dirksen named his Republican whip, Senator Thomas H. Kuchel of California, to floor manage the bill for the Republicans. Following their respective appointments, Humphrey and Kuchel met every day to plan strategy and tactics for getting the bill passed, frequently issuing joint press releases and always presenting a united bipartisan front in favor of the bill.

Hubert Humphrey and Thomas Kuchel were kindred political spirits. Although Kuchel was from Anaheim, California, one of the more conservative communities in the greater Los Angeles area, he was a committed Republican liberal and a consistent civil rights supporter. Kuchel was a strong political ally of Earl Warren, a former Republican governor of California who, in 1964, was chief justice of the United States Supreme Court. Kuchel was the acknowledged leader of a small but effective group of liberal Republicans in the Senate who, like their liberal Democratic counterparts, were ready to do everything possible to get the civil rights bill enacted. Senator Kuchel's efforts on behalf of the civil rights bill were recognized and appreciated by the White House staff. One White House staff memorandum described Kuchel as "a Senate Republican who is working his heart out for us on Civil Rights."[13]

Clarence Mitchell, Jr., recalled that he and Joseph Rauh, Jr., had a part to play in the naming of Humphrey and Kuchel as bipartisan floor managers for the bill:

> Joe Rauh and I went to see President Johnson and told him that Mansfield and Dirksen were too far removed from the civil rights struggle to be effective floor managers for the bill. We lobbied Johnson strongly to have two people really committed to civil rights, Humphrey and Kuchel, do the job.[14]

Clarence Mitchell, Jr., gave the following description of working with Humphrey and Kuchel on a daily basis:

142

Senator Humphrey was the real general and his cogeneral, if that's the proper title, was Senator Kuchel of California. This was a wonderful demonstration of bipartisan cooperation. We were together every morning with Mr. Kuchel and Mr. Humphrey. . . . All during the day we were in touch, each day, about tactical matters, and at the end of the day there was never a day that Senator Humphrey was not available for a meeting. Joe Rauh and I always met with him, I guess. We may well have worn out our welcome but he never showed it.[15]

A HIGH LEVEL OF DEBATE

Humphrey decided that he would place great emphasis on maintaining a dignified debate, working hard to not let the civil rights fight in the Senate degenerate into acrimonious confrontations and wild name-calling:

I made up my mind early that I would keep my patience. I would not lose my temper and, if I could do nothing else, I would try to preserve a reasonable degree of good nature and fair play in the Senate. I had good working relationships at all times with the Southerners, even on some of the more difficult days. . . . At all times I tried to keep the Senate on an equilibrium with a high degree of respect and friendliness."[16]

GETTING ORGANIZED

Most importantly, Humphrey believed that he had to organize the pro-civil rights forces in the Senate in such a way that they could oppose a 3 to 6 month filibuster without growing tired or starting to fight among themselves. This meant that all quorum calls would have to be answered promptly with a quorum of 51 senators, all weakening amendments to the bill would have to be promptly voted down, and all Southern arguments against the bill would have to be promptly refuted on the Senate floor.

The impression had to be created that, for just as long as the Southern Democrats could keep talking against the bill and thereby maintain the filibuster, the pro-civil rights forces would be able to go on meeting quorum calls and voting down weakening Southern amendments to the bill. Only under this condition -- that it was crystal clear the pro-civil rights forces could last just as long as the Southern forces could -- would uncommitted senators stop thinking about making a compromise with the Southerners and start thinking about voting for cloture. As Humphrey's legislative assistant expressed it: "It meant, in short, generating confidence among the bill's supporters that victory was possible and fighting the normal pressures for concession and compromise that were bound to spring up once the filibuster had run for several weeks."[17]

Humphrey knew that if weakness, discouragement, or disorganization ever appeared in the pro-civil rights camp, the probability of losing the support of those senators holding the balance of power in the Senate would greatly increase. Humphrey's legislative assistant noted:

> Dirksen, in particular, could be expected to assess carefully the desire of the civil rights forces to match their stirring words in behalf of racial justice with specific deeds. His judgments on cloture and the substance of the legislation could not help but be influenced by the commitment and tenacity demonstrated by the supposed advocates of the bill.[18]

With all of the above strategies and worries firmly in mind, Humphrey and civil rights supporters of both political parties in the Senate agreed on the following plan of action:[19]

144

1. Title Captains. If the Southern Democrats could make life easier during a filibuster by dividing up the work, so could the civil rights forces. Humphrey assigned responsibility for each title of HR 7152 to a different Democratic Senator who was strongly in favor of civil rights. At the same time, Kuchel appointed a Republican captain for each title. When a particular title came up for debate during the filibuster, only the particular bipartisan title captains and their legislative staff needed to be actively working on the Senate floor. Senators assigned to a different title could retreat to their offices and get much needed office work done.

This arrangement had two main purposes. First, it relieved Humphrey and his overworked legislative staff of the burden of mastering the details of each individual section of the bill. Second, it involved a large number of civil rights senators in the task of defeating the filibuster and gave them each an important role to play. As Humphrey later explained it:

> When our senators had a chance to debate the bill, title by title, they also had an opportunity to get some press for themselves, to be known as part of the team fighting for civil rights. This was good not only for the issue itself, but also for the senators and their public relations, and they seemed to like it. It involved them also in active floor duty, in constant and sharp debate with the opposition. They became ever more committed."[20]

Clarence Mitchell, Jr., and Joseph Rauh, Jr., of the Leadership Conference on Civil Rights were both present at the meeting where the idea of individual title captains was first suggested. Mitchell recollects that he either presented the idea or strongly supported it once someone else presented it. He explained:

> If it was my idea, I got it from the Southerners. They taught me more about legislative techniques

than any other group on Capitol Hill. I had nothing but respect for Richard Russell and the other Southern Democrats as legislative technicians.[21]

2. Quorum duty lists. If the civil rights forces were going to produce a quorum of 51 senators every time the Southerners demanded a quorum call, a special whip system would have to be established. As in the House of Representatives, the regular Democratic whip system in the Senate could not function because a number of the assistant whips were Southern Democrats. The result was a bipartisan "quorum duty list." The pro-civil rights Democrats pledged to have at least 35 senators on Capitol Hill each day to answer quorum calls while Republicans promised a minimum of 15. These 50 senators plus the Southern Democrat who made the quorum call would produce the 51 senators needed for a quorum. The system recognized the fact that some senators had to be away from Washington part of the time, particularly those who were up for reelection and had opponents in spring or early summer party primaries. On any day a senator had been assigned to quorum duty, he had to find and recruit a replacement if he could not be present as scheduled.

For the Democrats, the Senate Democratic Policy Committee set up and maintained a master chart which kept track of the daily whereabouts of all pro-civil rights Democrats. The Republican Senators supporting civil rights turned down the offer to be part of this Democratic quorum operation, preferring to operate their own civil rights whip system instead. "These special arrangements had but one objective: to produce 51 senators as quickly as possible whenever a filibustering Southern Democrat 'suggested the absence of a quorum.'"[22]

3. The Civil Rights Corporal's Guard. In addition to the title captains, Humphrey arranged for a small group of pro-civil rights Senators to be on the Senate floor each day. Their job would be to monitor the floor debate and guard against any sudden parliamentary maneuvers by the Southern Democrats.

They also were to occasionally pepper the filibustering senators with questions, particularly when the Southerners made questionable statements about the nature of race relations in the South and the protection of black rights in the South. Senators were assigned to this corporal's guard on a rotating basis, the assumption being that most senators not on duty would rarely choose to spend their time on the floor and would appear only to answer quorum calls.

In addition to the corporal's guard, Humphrey planned that he himself would spend several hours each day on the Senate floor personally debating the bill. Humphrey viewed this as probably the greatest legislative debate of his political career, and, as Democratic floor manager for the civil rights bill, he wanted to be present as much as physically possible. There also probably were some political motives at work here. If Humphrey were present on the Senate floor virtually every day and confronting the filibustering Southerners face-to-face with a strong defense of the civil rights bill, the view would certainly grow in the minds of the press and the public that Humphrey was the nation's chief protagonist for civil rights. Then, if a strong civil rights bill was enacted into law, Humphrey would get a major share of the credit.

4. <u>The Civil Rights Newsletter</u>. In an effort to further the impression that the civil rights forces really were well organized this time around, Humphrey and Kuchel decided to publish a daily newsletter to be distributed to Capitol Hill offices and to the press. This mimeographed single sheet provided friendly senators with a schedule of the day's activities on the Senate floor, a list of the day's corporal's guards, rebuttals to Southern Democratic arguments against the civil rights bill, and an occasional joke or two. The newsletter apparently served its purpose. Newspaper accounts of the filibuster were soon mentioning the existence of the newsletter as proof that the civil rights forces were much better organized and much more effective than in the past.

5. <u>Daily staff meetings</u>. Humphrey held a staff meeting approximately 15 minutes before the Senate convened each day.

Kuchel attended these meetings, as did the Democratic and Republican title captains, their staff assistants, and representatives of the Justice Department. Two mornings a week Clarence Mitchell, Jr., and Joseph Rauh, Jr., of the Leadership Conference on Civil Rights were allowed to attend. The purpose of the meetings was to keep the various leaders in close touch with what was going on and to debate the various tactics and strategies which could be adopted in order to get the civil rights bill through the Senate.

WHEAT AND COTTON

The record of these meetings in Humphrey's office, as well as other meetings that were being held at the same time, indicates that the civil rights supporters had many strategic options available to them and that which option to choose was often hotly debated. One of the first issues to cause dissension within the civil rights group was the administration's wheat and cotton bill.

President Lyndon Johnson had very skillfully arranged for the Senate to pass every piece of legislation he considered critical before the civil rights filibuster began. Thus the Kennedy tax cut bill had been moved out of the Senate before the civil rights bill came over from the House of Representatives. Joseph Rauh, Jr., explained the Johnson strategy:

> President Johnson had made it clear . . . that he would not care if the Senate did not do another thing for three months until the civil rights bill was enacted. This removed the filibusterer's greatest weapon -- that they could hold out until other needed legislation required the Senate to put aside the civil rights bill.[23]

In an off the record conversation with Clarence Mitchell, Jr., concerning the Southerners and their filibuster, President Johnson simply said, "Let them talk until summer."[24]

148

Still pending in the Senate, however, was an omnibus agricultural bill that would have provided market subsidies and other benefits to wheat and cotton farmers. Since cotton was the principal agricultural product in the South, several civil rights supporters argued that making the wheat and cotton bill wait until after the civil rights filibuster was concluded would put pressure on the Southerners to end the civil rights debate fairly rapidly.

The White House staff was particularly concerned that the wheat and cotton bill not be passed prior to the civil rights filibuster. A memorandum summarized the logic:

> It seems to me that if we permit . . . [the] cotton-wheat legislation ploy, we are taking away a really fine inducement to counteract a filibuster. Nothing speaks louder to Southern senators than cotton and wheat. If this legislation is passed before the civil rights bill is disposed of, the Southerners will have behind them the tremendous pressure which undoubtedly will build up for congressional action with each passing day of the filibuster.[25]

Other supporters of the civil rights bill pointed out, however, that preserving racial segregation was so much more important to Southerners than cotton farming that holding up the wheat and cotton bill would have virtually no effect at all on the civil rights filibuster. One of those holding to this point of view was Hubert Humphrey, who led the fight to clear the wheat and cotton bill out of the Senate before the civil rights filibuster began. Humphrey was from Minnesota, one of the largest wheat states in the nation, and he carefully pointed out that many of the Midwestern Republicans who they wanted to vote for cloture were also from large wheat states. Humphrey noted:

> I insisted [on taking up the wheat and cotton bill] because I felt there would be serious economic

149

consequences if we failed to take such action. The
president, however, was very adamant about taking
up civil rights, and so was Mansfield. However,
I pleaded the case for the cotton and wheat bill
over at the White House and finally was joined by
Mansfield, providing that the bill would not take
too long.[26]

Liberal Republicans supporting civil rights made
Humphrey and Mansfield "pay the price" for taking up wheat
and cotton prior to the civil rights bill. Senators Javits and
Keating of New York took to the Senate floor to chide the
Democratic leaders for missing the chance to pressure the
Southerners by holding up the cotton bill.[27] Republican Senator
Hugh Scott of Pennsylvania put the issue even more bluntly
when, at a civil rights rally in Philadelphia, he charged that
Humphrey and Mansfield were putting "cotton before people."[28]

CONCLUSIONS

The filibuster was a formidable obstacle. As Senator
Humphrey so plaintively noted, one needed to think long and
hard before setting out to defeat one. In many ways, getting
"psyched up" for the long ordeal was the most important part of
the process.

Shortly after the House of Representatives passed the
bipartisan civil rights bill, Senator Mansfield addressed the Senate
on the subject of civil rights and the tense legislative battle that
lay ahead:

Let me say at the outset that I should have
preferred it had the civil rights issue been resolved
before my time as a senator. . . . The senator
from Montana has no lust for conflict in
connection with this matter; yet this matter is one
which invites conflict, for it divides deeply. . . .
[But] the time is now. The crossroads is

150

here in the Senate.[29]

The Senate Democratic leader went on to say that he would not attempt to use obscure legislative rules or smooth parliamentary tricks to defeat the expected filibuster of the civil rights bill. Referring to himself, he said:

> The majority leader has no suave parliamentary tactics by which to bring legislation to a vote. He is no expert on the rules, and he is fully aware that there are many tactics which can forestall a vote. . . .
> Even if there were parliamentary tricks or tactics, the majority leader would not be inclined to employ them. I can think of nothing better designed to bring this institution into public disrepute and derision than a test of this profound and tragic issue by an exercise in parliamentary pyrotechnics.

Mansfield then called upon the Senate to stop arguing over rules and to begin dealing with civil rights as an issue. He concluded:

> For the truth is that we will not find in the Senate rule book even the semblance of an answer to the burning questions which now confront the nation and, hence, this Senate.
> We senators would be well advised to search, not in the Senate rule book, but in the Golden Rule for the semblance of an adequate answer . . . .

CHAPTER 8

RICHARD RUSSELL;
THE DEFENDING CHAMPION

The Southern Democrats opposed to the civil rights bill had little of importance to do before the bill reached the United States Senate. The Southern forces were clearly outnumbered in the House of Representatives, and even Howard Smith's House Rules Committee had only been able to slow the bill's progress rather than stop it. In the Senate, however, the strategic situation was completely different. As a result of the Senate rules and the "extended debate" which they permitted, the Southern Democrats in the Senate had a powerful weapon -- the filibuster -- with which to oppose the bill.

The leader of the Southern Democratic forces in the Senate was Richard Russell of Georgia. On his shoulders now fell the responsibility of stopping the civil rights bill, or at least amending it in such a way that it no longer threatened the white South and its traditional institution of racial segregation. A review of Russell's life and Senate career indicated that he was an unusually well qualified man for the job.

A TRUE SON OF THE SOUTH

Richard Brevard Russell, Jr., was born in 1897 in the small northern Georgia town of Winder. Located approximately 40 miles northeast of Atlanta, Winder was on the northern edge of the "black belt," a group of counties that contained most of Georgia's rural black population. Winder existed to serve the farms nearby, many of them less than fifty acres and farmed by

153

tenants or sharecroppers.

Russell's father, Richard Russell, Sr., practiced law and was active in Georgia politics. He became chief justice of the Georgia Supreme Court in 1922 and served in that office for the remainder of his life. Richard Russell, Jr., grew up on his father lands just outside of Winder. The Russell family owned several hundred acres of farmland and employed a number of sharecropping families.

Richard Russell, Jr., received a Bachelor of Laws degree from the University of Georgia in 1918. He served in the Naval Reserve during World War I, guarding a coastal battery. He returned to Winder and in 1920, at the age of 23, was elected to the Georgia House of Representatives. He became speaker of the Georgia House in 1927 and, in 1930, was elected governor. He was the youngest Georgian to ever sit in the governor's chair.

In 1932, when Russell was a relatively young 35, one of Georgia's two U.S. senators, William J. Harris, died. Russell was elected to serve out the remaining four years of Harris's term. By the spring of 1964, therefore, when the bipartisan administration civil rights bill arrived on the Senate floor, Russell had been in the U.S. Senate for more than 31 years.

Russell found a home in the U.S. Senate, a legislative body that revered tradition and custom as much as the South did. It was rumored that, upon arriving in the Senate, Russell memorized the Senate rulebook. Whether or not the rumor was true, the existence of the rumor symbolized the fact that Russell had solidly mastered the intricacies of parliamentary maneuvering. A lifelong bachelor, Russell worked long hours at the Capitol, devoting his life to attending committee meetings, serving the needs of his constituents, and, it was said, reading the Congressional Record every day the Congress was in session.

In 1936, when Russell's four year term in the senate neared its end, he was challenged for reelection by Eugene Talmadge, who had succeeded Russell as governor of Georgia. When Talmadge charged that Russell was supporting U.S. Government programs that forced "social equality" among the races, Russell had no choice but to firmly state his belief in white supremacy. "As one who was born and reared in the atmosphere of the Old South," Russell replied, "with six generations of my forebears now resting beneath Southern soil, I am willing to go as far and make as great a sacrifice to preserve and insure white supremacy in the social, economic, and political life of our state as any man who lives within her borders."[1]

The Russell-Talmadge battle for Russell's Senate seat was hard fought. When Talmadge attempted to get votes by charging that Southern white women had "associated" with blacks at the Democratic National Convention in Philadelphia, Russell responded with a strong statement of his belief in white supremacy coupled with the charge that Talmadge was stirring up racial prejudice for political purposes. "This is a white man's country, yes, and we are going to keep it that way," Russell said. Later, however, he noted that Talmadge was "doing what every candidate who is about to be beaten does -- he comes in crying nigger."[2]

When the votes were counted, Russell, with his somewhat more dignified approach to the race issue in Georgia, easily defeated Talmadge. It was the last serious challenge Russell ever faced for his Senate seat. He thus began to accumulate the untouchable political power of a veteran Southern senator. As a student of Russell's political career noted:

> In one way he was fortunate, since he was secure to direct his energies and emerging talents to fight the last battles against the modernization of the South over civil rights. On the other hand, he was unfortunate since he never had to continue the process of political reeducation every politician faces in each election year.[3]

RUSSELL IN THE SENATE

Richard Russell participated in his first filibuster of a civil rights bill in 1935. He and his fellow Southern senators easily

155

stopped an anti-lynching bill with 6 days of nonstop talking. When a similar bill came before the Senate in 1938, a 6 week filibuster by the Southerners was required to stop it. Russell was critical of lynchings, mainly because they disrupted the settled life of the South and disregarded the rule of law. He filibustered against the 2 anti-lynching bills, however, because he believed it was important to defend the principle that the United States Government should not interfere in the internal affairs of the Southern states.

Russell proved to be a skillful practitioner of the filibuster and an apt student of the Senate rules that make it possible. The leader of the Southerners at that time, Tom Connally of Texas, named Russell his second-in-command and had him organize filibuster strategy meetings. Similar to his behavior in his electoral campaigns in Georgia, Russell refrained in the senate from giving the harsh racial speeches characteristic of many deep South senators.

By the end of World War II, Richard Russell was the acknowledged leader of the Southern bloc in the U.S. Senate. No longer a student and helpful aide, Russell was in firm command of the Southern forces. When a fair employment practices (FEPC) bill reached the Senate floor in 1946, Russell altered the Southerner's filibuster strategy. Instead of giving long and unrelated speeches in the Senate on any subject that came to mind, the Russell led Southerners debated the fair employment bill on its merits. The provisions of the bill were attacked with relevant and reasonable arguments, and the filibusterers rarely if ever strayed from the subject matter of the bill.

Russell proved very able at keeping the Southern bloc in the Senate well organized. He became skilled in defending against parliamentary maneuvers on the part of the opposition, and he worked to set a high tone of debate for the Southern defense. No longer could social pundits and comedians make jokes about the irrelevant subjects discussed by Southern senators during a filibuster. Russell strove, with some success, to make the filibuster a more respectable parliamentary tool.

Russell faced a crucial career decision in 1951. Both the

Senate Democratic leader and the Senate Democratic whip had been defeated in the November 1950 general elections. Russell probably could have been elected Democratic leader in the Senate if he had sought the job. If he became part of the Democratic leadership in the Senate, however, he would have to take a "national" approach on the civil rights issue rather than remain a staunch defender of Southern racial segregation. Russell was unwilling to do this. He decided his role of being the Southern leader in opposing civil rights was more important than being Senate Democratic leader.[4]

Once he had decided not to seek the post of Senate Democratic leader himself, Richard Russell threw his support to a young Southern colleague, Senator Lyndon B. Johnson of Texas. The two men became close friends and allies in the Senate. Russell often spent his Sunday mornings at Johnson's home, and Johnson's daughters affectionately referred to Russell as "Uncle Dick." It was Lyndon Johnson, however, and not Richard Russell, who became a party leader in the Senate and thus began the process of moderating his views on race relations. As Senate Democratic leader, Johnson became a supporter of compromise on civil rights issues. Later, when he became president, Johnson evolved into a strong supporter of civil rights. Because Russell declined to become part of his political party's leadership in the Senate, Russell never had to change his views. He remained strongly committed to the twin Southern values of white supremacy and racial segregation.

Russell and Lyndon Johnson remained the closest of friends, but they opposed each other when civil rights bills would come before the Senate during the period that Johnson was Democratic leader. One time Johnson was trying to defeat a Southern filibuster with round-the-clock Senate sessions. It was late at night, and although he had a group of pro-civil rights senators guarding the floor, Johnson became worried that Russell might be about to pull a parliamentary trick or two. Johnson dressed and went down to the Senate chamber. He pushed open a swinging door to see what was going on. He could hear the Southerners speaking; he could see that his pro-civil rights colleagues were dutifully listening. He also could see that the swinging door at the other end of the Senate was pushed open, and Richard Russell was standing there. Russell had come down to make certain that Johnson did not try anything.[5]

Russell saw the filibuster as a genuine asset to the legislative process in the U.S. Congress. The filibuster enabled him and his Southern colleagues to delay any legislative proposal long enough for a number of senators from outside the South to come to see the flawed character of the particular proposal. Most of these converts to the Southern cause would be conservative Republicans, a group of senators who shared Southern concerns for states' rights and protecting the individual from strict government regulation.

Thus, as the bipartisan civil rights bill arrived in the Senate in the spring of 1964, Richard B. Russell, Jr., the senior senator from Georgia, could be characterized as "the defending champion." Since becoming the leader of the Southern bloc in the Senate during World War II, he and his colleagues had never lost a civil rights battle in the Senate. With Russell at the helm, the filibuster had become more respectable, and the Southerners had progressively improved their filibustering techniques. With his 30 years experience in the Senate and his firm ideological commitment to racial segregation, Russell was going to be a hard man to beat.

THE SOUTHERN IDEOLOGY

Throughout his years in the United States Senate, Richard Russell worked to clarify and justify the Southern point of view on race relations. Although Russell had no dislike for blacks personally, he was a staunch supporter of a hierarchical view of Southern society. Blacks were at the bottom of the society, whites were above them, and the white elite ruled over all. There was room for individual advancement for blacks, but only so long as black advancement did not disturb white control of the society. Russell believed that blacks were inferior to whites, both biologically and socially, and therefore blacks needed white guidance and control in order to survive and prosper. "He believed that blacks out of the control of whites would destroy Southern civilization as he knew it," and he fought all efforts to weaken the system of white supremacy that kept Southern blacks under strict white control.[6]

Over the years, Russell developed a standard response to any civil rights proposal that came up for debate in the U.S. Senate. He would begin by explaining how brave Southern soldiers had fought the Civil War to preserve the Southern way of life. He would describe the path of destruction across his home state of Georgia left by General Sherman's march to the sea. Defeated on the battlefield, the South was subjected to the tyranny of Northern Reconstruction. Fortunately, once Union troops were removed, the doctrine of white supremacy restored order to race relations in the South. That racial order had functioned well and remained undisturbed until outsiders, primarily communists and Northern liberals, attempted to come into the South and impose social change. It was the efforts of these outside groups, and not the doctrine of white supremacy, that was the main cause of racial discord in the South.[7]

Russell therefore portrayed himself as fighting for a way of life that he loved and cherished. He believed he was fighting to sustain social institutions which both the white man and the black man approved as being essential to harmony in racial relations in the South. "We will resist to the bitter end," Russell once told the Senate, "any measure or any movement which would have a tendency to bring about social equality and intermingling and amalgamation of the races in our [Southern] states."[8]

As the years went by and the doctrine of white supremacy came under increasing attack, Russell toned down his arguments that the white race was superior. He began to portray racial segregation as benefitting both races. Along with the other Southern senators, he began to oppose civil rights bills, at least publicly, on constitutional issues and states' rights issues rather than by defending white supremacy as a concept.

Yet the doctrine of white supremacy, and the strict racial

159

segregation that went with it, remained at the core of Russell's opposition to all civil rights bills. Richard Russell, after all, was the product of the South's plantation culture, a culture which still partly survived in the tenant farmers and sharecroppers of Russell's Winder, Georgia, home. In the minds and hearts of many of Russell's fellow Southerners, both rich and poor, it was this Southern culture that really mattered in life. This culture "forbade the slightest compromise with the 'evil' of social equality. For Russell and many of his contemporaries, white supremacy was more than a system of beliefs; it was vital to their identity as a society."[9]

THE SOUTHERN CRITIQUE OF THE BILL

When the bipartisan civil rights bill came before the Senate in March 1964, Russell and his Southern colleagues based most of their opposition on the idea that the bill was unconstitutional. The bill represented, they said, an unwarranted invasion by the United States Government of the property rights of those Americans who owned restaurants, motels, and swimming pools and who ought to be allowed to serve whomever they pleased. Exactly as there was a freedom not to buy at a particular store or restaurant, there was a freedom not to sell a commodity to a particular customer or a particular group of customers. There is a "natural right to discriminate," the Southerners concluded, and this right was just as important as the more traditional rights of life, liberty, and the pursuit of happiness.[10]

A second major Southern criticism of the bill was that it gave the United States Government too much power to interfere in state and local affairs. The bill, it was argued, would create a "Federal blackjack" under which U.S. Government officials could come into any community in the country and override the wishes of the local politicians and the local citizenry. Because the United States Constitution provided for a "territorial" separation of powers between the national and state governments, giving the national government the power to dictate racial policies to the states violated this territorial separation of powers and thus was unconstitutional.[11]

The Southerners also argued that basing the public accommodations section of the civil rights bill on the commerce clause of the Constitution was a complete misinterpretation of what the Founding Fathers had in mind when they put the commerce clause in the Constitution. The Founders were only thinking of goods moving in interstate commerce, this argument stated, and defining people driving down highways and stopping at restaurants and motels as articles of commerce was simply pushing the commerce clause much further than it was ever intended to go.[12]

It also was frequently hinted by the Southerners that the civil rights bill was mainly the result of "illegal" civil rights demonstrations, primarily those held in the South under the direction of Martin Luther King, Jr. Rather than rewarding these illegal demonstrations with legislation, the Southerners implied, the Congress should encourage local authorities to punish the demonstrators with sterner police measures and longer jail sentences.[13]

Last, but in many ways most important, the Southern Democrats repeatedly made the point that, once the American people learned about the many constitutional violations that were included in the civil rights bill, they would turn strongly against it. At one stage of the debate Senator Russell put the argument this way:

> I do not hesitate to predict that there will come a time when some of those . . . who are deceiving the American people with cries of "civil rights" so that they will not understand what is in the bill, will have an opportunity to explain to a number of outraged constituents the reasons that prompted this action.[14]

Russell was stating more than an argument here. In fact, he was explaining the entire philosophy of the filibuster. The

Southern Democrats' basic rationale for the extended Senate debate on the bipartisan civil rights bill was that time was needed to allow the American public to become fully informed about the actual effect of the bill and to register the negative opinion which, the Southerners believed, such knowledge would naturally create.[15]

THE SOUTHERN LEGISLATIVE STRATEGY

Early in March 1964 Richard Russell gathered the Southern senators together for the first of many strategy conferences on how best to oppose the civil rights bill. After the meeting ended, Russell told the press that the he and the Southerners "intend to fight this bill with all the vigor at our command."[16] What Russell was really saying was that the Southerners were ready to tie up the Senate for weeks and weeks with "extended debate" until the civil rights forces were ready to make major concessions.

Russell's strategy was that, as the Southern filibuster continued over a long period of time, public sentiment would rise against the civil rights bill. Russell believed that the increasing violence and the confrontational character of the continuing racial demonstrations throughout the nation would soon produce an anti-civil rights reaction in the American people. He also hoped the proponents of the legislation, an uneasy coalition of liberal Democrats and moderate Republicans in the Congress, soon would begin fighting among themselves. There also was the possibility that church and civil rights groups, in their all-out drive for votes for cloture, might overpressure uncommitted senators and "turn them off."

Russell possibly could benefit from the frequent statements by Ohio Representative William McCulloch and other pro-civil rights Republicans in the House of Representatives that they would not accept major amendments to the bill while it was before the Senate. If Russell could keep the filibuster going long enough to gain some major Senate amendments to the bill, such as eliminating the funds cutoff or the equal employment opportunity provisions, then possibly McCulloch and his band of House Republicans would drop their support of the bill. Stalled by a serious disagreement between the Senate and the House, the bill might ultimately die a quiet death.

There also was the external political situation to consider. The year 1964 was a presidential year. Both Democratic and Republican presidential primary elections would be taking place. Certainly the civil rights bill would become an issue in the presidential nominating campaigns in both parties, some candidates committed to the bill and other candidates strongly opposed to it. Who could say what effect the campaign would have on public attitudes toward the civil rights bill? It certainly made sense to keep the filibuster going long enough to find out. If necessary, Russell might be able to keep the filibuster going until the Republican and Democratic national nominating conventions in the summer of 1964. Who knew what might occur at those two nationally publicized political events? Something might happen to damage the civil rights movement, which would have the effect of weakening the chances of getting cloture on the civil rights bill.

It also was important to keep in mind that the arithmetic was all working in Russell's favor. He had 18 Southern Democratic senators filibustering. Also on the filibuster team was John Tower, the Republican senator from Texas. That totaled 19 certain votes against cloture. Russell only needed 1/3 of the Senate, 34 votes, to defeat a cloture vote. If he could convince only 15 more senators, probably conservative Republicans and conservative Mountain West Democrats, to not vote for cloture, he could continue the filibuster indefinitely.

Russell and his Southern colleagues thus appeared to have much in their favor as the filibuster of the bipartisan civil rights bill began. Based on the experience of the past, civil rights supporters would not be able to get the necessary 2/3 vote for cloture and would, in the end, come to Russell to "make a deal." The result would be a severely weakened civil rights bill. If the pro-civil rights drive for cloture really bogged down, the end result might be no civil rights bill at all.

MAINTAINING THE SOUTHERN COALITION

Exactly as Senator Humphrey would have to keep the pro-civil rights senators organized and cooperating, Russell would have to keep the filibustering Southerners working together. The Southern senators were unanimous in their opposition to the civil rights bill, but there were varying degrees of anti-civil rights commitment. Some of the Southern senators could be characterized as moderates. They would be willing to end the filibuster in return for major amendments to the civil rights bill. Others, such as Strom Thurmond of South Carolina, might oppose any compromise whatsoever and urge that the Southerners fight the civil rights bill to the bitter end. Similar to any party leader in a legislative setting, Russell would have to adjust his strategy and tactics to meet the needs and demands of his closest colleagues and supporters.

Russell took advantage of every opportunity to state the Southern position on the civil rights bill. In a letter to a constituent, he expressed his concern about the U.S. Government forcing the integration of the races:

> I believe that the Negro is entitled to equal and exact justice before the law and that he is entitled to every right that I enjoy. There is nothing in our Constitution . . . , however, that says we must enjoy these rights together at the same time and in the same place. . . . I cannot believe that anyone who supports this iniquitous legislation has any real understanding of the extent to which it destroys the Constitution . . .[17]

He developed this idea further in a subsequent letter:

> The legislation now before the Congress is so drastic that I cannot support it. I do not believe that Federal compulsion can be properly employed under our Constitution to compel one group to

share its rights with another at the same time and in the same place against its will. This is, in my opinion, an unconstitutional infringement upon one's right to choose his associates . . .[18]

Russell repeatedly argued that no bill had ever been submitted to the American Congress that posed a greater threat to the American form of government. In place of a government of laws, Russell contended, the civil rights bill threatened to substitute a government of men -- men clothed with an official title but operating without the restraint of law. "The American people," Russell concluded, were "completely unaware of what they are doing to themselves and their own rights as American citizens."[19]

Similar to Russell, Strom Thurmond of South Carolina was a well-known spokesman for the Southern opponents of the civil rights bill. "It is my firm conviction that every weapon available in the legislative book of procedures should be employed to kill these obnoxious proposals," Thurmond told his constituents in a televised statement when the civil rights bill was first introduced in Congress.[20] Thurmond was particularly concerned about the problem of the U.S. Government interfering in social relationships. In a constituent newsletter he noted:

Even many who favor integration indicate in correspondence to me that they oppose this legislation because it would give unprecedented power to Washington bureaucrats to try to force changes in human attitudes on the selection of associates, both in private as well as in public life.[21]

Senator Thurmond expressed his views in opposition to civil rights so forcefully that one senator once said of him: "Just listen to 'ole Strom. He really believes all that stuff."[22]

In a radio broadcast early in the struggle over the civil rights bill, Thurmond quoted a Supreme Court opinion that ably summed up his viewpoint and the general Southern viewpoint on racial integration:

> Freedom of the individual to choose his associates or his neighbors; to use and dispose of his property as he sees fit; to be irrational, arbitrary, capricious, even unjust in his personal relations are things all entitled to a large measure of protection from government interference.[23]

CONCLUSIONS

As Senate debate on the civil rights bill began, Richard Russell was aware that he was in for one of the toughest battles of his long and, heretofore, successful career. His longtime friend from the Senate, Lyndon B. Johnson, was president, but Johnson now was committed to civil rights and, on this issue, a skilled opponent of Russell. Russell also faced a well organized bipartisan coalition of civil rights supporters.

Senator Russell could see exploitable weak spots in his opponents' armor, however, and he meant to exploit those weak spots to the very best of his ability.[24] During his time as Southern leader, Russell had defended the white South successfully every time a civil rights bill had come before the Senate. Many believed he would successfully defend the white South this time also.

CHAPTER 9

FILIBUSTER #1;
THE MOTION TO CONSIDER

On 17 February 1964, one week after the bipartisan administration civil rights bill passed the House of Representatives, Senate Democratic Leader Mike Mansfield of Montana was standing on the Senate floor, quietly and patiently waiting. Through the door and down the aisle came a clerk from the House of Representatives, carefully carrying the House approved civil rights bill from the House to the Senate.

Ordinarily the House clerk would have quietly handed the bill to the Senate clerk. Then the Senate clerk would have routinely read the title of the bill, seen that it concerned civil rights, and sent the bill to the Senate Judiciary Committee.

But routine was not what Mike Mansfield had in mind for this particular day in the Senate.

The Constitution provides for the vice-president of the United States to serve as president of the Senate, therefore senators traditionally address the chair as "Mr. President." In actual practice, the vice-president sits as president of the Senate only on rare occasions. During most sessions a junior senator from the majority party (the Democratic Party in 1963-1964) sits in the "president's" chair and performs the routine task of recognizing senators who wish to speak.

Therefore, when Democratic Leader Mansfield wanted to speak to the Senate, he addressed the junior senator in the chair with the customary title of "Mr. President."

"Mr. President," said the Democratic leader, "I request that House bill 7152 be read the first time." The Senate clerk quickly read the bill's title. "Mr. President," Mansfield then said, "I object to the second reading of the bill today."[1]

With these two sentences, Mansfield took the first step in an elaborate three-step parliamentary maneuver aimed at bypassing the Senate Judiciary Committee and its chairman, Senator James Oliver Eastland of Mississippi.

By objecting to the second reading of the House passed civil rights bill, Mansfield had stopped the bill at the presiding officer's desk. In effect, the Democratic leader had taken the bill under his own direct control. He next announced that the Senate would take up the administration farm bill (wheat and cotton) and then would take up the civil rights bill, probably getting to civil rights about the first week in March.

Mansfield then gave his fellow senators and the press and public a preview of exactly how he planned to handle the obstructionism of Senator Eastland:

> Mr. President, in the near future, the leadership will propose to the Senate that this measure be placed on the calendar without referral to committee, and that, subsequently, the Senate as a body proceed to its consideration.

Mansfield carefully explained to the Senate that he was treading a familiar path, and that everyone knew the reason why the civil rights bill could not be forwarded to the Judiciary Committee for public hearings and committee mark up. "The procedures which the leadership will follow are not usual," Mansfield noted, "but neither are they unprecedented. And the reasons for unusual procedures are too well known to require elaboration."[2]

BYPASS OR REFER WITH INSTRUCTIONS

Over the following three weeks, which was the period of time required for the Senate to finish the wheat and cotton bill, a serious strategy argument broke out among the liberal senators

168

supporting the civil rights bill. Should the civil rights bill bypass the Senate Judiciary Committee completely, or should the bill be referred to the Judiciary Committee with instructions to report it back, <u>unamended</u>, after a specified period of time?

Senator Wayne Morse of Oregon, a strong civil rights supporter, was the principal advocate of referring the bill to committee with strict instructions to report the bill back unchanged. Morse argued that every single sentence of the bill would be litigated. He believed that committee hearings and a committee report would give the courts much needed information about the intent of Congress, information which would be essential when, as inevitably would happen, the courts were called upon to find various parts of the civil rights bill constitutional. The Senate Judiciary Committee should, Morse repeatedly told the Senate, "sit down and write a scholarly majority report that the courts can use in the hotly contested litigation that will take place in innumerable cases in the next decade."[3]

Furthermore, Morse noted, since the Southern Democrats could filibuster the motion to take up the civil rights bill without the bill having first gone to committee, it would save time in the long run to send the bill to the Judiciary Committee for a specified period of time.

Hubert Humphrey was the principal voice for bypassing the Judiciary Committee completely. He constantly repeated the civil rights slogan that "121 consecutive civil rights bills died in the Senate Judiciary Committee from 1953 to 1963." In meeting after meeting Humphrey argued that referral to the committee with orders to report back would add nothing to the legislative history of the bill and would simply waste more time.

A "BORE-ATHON"

Subsequent debate on the Senate floor gave those senators who opposed sending the civil rights bill to the Judiciary Committee (with orders to report back the bill unchanged) an opportunity to further state their case. Senator Joseph S. Clark, a Democrat from Pennsylvania, gave a graphic description of what would happen to the bill once it fell into the hands of committee chairman Eastland:

> He will never even poll the committee. There will be no report, so that in the end we will have some testimony which will merely reiterate much of the testimony already taken in two other [Senate] committees and in the House, and we shall have wasted 10 days.[4]

Clark's remarks were strongly seconded by Senator Keating of New York:

> Speaking as a member of [the] committee, I must question the premise that sending this bill to the Judiciary Committee -- the traditional graveyard for civil rights legislation -- will somehow add to the body of knowledge in this area. . . . The chairman of the Judiciary Committee has decided that the rules of the Senate [unlimited debate] are also applicable to the committee. This means that a "bore-athon" is not only possible, but predictable in the committee. It has happened before and, I assure you, it will happen again.[5]

The NAACP was strongly opposed to sending the civil rights bill to the Judiciary Committee. Clarence Mitchell, Jr., told Democratic leader Mike Mansfield that he (Mitchell) and the NAACP would regard referral of the House passed bill to the Senate Committee on Judiciary "as betrayal."[6] Mitchell subsequently made public a telegram he sent to Senator Morse urging him to end his support of Judiciary Committee hearings. The telegram read:

> If there is any one thing that strains the faith of citizens, it is a persistent effort to give an aura of

170

respectability to committee hearings on civil rights
[run by Senator Eastland]. To the man in the
street, this is the equivalent of the stacked deck,
the hanging judge, and the executioner who enjoys
his work.[7]

Humphrey felt personally vexed that a strong civil rights
supporter like Wayne Morse would be pressing him so hard to
send the bill to the Judiciary Committee. "The only time I see
Wayne anymore," Humphrey lamented at a civil rights strategy
meeting, "is to take the body blows as he goes by."[8]

THE MANSFIELD SURPRISE

At first it appeared that Senate Democratic Leader Mike
Mansfield would side with Humphrey and attempt to bypass the
Judiciary Committee completely. On 26 February 1964, just
before the Senate took up the wheat and cotton bill, Mansfield
moved that the civil rights bill be placed on the Senate calendar
(from which it could be motioned up for Senate debate at a later
date).

Following the successful completion of this piece of
routine business (only slightly delayed by a Southern Democratic
point of order), Mansfield asked unanimous consent that "House
bill 7152 be referred to the Judiciary Committee with instructions
to report back, without recommendation or amendment, to the
Senate not later than noon, Wednesday, March 4."[9]

Humphrey and Kuchel were perplexed by this attempt on
Mansfield's part to placate Senator Morse and respond to at least
a portion of the Southern demand for Judiciary Committee
hearings. The bipartisan floor leaders for the civil rights bill had
been given a minimum of advance notice that Mansfield was
going to make this motion,[10] and Republican Senator Jacob Javits,
learning about Mansfield's motion when Mansfield presented it
on the Senate floor, jumped to his feet to object, thereby
blocking the Democratic leader's request for unanimous consent.
Javits did suggest, however, that Mansfield make his motion

171

again the next day when Javits and other senators backing the bill would have had more time to think about it.

Mansfield did make his motion again the following day, only this time it was Judiciary Chairman Eastland who objected to the unanimous consent request. Eastland then proceeded to portray the request as a near insult to his Committee:

> The net result would be that we would be handcuffed. . . . I will not be a party to sending a bill to the committee when it cannot amend it and cannot make a recommendation. . . .
> Therefore, Mr. President, I object.[11]

The episode illustrated that there was something of a difference between what Humphrey and Kuchel were trying to do and what Mansfield was trying to do. Humphrey and Kuchel were endeavoring to pass the strongest civil rights bill possible. Mansfield wanted a civil rights bill, but, as Democratic leader, he was ready to try to placate maverick civil rights supporters such as Wayne Morse and, if possible, the Southerners. For the remainder of the Senate debate on the bipartisan civil rights bill, Humphrey and Kuchel were somewhat tense and worried about what other moves Mansfield might make to keep in the good graces of all the senators, including the Southerners.

THE MOTION TO CONSIDER

By Monday, 9 March 1964, the Senate had disposed of the wheat and cotton bill. On that day Mansfield planned to offer his motion that House bill 7152, the bipartisan administration civil rights bill, be taken from the calendar and be considered as the next item of business for the United States Senate.

Under ordinary conditions such a motion to consider is debatable, which means the Southern Democrats could filibuster both the motion to consider and the civil rights bill itself. The prospect, therefore, was for two filibusters, which led to the prospect that two cloture votes might be required to overcome the two filibusters.

Mansfield's one hope to avoid a double filibuster was a Senate rule providing that a motion to consider is not debatable during the morning hour. The morning hour is the period from 12 Noon, when the Senate customarily goes into session, until 2 P.M., when the Senate gets down to hard legislative work. The morning hour is set aside for senators to make speeches on current political issues, put newspaper articles from hometown newspapers in the Congressional Record, and take care of other matters that really do not require the other senators to be in attendance.

Unfortunately for Mansfield, the Southern Democrats knew all about the rule that a motion to consider is not debateable during the morning hour. They could easily foil Mansfield's use of the rule by filling time during the morning hour, thereby denying Mansfield the opportunity to make his motion to consider until after 2 P.M. (when the morning hour would be over and the motion would be debateable).

Mansfield's staff had developed some complicated parliamentary moves which might have enabled the Democratic leader to present his motion during the morning hour. Mansfield reviewed these maneuvers and, in typical Mansfield style, pronounced them too "tricky." He resolved to offer his motion as soon as he could get the Senate floor in the regularly approved manner, and, if that were after the morning hour, then he would simply accept a Southern filibuster of his motion to consider.[12]

As the Senate went into session on 9 March 1964, Senator Richard Russell of Georgia, the leader of the Southern Democrats, was well prepared to see that Democratic Leader Mansfield would not get the Senate floor during the morning hour. The day began with the customary unanimous consent request that the Senate dispense with the reading of the Journal (Congressional Record) from the previous day. Senator Russell promptly objected and then announced that he would offer amendments to the record. Following the long and laborious

173

reading of the Journal, Russell asked that it be amended to include some statements that Senator Mansfield had made about the civil rights bill the previous Friday. Russell then gave a long speech supporting his proposed amendment to the Journal, citing a number of the legal arguments that had been used against the civil rights bill in the House Judiciary Committee and on the House floor.

The Southern leader then moved on to a general discussion of civil disobedience, reading into the record several recent newspaper stories on the topic. A number of the newspaper articles contained reports of attacks on teachers in urban schools, a phenomenon which Russell associated with the activities of a prominent civil rights group (CORE, the Congress of Racial Equality). As 2 P.M. came and went and the morning hour was safely behind him, Russell concluded by reading an article from the Washington Star regarding the activities of pressure groups during House passage of the civil rights bill.[13]

When Senator Mansfield finally obtained the Senate floor, he expressed the hope that eventually the Senate would have a chance to vote the bipartisan civil rights bill up or down. He then tried to impress upon his fellow senators the importance of what they were about to do:

> There is an ebb and flow in human affairs which at rare moments brings the complex of human events into a delicate balance. At those moments, the acts of governments may indeed influence, for better or for worse, the course of history. This is such a moment in the life of the Nation. This is that moment in the Senate.[14]

Mansfield then made his motion, which was strictly procedural: "Should the Senate proceed to the consideration of HR 7152, the Civil Rights Act of 1964?" Immediately Sam Ervin of North Carolina, Lister Hill of Alabama, Russell Long of Louisiana, and John McClellan of Arkansas took the floor and began discussing Mansfield's motion to consider. Filibuster #1 had begun.

NATURE OF THE DEBATE

The Senate debate on the motion to consider was highly disorganized. Rather than staying on the narrow subject of the motion to consider, pro-civil rights senators and anti-civil rights senators alike made extensive comments about the substance of the civil rights bill. Some of the speeches did not refer to either the motion to consider or the civil rights bill, but were on entirely extraneous subjects. Also there was little correlation between one speech and another, even when the speeches were consecutive. The various senators who spoke during the debate on the motion to consider appear to have mainly been stating their views for the record rather than trying to build a logical case for or against civil rights that would sway their colleagues.[15]

Humphrey and Kuchel had a decision to make when it became clear that the Southerners were going to debate the merits of the bill as well as the propriety of the motion to consider. Originally the civil rights forces had planned to withhold their substantive arguments until the bill itself was pending. However, when the Southerners began debating the bill on its merits, Humphrey decided "to take on the Southern Democrats without delay in order to avoid a blackout of news favorable to the bill."[16]

Humphrey adopted a strategy of immediate answer. Whenever the Southerners inserted a substantive criticism of the bill into the debate on the motion to consider, the pro-civil rights forces would immediately take the Senate floor and give a vociferous reply. As a legislative aide to Senator Kuchel expressed it, the idea was "to create an atmosphere of winning by being aggressive."[17]

On many occasions the strategy of immediate answer worked effectively for the civil rights senators. At one point, Humphrey maneuvered Senator Allen Ellender of Louisiana into admitting that blacks were prevented from voting in certain parts of the South because whites feared the prospect of being governed by black elected officials. The exchange of remarks on the Senate floor went like this:

> Mr. ELLENDER. It is true that in some states there are counties where the ratio of Negroes to whites is 2 to 1. There may be registration difficulties in those counties. But why? . . . It is because the few whites in those counties would be scared to death to have Negroes in charge of public office without qualification.
>
> Mr. HUMPHREY. What the Senator from Louisiana is saying is that although the whites are in the minority, they prevent the colored majority from registering to vote? . . .
>
> Mr. ELLENDER. Well --
>
> Mr. HUMPHREY. The Constitution is rather explicit on that subject.
>
> Mr. ELLENDER. I understand that. I am not saying they should not be registered, but I am giving the Senator the reason why. If this happened in the state of Minnesota, the Senator from Minnesota would do the same thing.
>
> Mr. HUMPHREY. Not at all. Not at all.
>
> Mr. ELLENDER. The Senator from Minnesota has not lived in the South. The situation does not exist in the state of Minnesota that has existed in the South. In some counties in the state of Mississippi, the ratio of Negroes to whites is 3 to 1.
>
> Mr. HUMPHREY. I appreciate that. . . .
>
> Mr. ELLENDER. I am frank to say that in many instances the reason why the voting rights were not encouraged is that the white people in those counties who are in the minority are afraid they would be outvoted. Let us be frank about it. . . .
>
> Mr. HUMPHREY. It is a fact, is it not,

that the large numbers of colored people who are citizens of the United States, many of whom pay taxes, many of whom are called upon to perform all the duties of citizenship, in peace and war, are denied the right to register and thereby denied the right to vote?

    Mr. ELLENDER. That has been done in many places.[18]

Senator Sam Ervin of North Carolina stepped in at this point to aid Ellender, trying to make the traditional Southern Democratic point that it was the black people's own fault that they could not vote because they did not "bother" to register. But the damage to the Southern cause had already been done. Humphrey's aggressive exchange with Ellender had effectively drawn the attention of the press to Senator Ellender's admission. National network television news and the following day's morning papers carried the story that a Southerner had admitted that some Southern whites were "scared to death to have Negroes in charge of public office." From the point of view of civil rights advocates, the need for a national voting rights law had been underscored. Humphrey's policy of immediate answer had worked.

TO CLOTURE OR NOT TO CLOTURE

Mansfield and Humphrey had thought the Southerners would filibuster the motion to consider for about one week. Suddenly the debate had been going on for a full week and was well into its second week. Political wags around Capitol Hill, comparing this preliminary filibuster to the short "miniskirts" that were popular in women's fashions at the time, began describing it as a "minibuster."[19]

Suddenly the main topic of conversation in civil rights strategy meetings was what to do about the ever lengthening debate on the motion to consider. Initially Hubert Humphrey had argued in favor of a cloture vote after only five days. "Five days of [Southern] snorting is enough," Humphrey said, "and then we should get the bill up." Humphrey was opposed, however, by Thomas Kuchel. "We ought to permit the Southerners to filibuster since the American people will get disgusted with them," Kuchel said. "A prolonged filibuster on the motion to set the legislation for action works to our advantage." Clarence Mitchell, Jr., of the NAACP agreed with Kuchel that the best advice was to "let the Southerners talk."[20]

On 17 March 1964 the New York Times carried a major story that Mansfield, Dirksen, Humphrey, and Kuchel had decided to seek a cloture vote the following week if the Southerners continued to debate the motion to consider. In point of fact, it was only Mansfield and Dirksen who were talking cloture at such an early point in the proceedings. By this time Humphrey and Kuchel, particularly Kuchel, were strongly opposed to it. The bipartisan floor managers wanted to withhold a cloture vote until (1) it could be invoked on the civil rights bill itself, and (2) they were certain they had enough votes to win the cloture vote. A legislative aide to Senator Humphrey summarized the reasons for this strategy:

> To attempt cloture and to fail would seriously cripple the civil rights forces in their campaign to generate confidence and momentum behind the legislation. And those senators who voted against cloture once would be that much more difficult to win later in the debate.[21]

It was disturbing to Humphrey and Kuchel that Mansfield and Dirksen had let the New York Times hear of a cloture effort on the motion to consider. The whole affair hinted at a greater inclination by both Mansfield and Dirksen to think in terms of a compromise settlement. There was little disagreement among political observers that, once cloture had been tried and had failed, the bill would then become far more vulnerable to major concessions in the pattern of earlier civil rights debates. Humphrey's legislative aide gave this analysis of the situation:

178

From Mansfield's perspective, however, this possibility was much less a disaster than it would have been for Humphrey or Kuchel. Partially due to a less intense involvement over the years in the civil rights effort, and partially due to a perspective which necessarily considered the civil rights bill as one among many bills that would have to pass under his general direction, Mansfield gradually emerged as less of an absolute proponent than either floor manager, less willing to think only in terms of demolishing the filibuster as the essential step toward total victory.[22]

The day after the New York Times story concerning a possible cloture vote, Mansfield abandoned the plan completely. Apparently heavy pressure from Humphrey and Kuchel caused the Democratic leader's change in view on the issue. Senator Kuchel told his legislative assistant that Mansfield backed down from the cloture plan after Kuchel had "vigorously" objected to it.[23]

In fact, Kuchel's legislative assistant actually theorized at this time that Mansfield's early pressure for cloture on the motion to consider was a plot by President Johnson to shame the Republicans. The legislative assistant wrote in his daily notes:

> My cynical mind tells me that this might be a Lyndon Johnson attempt to embarrass the Republicans since we would be shy the 25 votes the GOP needs to deliver for cloture. Those votes will be available five or six weeks from now, but not if the vote is held now.[24]

As strategy making was going on in the meeting rooms of the Senate side of the Capitol, the minibuster continued unabated. When Senator John Stennis of Mississippi heard about the publication of a civil rights newsletter, he revealed his displeasure on the Senate floor. "I should like to ask," Stennis

179

intoned, "who writes these mysterious messages, which come to senators before the <u>Congressional Record</u> reaches them, and in them attempts to refute arguments made on the floor of the Senate?" Hubert Humphrey was only too pleased to respond to Stennis and simultaneously publicize the organizational efforts of the civil rights forces. "There is no doubt about it," Humphrey readily admitted. "The newsletter is a bipartisan civil rights newsletter. . . . For the first time, we are putting up a battle. Everything will be done to make us succeed. . . . I wish also to announce that if anyone wishes to have equal time, there is space on the back of it for the opposition."[25] As Humphrey surely knew would be the case, the Southern Democrats declined to contribute any material to the "back" of the civil rights newsletter.

Exactly as they had intended, Mansfield and Humphrey were able to keep the debate on the Senate floor polite and friendly. At the end of one long day, for example, Willis Robertson of Virginia, having just ridiculed every title in the bill, walked over to Humphrey and offered him a small Confederate flag for his lapel. Humphrey accepted the "Stars and Bars" graciously and then gave a speech praising Robertson for his "eloquence and his great knowledge of history and law, but also for his wonderful . . . gentlemanly qualities and his consideration to us at all times."

Senator Robertson then delivered a Southerner's ultimate compliment to a Northerner by telling Humphrey that it was Union soldiers from Humphrey's home state of Minnesota that successfully invaded Virginia in the Civil War. Robertson said: "I told the Senator [Humphrey] that if it had not been for the men from Wisconsin and Minnesota, when Grant finally came down into Virginia, we would have won." Robertson then jokingly took back some of his praise by noting that the Wisconsin and Minnesota soldiers took Virginia only because most of them were former Virginians. "They formerly belonged to Virginia," Robertson concluded. "We could not whip them . . . ." Arm in arm, Humphrey and Robertson retired to Humphrey's office "for some early evening refreshment."[26]

THE END OF THE MINIBUSTER

Completely stymied by the apparent willingness of the Southern Democrats to debate the motion to consider until forced by external forces to stop, Humphrey and Kuchel began thinking of various steps that might be taken to dramatize the obstructionism of the filibusterers. One plan was to have Mansfield make daily requests on the floor of the Senate that the motion to consider be voted upon. Another idea was to constantly talk about the "threat" of a cloture vote to the press. The hope here was that serious press coverage of such a threat might convince the Southerners that the civil rights senators actually had the votes for cloture, and that the Southerners were thereby taking great risks in continuing to block the Senate from taking up the bill.[27]

As it turned out, none of these plans were necessary. Richard Russell, the leader of the Southern Democrats, concluded that two weeks was about as far as he could push his luck in continuing the filibuster against the motion to consider. It was not in his interest to provoke senators into the successful application of cloture so early in the game. A legislative aide to Senator Humphrey gave the following explanation of why Russell ended the filibuster of the motion to consider:

> Recognizing that to continue [filibuster #1] further would eventually incur those risks, Russell passed the word quietly to Mansfield that a vote on the preliminary motion could occur. . . . Both sides, in short, concluded that it was in their respective best interests to avoid a showdown over cloture at this stage of the debate.[28]

Senator Russell never announced his decision to end the minibuster publicly. The Southerners just stopped talking at the agreed upon time and the vote took place. Mansfield, of course, would not discuss the agreement in public either. As Hubert Humphrey's legislative aide noted:

[Such an action] would have embarrassed Russell and probably forced him to continue the filibuster [of the motion to consider] regardless of the consequences. Indeed, the principals to the decision talked little about it [the informal agreement to end the minibuster] even in private.[29]

With absolutely no warning to the public that things had changed, the Senate met on the morning of Thursday, 26 March 1964, and promptly voted, 67 to 17, to proceed to the consideration of H.R. 7152, the bipartisan civil rights bill.[30] Only Southern Democrats voted against the motion to consider. After considerable delay, the civil rights bill was officially before the Senate.

The fact that 67 Senators voted for the motion to consider did <u>not</u> indicate that Humphrey and Kuchel had 67 votes (the requisite number) for cloture. Several senators who voted to take up the bill either opposed cloture or had not yet committed themselves to support cloture.

In a final effort in behalf of his plan to get at least some committee consideration of the bill, Senator Morse moved to refer the bill to the Senate Judiciary Committee with instructions to report the bill back by 8 April 1964. After a brief rehash of all the previously stated arguments on this issue, Mansfield moved to table Morse's motion (in effect, killing it). Although the news media had carried reports that the vote on Morse's motion would be close, Mansfield's tabling motion passed easily by a vote of 50 to 34.[31] The last obstacle in the path of Senate consideration of the bill itself had been removed.

CONCLUSIONS

The 2 and 1/2 week debate on the motion to consider mainly revealed that the civil rights forces were short the necessary 2/3 vote for cloture. When it became apparent that an early cloture vote might be required to end the minibuster, an informal whip count showed the civil rights forces more than eight votes shy of the 67 votes needed.

It is interesting to note the performance of the 12 Republican senators who the civil rights forces hoped would eventually provide the additional votes for cloture. Of these 12 Republicans, now referred to as "The Crucial Twelve," 7 had supported Senator Morse's motion to send the bill to the Senate Judiciary Committee with instructions to report the bill back unamended. Although a vote for Morse's motion did not necessarily mean a senator was against cloture or anti-civil rights, it did mean that Humphrey and Kuchel did not, as yet, have that senator firmly supporting their point of view and their particular brand of civil rights leadership. Clearly a long and indecisive period of bidding for the cloture votes of these 7 senators lay ahead.

Civil rights floor leaders Humphrey and Kuchel were very concerned about the performance of Senator Everett Dirksen. The Republican leader had not only voted for Morse's motion but had given a strong speech in support of it. Dirksen told the Senate:

> If this [bill] is as important as the zealots would have us believe, that is all the more reason why the Senate should be most careful [and refer the bill to the Judiciary Committee]. . . . This bill would remake the social patterns of this country. Let no one be fooled on that score. Its impact would be profound. . . . I desire a civil rights bill. . . . But I want it to be fair, equitable, durable, and workable . . . .[32]

During his speech, Dirksen had continued to articulate his strong reservations about crucial parts of the legislation, particularly equal employment opportunity. As for equal access to public accommodations (to many observers the most important part of the bill), Dirksen announced his intention to introduce, at a later date, substitute language for the public accommodations section that had passed in the House of Representatives.[33]

The pro-civil rights forces were unnerved by the thought that Dirksen was going to introduce such a major amendment. Their concern was compounded by the fact that Dirksen had given no indication whatsoever as to what form his public accommodations amendment was going to take. The atmosphere of mystery which Dirksen had successfully created about his proposed amendments produced a general feeling of tension and malaise in the civil rights camp.

The civil rights forces had made some gains as the minibuster came to an end, however. Humphrey's strategy of immediate answer had produced the desired amounts of favorable publicity for the civil rights bill. Furthermore, the civil rights "quorum duty list" had functioned very effectively and, so far at least, all quorum calls had been answered quickly and in good order. Most importantly, the press had been impressed with the efficient organization of the civil rights forces and was spreading that impression throughout the nation. As the New York Times put it:

> Civil rights forces, not to be outdone by Southern opponents, have thrown up their own well manned command post in the Senate. . . . As militarily precise as the Southerners' three platoon system, the Humphrey forces are organized down to the last man . . . .[34]

As for the Southern Democrats, they had demonstrated just how effectively a filibuster can tie up the Senate. Humphrey and Kuchel had been totally unable to come up with any way to end the minibuster other than cloture -- and they clearly did not yet have the votes for cloture. Although it was never officially announced, insiders knew that the debate on the motion to consider had ended only because Richard Russell had decided to let it end, not because of any power of the civil rights forces.

Russell thus emerged from the debate over the motion to consider in a confident mood. "We have lost a skirmish," Russell told the Senate after the Morse motion (to refer the bill

184

to the Judiciary Committee with instructions to report back unamended) had failed. "We shall now begin to fight the war."[35]

Filibuster #1, the filibuster of the motion to consider, thus came to an end. Filibuster #2, the actual filibuster of the civil rights bill itself, was about to begin.

CHAPTER 10

FILIBUSTER #2;
THE BILL ITSELF

When the 1957 and 1960 civil rights bills were being filibustered in the Senate, the Southern Democrats had been allowed to speak at length while the pro-civil rights senators said little or nothing. This strategy had been based upon the hope, subsequently unrealized, that the Southerners would eventually run out of things to say. Knowing full well that this old strategy did not work, Senators Humphrey and Kuchel, the bipartisan floor managers for the 1964 civil rights bill, worked out a completely new strategy. They decided to begin the formal debate on the bill itself with a series of major speeches defending the bill.

Thus on 30 March 1964 Hubert Humphrey took the Senate floor and began an impassioned speech in favor of the bill. Humphrey later explained:

> I opened the debate followed by Kuchel. Each day a team of our people would take a title, so that for better than 12 days we held the floor giving detailed information about the bill and being able to get the public's attention as to what was in this bill.[1]

Humphrey's opening speech in favor of the bill lasted for over 3 hours. He began by telling the Senate that legislation was the best alternative to the civil rights unrest that had been sweeping the United States:

TO END ALL SEGREGATION

Within the past few years a new spirit has arisen
in those people who have been so long denied
[their basic civil rights]. How will we respond to
this challenge? The snarling dogs of Birmingham
are one answer. The force of equality and justice
is another. That second choice is embodied in the
bill that we are starting to consider.[2]

Humphrey illustrated his talk with examples of segregation
and its effects. At one point he made a comparison of
guidebooks published for people motoring across the country.
One guide book was for families traveling with dogs; the other
was for blacks. Humphrey noted:

It is heartbreaking to compare these 2 guidebooks.
In Augusta, Georgia, for example, there are 5
hotels and motels that will take dogs, and only 1
where a Negro can go with confidence. In
Columbus, Georgia, there are 6 places for dogs and
none for Negroes. In Charleston, South Carolina,
there are 10 places where a dog can stay, and none
for a Negro.[3]

Humphrey also cited evidence, compiled by the Senate
Commerce Committee, which revealed that, for a black family
traveling from Washington, D.C., to Miami, Florida, the average
distance between places where they could find sleeping
accommodations was 141 miles.

Another major point in Humphrey's opening address was
the fact that, in order to use public facilities such as parks,
swimming pools, and art museums, blacks had to file expensive
and time-consuming law suits. Humphrey said:

It is almost unthinkable to me that a citizen should
have to spend three years in litigation and take a
case to the U.S. Supreme Court, at a cost of
thousands of dollars, in order to be able to walk in

a city park that he helped pay for; to play on a city golf course that he helped pay for; to enter a city art museum that he helped pay for . . . .[4]

Humphrey concluded his opening address by calling on the Senate to pass the civil rights bill:

The goals of this bill are simple ones: to extend to Negro citizens the same rights and the same opportunities that white Americans take for granted. . . . We know that until racial justice and freedom are a reality in this land, our Union will remain profoundly imperfect. That is why we are debating this bill. That is why this bill must become law.[5]

Humphrey and Kuchel had several reasons for arranging a title by title discussion of the civil rights bill by its proponents. The speeches built a public record for the bill, thus compensating somewhat for the fact that the bill had not been reviewed by the Senate Judiciary Committee. The speeches also gave the Southern Democrats a chance to question the civil rights senators about what was in the bill and how it would all work when finally passed into law. The real goal, however, was to convince senators who were uncommitted about voting for cloture that there had been more than adequate debate and deliberation on the contents of the bill.

Little debate took place during this introductory period, however. The Southern Democrats seemed content to bide their time and enjoy a respite. The uncommitted senators simply stayed away from the Senate floor. It soon became clear that this initial formal defense of the bill by the civil rights senators was being listened to only by the press. When Senator Javits of New York, one of the Republican title captains, had finished his major presentation on the bill, not one senator rose to debate or discuss his talk. As Senator Joseph Clark of Pennsylvania later summed up the situation: "It damn near killed Javits when nobody asked him a question after his speech."[6]

In addition to the speeches by the title captains, other senators supporting civil rights gave speeches in favor of the bill during this period. Edward M. Kennedy of Massachusetts, the brother of the recently assassinated president, rose at his desk to give his maiden speech in the Senate. After a strong defense of the bill, he concluded with these words:

> My brother was the first president of the United States to state publicly that segregation was morally wrong. His heart and soul are in this bill. If his life and death had a meaning, it was that we should not hate but love one another. . . .
>
> It is in that spirit that I hope the Senate will pass this bill.[7]

A SLEEPY AND DREAMY SENATE

Once the title by title presentations by the pro-civil rights senators were over, the floor reverted to the Southern Democrats, who assumed the main burden of carrying the debate. Humphrey and his corporal's guard continued their strategy of immediate answer, but soon the Southerners were repeating themselves and there were no new charges to which to react. The pattern of argument became completely random, and on any given day it was impossible to know ahead of time exactly what was going to be discussed. One analyst wrote that the Senate chamber had become almost a sleepy and dreamy place where there were only the slightest indications that anything significant was taking place:

> It was almost absurd for a visitor to the United States Senate in the late winter or early spring of 1964 to think of himself as witness to a ceremony of revolution. What he could see from the press or visitors' gallery was so unutterably commonplace. . . . By half an hour after the noon

190

opening, normally, there would remain on the floor only four out of the one hundred senators of the United States -- two Southerners and two Northerners, each pair watching the other, while the business of the nation was suspended in the longest filibuster in American history. An Ervin and an Ellender for the South against a Javits and a McGee; a Russell and a Long against a McIntyre and a Keating; a Talmadge and an Eastland against a Case and a Kennedy, assigned by their leaders to patrol the floor, two against two . . . .[8]

THE SATURDAY DEBACLE

This atmosphere of boredom and inactivity dominated the Senate floor throughout the month of April 1964 and was broken only once. On Saturday, 4 April 1964, only 39 Senators answered the first quorum call of the day. For approximately the next hour, aides to pro-civil rights senators frantically dialed their telephones in an effort to find the 15 or so senators whose names were on the "quorum duty list" but who were not present in the Senate chamber. Then the aides were all called together for a meeting in Hubert Humphrey's office.

Looking simultaneously somber and exasperated, Hubert Humphrey sat down and read aloud the names of the absent senators and why, despite being on the "quorum duty list," they were not in Washington that morning.[9] Democrat Henry Jackson was back home in Washington state dedicating a new forest service laboratory. Clinton Anderson, a Democrat from New Mexico, was in Albuquerque meeting with state Native American organizations. Democrat Frank Moss and Republican Wallace Bennett of Utah were at the annual conference of the Church of Latter Day Saints (Mormon Church) in Salt Lake City. Nebraska Republican Roman Hruska was attending Republican Founders Day ceremonies in Omaha. And so it went through the list of missing Senators. This particular senator was up for reelection and had gone home to campaign; that particular senator had left

Washington to give a luncheon speech to a key lobby group. As a Senate aide quietly explained it to the press: "When the siren song of politics calls, they can't resist."[10]

After Humphrey had finished detailing the exact reasons for the failure of the civil rights forces to produce a Saturday quorum, he told Democratic Leader Mansfield there was no hope and, for that day at least, the cause was lost. As grinning and chuckling Southern Democrats put away their speeches and congratulated themselves on a major victory, Mike Mansfield recessed the Senate until the following Monday and called the entire situation "a sham and an indignity upon this institution."[11] Later in the day Hubert Humphrey bluntly asserted: "The only way we can lose the civil rights fight is not to have a quorum when we need it."[12]

The press gave extensive publicity to this Saturday debacle. The names of those senators who should have been present and were not present were run on the front pages of all the major newspapers. The unexcused absentees received particularly rough treatment from the media in their home states. Furthermore, after everyone was back in Washington the following Monday, Senator Mansfield called all the Northern and Western Democrats together and stressed that the final outcome of the debate depended primarily on their behavior. He emphasized that he possessed no more power than the most freshman senator to compel their attendance, and he ended his tongue-lashing by noting: "We have leaned over backwards to accommodate senators in this debate; now you have to meet us halfway."[13]

To reinforce Mansfield's words, Humphrey "turned the Leadership Conference operatives loose to impress upon negligent senators the importance of their making future quorum calls."[14] The major share of this particular burden fell on lobbyists from the AFL-CIO.

STAGED FAILURE

Although it appeared to the press and the public that

Humphrey and Kuchel had lost control of the civil rights forces during the Saturday debacle, actually the two men were reasonably well in control of the situation. Whip counts of the senators on the "quorum duty list" had shown the two floor managers as early as the previous Thursday that they were not going to make the Saturday quorum, and for a few hours the possibility of not scheduling the Saturday session was considered. It was decided, however, to go ahead and hold the Saturday session, letting the adverse press from the failed quorum call serve as a device for disciplining the errant civil rights senators. As a lawyer on the Senate Democratic Policy Committee staff put it, a failed quorum call on Saturday would be "fine since it will let us shape up the pro-civil rights forces early." A Republican staffer was most happy to support this point of view, mainly because his figures showed that Republican senators had been doing much better than Democratic senators at meeting quorum calls and therefore the Democrats would get the major portion of the heat from the press following a cancelled Senate session.[15]

This "staging" of the Saturday debacle to "shape up" the pro-civil rights senators apparently worked because the situation with quorum calls quickly improved. Although some frantic Friday night telephoning was required for the Saturday session one week following the Saturday debacle, a quorum was assembled in just ten minutes.

THE OLD BALL GAME

The following Wednesday afternoon a small group of senators assembled at D.C. Stadium (subsequently renamed Robert F. Kennedy Stadium) to watch President Johnson throw out the first ball in the opening game of the 1964 baseball season. The hometown "baseball" Senators were well on their way to their first loss of the season when, at the end of the third inning, the public address system suddenly blared out the following message: "Attention, please, there has been a quorum call in the United States Senate. All U.S. senators are requested

193

to return to the Senate chamber immediately." Back on the Senate floor, Spessard Holland of Florida had observed "the absence of a quorum."

The moment the announcement of the quorum call was made in D.C. Stadium, half a dozen senators, including Democratic Leader Mike Mansfield, Democratic Whip Hubert Humphrey, and Republican Leader Everett Dirksen, left their seats. The only senator remaining (other than those on the playing field) was Georgia Democrat Richard Russell, who, according to a colleague, "never moved."[16]

For this particular quorum call, however, the civil rights forces were well prepared. A group of black limousines, complete with a sirens blaring police escort, had been specifically arranged for such an eventuality. The missing senators were raced back to the Capitol building in less than 20 minutes. The quorum call was met, and the pro-civil rights forces had the day's top civil rights news story.

That evening a similar summons was sent out to senators attending a special Shakespeare presentation cohosted by the president's wife, "Lady Bird" Johnson, and Stewart Udall, the secretary of the interior. Udall intercepted the telephone call, however, and refused to interrupt the cultural performance to announce the quorum call of senators. Pointing out that these particular senators had been given permission to leave the Senate for the evening, Udall grumbled, "They [the civil rights floor leaders] ought to organize their work better." The dispute became academic, however, because other senators were found and the quorum call was successfully met.[17]

As the Senate proceeded with the ever lengthening filibuster, national attention shifted from the floor of the Senate to civil rights events taking place outside the Senate. In fact, it can be argued that, during April and early May, both sides were wasting time on the Senate floor while pursuing their objectives elsewhere and in other ways. The civil rights forces were mainly working on bringing organized pressure to bear on Everett Dirksen and the small handful of Republican Senators who were still uncommitted on the question of voting cloture.

194

The Southern Democrats, on the other hand, were wasting time in hopes that national public opinion would turn against civil rights and thereby convince the uncommitted senators <u>not</u> to vote for cloture.

A STATEMENT A WEEK

President Johnson led the public relations campaign in favor of the civil rights bill by making virtually a statement a week calling for passage of the bill. One week the president was quoted by congressional leaders as saying he was "committed" to the bill with "no wheels and no deals."[18] Another week he stated: "The civil rights bill which passed the House is the bill that this administration recommends. . . . Our position is firm and we stand on the House bill."[19] A week after that, the president told a news conference: "I think we passed a good bill in the House. I hope the same bill will be passed in the Senate. . . . I hope it [the Senate] stays on the subject until a bill is passed that is acceptable."[20]

In a special press interview marking Lyndon Johnson's first hundred days in office, the president said:

> I think that when the Senate acts upon the civil rights bill, that we will have the best civil rights law that has been enacted in 100 years, and I think it will be a substantial and effective answer to our racial problems. . . . I don't want to predict how long it [the Senate] will be discussing this bill. I am hopeful and I am an optimist and I believe they can pass it and I believe they will pass it and I believe it is their duty to pass it, and I am going to do everything I can to get it passed.[21]

As the filibuster wore on, Johnson began directing his remarks somewhat pointedly at the Senate and its failure to act:

> Well, they have been debating [the civil rights bill]

195

for a good many days, and obviously there will be much debate yet in the offing. . . . But I believe, after a reasonable time, the majority of the senators will be ready to vote, and I hope that a vote can be worked out.[22]

A week later the president reiterated the point that the Senate would be a long time passing the bill, but a bill would be passed:

I think it [the filibuster] will go on for some time yet, but I believe at the proper time, after all members have had a chance to present their viewpoints both pro and con, the majority of the Senate will work its will and I believe we will pass the bill.[23]

A week after that Johnson was still hammering away at this now familiar theme:

We need a good civil rights bill, and the bill now pending in the Senate is a good bill. I hope it can be passed in a reasonable time.[24]

By mid April, however, even the president appeared to be getting exasperated with the torpor that had gripped the Senate. Giving a prepared address to the American Society of Newspaper Editors, Johnson said:

Our nation will live in tormented ease until the civil rights bill now being considered is written into the book of law. The question is no longer, "Shall it be passed?" The question is, "When, when, when will it be passed?"[25]

Commenting retrospectively several years later, Deputy Attorney General Nicholas Katzenbach suggested that President

196

Johnson made these strong statements with little confidence in his own mind that the civil rights bill could be passed without major amendments. In fact, it was Katzenbach's recollection that it took considerable persuading to get President Johnson to believe that a cloture vote could be achieved on the House passed civil rights bill without significantly changing it. Katzenbach said:

> I think that President Johnson really felt that we were nuts in trying to think that we could get cloture in the Senate on this. I had a long talk with him about it. . . . The president said that he just didn't see how you could get 67 votes. . . . We went through them [the list of Senators] one by one, and I think I was a little more optimistic than he was, but I said to him, "If you do anything publicly but indicate that we're going to get cloture on this bill, we can't possibly get cloture on this bill. And the only way we can get it is for you with your experience to express absolute confidence publicly and privately that we're going to get cloture on this bill," which was putting his neck right on the line. And then he did that. . . . [It was a] very courageous public attitude for a man who was not really persuaded that cloture could not be gotten, but who was willing to put his neck right out, and if you'll look through that period you'll find he said constantly, "Yes, we'll get it."[26]

"ACTIVE, AT NO TIME PASSIVE"

In the Senate itself, Hubert Humphrey was pressuring the civil rights senators to make maximum use of their public positions as Senators to gain additional press and publicity for the civil rights bill. Humphrey noted:

197

It is fair to say that for about one month the proponents of the legislation were able to demand press attention more often than the opponents. We encouraged our people, that is, the pro-civil rights senators, to be on radio and television. I wrote to each senator suggesting radio and television programs, suggesting newsletters [to constituents], enclosing sample copies of newsletters that other senators had prepared. We encouraged reprints of key material that had been put in the [Congressional] Record so that there could be answers to the questions of the people back home. We answered the propaganda of the anti-civil rights groups. In other words, we were active, at no time passive, and at all times challenging the opposition.[27]

Humphrey himself embarked on a systematically designed public speaking schedule in favor of the bill. He chose the audiences for these public speeches very carefully, speaking only to groups that were known to be strongly in favor of civil rights. Humphrey wanted to make sure he was not greeted by pro-segregation protestors and demonstrators as he went about the nation defending the civil rights bill. A conscious effort was made to see that, whenever and wherever Humphrey went and spoke, he was surrounded by cheering throngs and avid supporters. Newspaper and television coverage of Humphrey's speeches would thus give the impression that there was overwhelming support for civil rights in the nation at large.[28]

With his long record of support for civil rights and other liberal causes, Humphrey could count on drawing a strongly committed liberal audience, and by choosing to speak only to committed liberal groups, he guaranteed the most favorable and positive of speaking environments. The result was a series of public addresses that were, in reality, well staged political love feasts. Humphrey would shout carefully phrased slogans supporting civil rights, and the audience would respond with enthusiastic cheers and applause.

Humphrey thus spoke to the American Jewish Congress, the Lutheran Brotherhood League, and the American Baptist Convention. All of these religious groups had endorsed the civil rights bill, and all of them were urging their ministers and rabbis to visit their senators and lobby them to vote for cloture. Humphrey even personally thanked the Baptists for their support of the bill: "The fight was waged by you and other religious bodies during the past few months, and it has been magnificent."[29]

Speaking to a convention of Americans for Democratic Action in Pittsburgh, Humphrey took the group immediately into his confidence: "I want to emphasize civil rights tonight because, frankly, it is a subject that is uppermost in my mind these days." Humphrey then built the main body of his talk around the concept of the "citizenship gap," the idea that there was a tremendous "gap" between the rights of white Americans as citizens and the rights of black Americans as citizens. Humphrey also emphasized the economic hardships placed on blacks by discrimination in hiring and job training. He finally concluded that there were two citizenship gaps, "the gap between the promise and fulfillment of the Constitution, and the gap between the promise and fulfillment of our great free enterprise system."[30] Humphrey's use of the word "gap" in this speech was intentional in view of the extensive use at the time of the phrase "missile gap," a reference to an alleged gap between the number of intercontinental ballistic missiles possessed by the United States compared to a larger number possessed by the Soviet Union.

In an address to the California Democratic Club Convention in Long Beach, California, Humphrey received the expected enthusiastic round of applause by hammering home one of his favorite civil rights slogans. This nation must, he said, "walk out of the shadows of state rights and walk forthrightly into the bright sunshine of human rights."[31]

No matter what sort of group he might be speaking to, Humphrey worked to relate their principal interests and concerns to the civil rights bill. Addressing the National Association For Mental Health in Washington, D.C., Humphrey worked in extensive comments about the mental anguish caused by poverty, deprivation, and racial discrimination:

> Psychiatry tells us to give a child or a man or a woman room to grow, to develop, to fulfill themselves. We are not giving the tenth of America represented by our Negro citizens the "room" to make their fullest contributions to our democracy.

Humphrey concluded his speech on mental health by noting that black Americans could not be expected to quietly accept the psychological limitations placed upon them by racial discrimination:

> We cannot expect almost 20 million Americans to be contented with living for the most part in the filth of slums, or with being denied the jobs their brains and skills qualify them for, denied the respect and equal treatment they deserve from their fellow citizens.[32]

Along this same line of fitting the speech to the particular interests of the group involved, Humphrey spoke at the annual dinner of the Four Freedoms Awards Foundation in New York City. After reminding the audience of the importance of the original four freedoms -- freedom of speech, freedom of worship, freedom from want, and freedom from fear -- Humphrey proposed the creation of a fifth freedom -- the freedom of human dignity. But human dignity could hardly be said to exist, Humphrey noted, when black children are repeatedly told to stay in their place:

> And what place? The bottom of the scale, the worst of everything. The lowest, the last, the

200

shoddiest, the back of the bus, the worst of the
tenements, the most crowded school. Never mind
if the child has the potential of a George
Washington Carver . . . or a Martin Luther King.
I ask you, how long are 20 million Americans
supposed to take all this?[33]

In an address at Johns Hopkins University, Humphrey
highlighted the international implications of racial discrimination:

Internationally it is imperative that we come to the
world with clean hands. How, I ask, can a nation
that denies or ignores the rights of its colored
citizens continue to be the leader of a world that
is more than half colored? Our role of world
leadership demands that we set an example for the
world, an example of respect for human dignity,
of equal rights for all Americans.[34]

RELIGIOUS SUPPORT

On 13 April 1964 the National Conference on Religion
and Race, a subgroup of the National Council of Churches,
called upon clergymen throughout the nation to support the civil
rights bill. Two weeks later, on 28 April 1964, an Inter-religious
Convocation on Civil Rights brought more than 5,000 clerics and
lay leaders of all faiths to Washington to discuss the role which
religious leaders should play where civil rights was concerned.
Held at Georgetown University, the convocation had been
specifically scheduled to occur at the moment when the Southern
filibuster of the civil rights bill would be reaching its peak in the
Senate.

Every member of Congress was invited to attend the
convocation, and those members of Congress who did not attend
were called on personally by convocation attendees from their
home states and of their own particular religion. The influence
of this kind of "religious lobbying" was thought to be particularly

useful for reaching uncommitted Republican senators from the Midwest and the Rocky Mountain West. Having few black constituents, these senators did not feel very much hometown pressure to vote in favor of civil rights. They did, however, have large numbers of constituents who were deeply religious, and it was considered important to show these senators that, for religious reasons, large numbers of their constituents wanted them to vote for cloture on the civil rights bill. After being on the receiving end of such heavy religious lobbying, one senator commented to Hubert Humphrey in exasperated tones: "Every time I'd try to argue about Title VII, they'd get down on their knees and start to pray. How can you win an argument against God?"[35]

On 19 April 1964 theological students representing the three major religions -- Catholic, Protestant, and Jewish -- began a vigil at the Lincoln Memorial in behalf of the civil rights bill. Every day, 24 hours a day, three divinity students from each of the faiths stood before the monument to Abraham Lincoln as a "dramatic witness to the moral cause of civil rights."[36]

Over 400 members of the Southern Presbyterian Church signed a petition urging passage of the civil rights bill. The press was quick to publicize the fact that one of the signers was the Reverend W. D. Russell, a nephew of Georgia Senator Richard D. Russell, the leader of the Southern Democratic opposition to the bill.[37]

THE CHANGING CHARACTER OF
THE CIVIL RIGHTS DEMONSTRATIONS

As Lyndon Johnson and Hubert Humphrey were going about their business speaking in favor of the civil rights bill, a change was taking place in the character of the civil rights demonstrations around the country. As the more established civil rights organizations such as the Southern Christian Leadership Conference and the National Association for the Advancement of Colored People moved to tone down the demonstrations while legislation was being considered in Congress, other groups were becoming much more strident and increasingly militant in their demands.

Of particular concern was the fact that these new kinds of civil rights demonstrations were taking place in the North and the Border States rather than in the South. Also the goals of these demonstrations were different and somewhat more controversial. Instead of demonstrating for the simple right to eat in a public restaurant and swim in a public swimming pool, these Northern demonstrations were aimed at increasing employment opportunities in private businesses and ending de facto school segregation, i.e., segregation that was caused, not by school systems being officially segregated, but by all the children who lived near the schools being either all white or all black. Also, there was less commitment to keeping these Northern demonstrations nonviolent, and the result was often unpleasant rock throwing and insult shouting incidents in which the demonstrators rather than the police appeared to be the aggressors.

THE CLEVELAND BULLDOZER INCIDENT

An example of this new type of demonstration occurred in Cleveland, Ohio, in early April 1964. The Cleveland school board had begun constructing three new elementary schools in predominantly black neighborhoods. Although the new schools would relieve overcrowding among black elementary school students, local civil rights leaders saw them as promoting "resegregation" since they would be in all black neighborhoods and would only be for black students. The result was a series of demonstrations at the building sites of the new schools in an effort to halt construction and, it was hoped, get the new schools constructed in areas where they would attract an integrated student body.

One afternoon about 100 demonstrators, both white and black, gathered at the edge of the muddy lot on which one of the three schools (Lakeview) was being built. Suddenly the demonstrators broke out of their picket line, raced on to the construction site itself, and threw themselves in the path of bulldozers, power shovels, trucks, and concrete mixers. They placed themselves as close as possible to the wheels and treads of the machinery. A woman five months pregnant and five other demonstrators leaped into a ditch and lay down prone just beneath a power shovel's steel clawed jaws. Cleveland police were called to the scene and began to disperse the demonstrators, but many of the protesters fought and tussled with police officers. Two demonstrators were slightly injured in the battle and 21 had to be arrested when they would not leave the construction area peacefully.

One of the civil rights leaders was a white minister, the Reverend Bruce W. Klunder, 27, who was a graduate of the Yale University Divinity School and the assistant executive secretary of the Student Christian Union at Case Western Reserve University. Following the first day's demonstration and arrests, Klunder vowed that he and his group would return. "We are dedicated and committed to continue," he told the press, "and we will not stop short of having the school board revise its plans. This can be done by placing our bodies between the workers and their work."[38]

The next day the Reverend Klunder returned to the Lakeview school site with over 1,000 demonstrators, 10 times more than the previous day. Awaiting them were large numbers of Cleveland police officers forming a cordon around the construction area. The protesters threw rocks, bottles, bricks, and large chunks of cement at the policemen. Charging under a hail of stones, the civil rights demonstrators repeatedly tried to break through the police lines. This time thirteen persons were injured, five demonstrators and eight policemen. Twenty-six demonstrators were arrested.

At this point Klunder gathered a group of supporters around him and planned a sneak invasion of the construction site through nearby backyards. Shortly thereafter the minister, two women and a man ran across the school lot toward a bulldozer. Three of them lay down in front of the machine. Klunder lay down behind it. The driver immediately stopped when he saw the three in front, looked around, and then began slowly backing

204

his heavy machine. He had not seen Klunder. When he finally brought his machine to a halt, the dead body of Bruce Klunder lay in the mud. The bulldozer treads had gone over his chest.

In the frenzy that followed Klunder's death, six men charged past police and attacked the bulldozer driver. He had several teeth knocked out before police were able to rescue him. The mayhem lasted for almost two hours and was carefully recorded by newspaper photographers and television cameramen. As darkness came on, gangs of black youths returned to the neighborhood and smashed car windows, overturned a truck and beat the driver, smashed shop windows, and looted stores.

Cleveland school officials gave in when faced with such an uncontrolled and uncontrollable situation. All construction work at the school site was halted, and a committee was named by the school board and the civil rights groups to make a study of possible solutions to the problem of de facto school segregation in Cleveland.

"POINTLESS . . . DESTRUCTIVE . . . DANGEROUS"

Suddenly almost all of the civil rights news stories were worrisome to those working in Washington for passage of the civil rights bill. In Berkeley, California, demonstrators seeking more minority jobs filled supermarket carts with food, much of it perishable, and then abandoned them in the store, leaving unrefrigerated items to spoil before store employees could get them back into the freezer. In New York City, militants publicly threatened to protest racial problems in the city by leaving their faucets open and thereby reducing water pressure and perhaps causing a water shortage. In Atlanta, Georgia, blacks entered a segregated restaurant and urinated on the floor. The white mayor of Atlanta reacted strongly and gave a stinging speech entitled, "Is Urination Nonviolent?" Time Magazine concluded that, increasingly, "local civil rights demonstrators seem to employ pointless, often destructive, and sometimes dangerous tactics."[39]

THE WORLD'S FAIR STALL-IN

The changed character of the civil rights demonstrations reached a peak of publicity when the Brooklyn chapter of the Congress of Racial Equality announced it would stage a "stall-in" on the opening day of the New York World's Fair. The fair, located on Long Island and accessible to New York City by both subway and freeway, was scheduled to open on 22 April 1964. President Johnson was scheduled to speak at the opening day ceremonies. Because the World's Fair had been so vigorously promoted in the news media, the threat to ruin opening day with a disruptive civil rights demonstration became the top civil rights news story of the week.

Day after day the newspapers and television stations reported the plans of the demonstrators to the nation. Large numbers of automobiles would be intentionally stalled on the heavily trafficked freeways and streets leading to the fair site. Demonstrators would pretend to have a flat tire, or an overheated engine, or just defiantly stop their car in a lane of traffic and refuse to move on.

The plan appeared highly disruptive to anyone who knew about New York traffic. New York was a city where a single stalled car on the Long Island Expressway could cause a miles long traffic jam. As one commentator expressed it:

> To plan a deliberate stall-in, with fifty cars clogging the expressways, meant to reach for the nerve centers of the enormous, delicate megalopolis which is the most technically sensitive in the world. To reach for the Douglaston Interchange, the Van Wyck Interchange or the Triborough Bridge is to grab at the groin of a community of 10 million people.[40]

The demonstrators also had plans for the subway trains running to the fairgrounds. Black radicals openly urged civil rights protesters to pull the emergency brake cords of subway trains as they raced toward the fair at speeds in excess of 35 miles per hour. The local press quickly pointed out that pulling the emergency cord instantly locks the wheels of the subway train, causing the train to stop with a sharp jerk, almost as if the train had run into a brick wall. The chances of severe injury to passengers, and possibly fatalities, were said to be very great.

The news media picked up and publicized virtually every threat the demonstrators made. It was reported that cars and drivers for the stall-in would be coming to New York in motorcades from Maryland, Pennsylvania, and even Chicago, almost 1,000 miles away. Leaders at the Brooklyn CORE office boasted that over 2,000 cars would stop dead on the highways, thereby creating the greatest traffic jam in New York history. Even the ticket booths to the World's Fair itself were targeted for delay. Demonstrators would create long ticket lines by slowly laying out 199 pennies for the $2 admission, then would return to the end of the line when they "discovered" that they did not have enough money to get in.

As opening day approached, still more stall-in plans were announced. Allegedly an airplane was going to fly over the fairgrounds and drop leaflets detailing and protesting racial discrimination in New York. It was even stated that a Harlem group would trap hundreds of live rats in the slums, bring them to the fairgrounds, and release them into the crowds during President Johnson's speech.[41]

In many ways, the tone of the statements of the new civil rights militants was more disturbing than their actual plans. A well-known political commentator described the thoughts of a black militant the night before the stall-in:

> The stall-in . . . would open a new world. . . . The United States owed the Negroes for three hundred years of unpaid labor as slaves; the reparations bill was going to be presented tomorrow; New York would be paralyzed.[42]

If the plans for the stall-in were a good news story, the

plans of New York City and New York State officials for handling the stall-in were an equally good news story. There were hasty conferences of City officials at Gracie Mansion, the official residence of the mayor of New York. All police leaves were cancelled. Emergency command posts were established at key points on the highway system and the subway system leading to the fair. Long lines of tow trucks were assembled and parked adjacent to key bridges and intersections. Police helicopters were scheduled to hover overhead to spot traffic jams and, by short-wave radio, dispatch tow trucks and police cruisers as needed. The city, along with the entire nation, nervously awaited the great confrontation.

"CIVIL WRONGS DO NOT BRING CIVIL RIGHTS"

Back on Capitol Hill, the death of Reverend Klunder in Cleveland and press coverage of the planned New York World's Fair stall-in were causing great concern at civil rights strategy meetings. At a 14 April 1964 session in Hubert Humphrey's Capitol office, Humphrey's top legislative aide asked Assistant Attorney General Nicholas Katzenbach what his thoughts were on the World's Fair excesses of Brooklyn CORE. Katzenbach replied:

> Of course there will be excesses in the civil rights
> movement, just as there are excesses on the other
> side. Our job is to get the law through, not sit in
> judgment on each demonstration.

Katzenbach later pointed out that he did not believe one should refuse to vote for the bill, if it is a good bill, just because there may be unwise picketing or inappropriate demonstrations.[43] At this point Senator Kuchel's legislative assistant proposed a joint declaration by members of both political parties condemning the current wave of excesses in the civil rights movement. He was supported in this sentiment by the Humphrey people, and the major staff assignment for the remainder of the day was the fashioning of just such a statement.[44]

The next day, 15 April 1964, Humphrey and Kuchel issued the joint statement. "Civil wrongs do not bring civil rights," the bipartisan civil rights floor managers told the nation. "Civil disobedience does not bring equal protection under the laws." They went on to condemn "unruly demonstrations and protests that bring hardships and unnecessary inconvenience to others," and they warned that "illegal disturbances and demonstrations which lead to violence or injury" would hamper the current effort to enact a strong civil rights bill.[45]

Humphrey and Kuchel were joined by a chorus of other voices pointing out the damage which the new kinds of demonstrations were doing to the civil rights movement. Attorney General Robert Kennedy told the press that he had conferred privately with Humphrey and Kuchel before they issued their statement warning against violent demonstrations, and the attorney general himself noted that "these activities, whether actions of violence or some of the other irresponsible actions, deter the efforts to obtain passage of the legislation."[46] National leaders of the National Association for the Advancement of Colored People, the Congress of Racial Equality, and the National Council of Negro Women condemned the planned stall-in at the New York World's Fair, and James Farmer, National Director of CORE, suspended the Brooklyn chapter of CORE when its officers insisted on going through with the stall-in proposal. The Denver Post charged editorially that the new wave of demonstrations had "managed to do what Bull Connor, Governor Wallace, Governor Faubus, Governor Barnett and the Grand Kleagle of the Ku Klux Klan could not do -- it has made the cause of human rights look silly."[47]

The real concern on the part of civil rights advocates was that the changing character of the demonstrations would cause a "Birmingham in reverse." Hubert Humphrey put the idea this way:

> The scenes [in Birmingham] of police dogs and
> policemen with clubs being used against peaceful

demonstrations caused great public outcry. But if the extremists in the civil rights movement decide to inconvenience hundreds of thousands of people, it's going to have the same reaction in reverse.[48]

As it turned out, the proposed stall-in at the New York World's Fair did not materialize. A brief attempt at blocking the doors of fairbound subway trains was broken up by a flying squad of Transit Authority policemen, and less than a dozen demonstrators actually tried to stall their cars on the freeways leading to the fair site. President Johnson helicoptered in for the opening day ceremonies without incident. One public official, Senator Jacob Javits of New York, decided to go to the fair on the subway and, if necessary, directly confront the demonstrators who were doing so much damage to his civil rights efforts in the Senate. As he and his wife arrived at the subway station and boarded the train, however, there was no one there to confront them.[49]

Just the threat of the stall-in had been enough to draw press criticism, however. Time Magazine commented that only one conclusion could be drawn from the entire unhappy affair: "A tiny minority in the civil rights movement had managed to make a lot of people mad without achieving a single thing for the cause."[50]

There was another press reaction to Reverend Klunder's death in Cleveland and the threatened stall-in at the World's Fair in New York. Newspapers and national magazines began speculating about the threat of a "white backlash," the fact that many whites previously favorable to civil rights might turn against it if demonstrations became increasingly violent and demands started to appear unreasonable.

At one point during the long spring of 1964, Representative William McCulloch told a House of Representatives aide that the disturbing character of these new civil rights demonstrations in the North was costing the civil rights bill considerable support in the House. The aide said:

Representative McCulloch is getting progressively worried. He claims they would lose 25 percent of the votes they had if a vote were now to occur in the House on the civil rights bill.[51]

THE GOLDWATER CAMPAIGN FOR PRESIDENT

Another event outside the Senate which began to have an impact on the civil rights bill was the increasingly bitter campaign for the Republican nomination for president of the United States. Initially there were only two announced candidates, Senator Barry Goldwater of Arizona and Governor Nelson Rockefeller of New York, and the race between them was essentially ideological. Goldwater was an outspoken Western conservative; Rockefeller was a dedicated Eastern liberal.

Although both men claimed to be supporters of civil rights, their public positions on the civil rights bill were quite different. Rockefeller was an all-out supporter of the strong civil rights bill passed by the House of Representatives. Goldwater, on the other hand, continually expressed reservations about the bill and began to announce to the press and public those provisions of the bill he believed should be deleted.

Although Goldwater had at one time been a member of the NAACP and frequently expressed his support for the concept of equal rights for all Americans, he often stated that he was opposed to legislative action at the national level in this field. In a major campaign address in Chicago he said he would vote for the civil rights bill only if the public accommodations and the equal employment opportunity sections were removed.[52] To anyone who knew the details of the legislation then being debated in the Senate, such a major deletion would "cut the heart out of the civil rights bill."[53]

The battle between Goldwater and Rockefeller began with New Hampshire's "First in the Nation" presidential primary election on 10 March 1964. The outcome of the New Hampshire Republican primary was a surprise. An unannounced candidate, former Senator Henry Cabot Lodge of Massachusetts,

211

won both the popular vote in the primary and all of New Hampshire's delegates to the Republican National Convention. Lodge's victory was considered doubly surprising because his name had not even been printed on the election ballot (his supporters had to "write-in" his name in order to vote for him). Also unusual was the fact that Lodge was currently 10,000 miles away from New Hampshire serving as U.S. ambassador to South Vietnam. Goldwater finished a distant second to Lodge, and Rockefeller finished third but close behind Goldwater.

The Lodge "write-in" victory in New Hampshire and the accelerating "Draft Lodge" campaign that grew out of it were seen as a disaster for the Rockefeller forces. The main Rockefeller strategy had been to win big in the Republican presidential primaries and thereby demonstrate that Goldwater was not the popular choice of moderate, "mainstream" Republicans. Unfortunately for Rockefeller, Lodge appealed to the same moderate to liberal wing of the Republican Party that Rockefeller represented. Lodge's surprise entrance into the campaign meant that Lodge and Rockefeller would split the moderate to liberal vote in the Republican primaries, thereby allowing Goldwater's bloc of conservative supporters to look more powerful than they actually were.

The Rockefeller forces tried to put the best possible face on the New Hampshire primary. Rockefeller told the press that Lodge's big win was "a victory for moderation" and a repudiation of the "extreme" conservative stands taken by Senator Goldwater.[54]

As the battle for the Republican nomination for president continued through late March and into April, Lodge and Rockefeller continued "to knock each other out," and Barry Goldwater quickly took the lead in terms of the number of delegates to the Republican convention committed to vote for him. As Goldwater himself expressed it after he captured all 58 convention delegate votes in Illinois in mid April: "The polls all talk about Lodge, but everybody overlooks the fact that I'm getting the delegates."[55]

By the end of April 1964, political commentators were

looking to the 15 May 1964 Oregon primary as the next crucial skirmish in the battle for the Republican presidential nomination. Lodge, Rockefeller, and Goldwater would all be running against each other in one of the best publicized presidential primaries in the nation. Early polls, as usual, had shown Lodge with a commanding lead with Goldwater second and Rockefeller third.

After Oregon, political attention would shift to the California Republican presidential primary in early June. Only Goldwater and Rockefeller would meet in that major struggle (the Draft Lodge forces had not organized in time to meet California's early filing deadline). In 1964 California election laws called for a "winner take all" primary. If Goldwater won he would get all of California's sizable delegation to the Republican Convention. If Rockefeller won, he would get all the delegates.

But in late April 1964 practically no one was expecting Nelson Rockefeller to have much of a chance in the California primary. The prevailing prediction was that, after Lodge scored his expected victory over Goldwater and Rockefeller in Oregon, there would be no momentum left in the Rockefeller campaign. The result would be a Goldwater victory in California and a guaranteed Goldwater nomination at the Republican National Convention in July.

The Lodge-Rockefeller-Goldwater battle was having several effects on the Senate filibuster of the civil rights bill. One effect was that Senator Kuchel, the Republican floor manager for the bill, was a strong backer of Nelson Rockefeller for the Republican presidential nomination and was actively campaigning for Rockefeller against Goldwater in the California primary campaign. Kuchel flew to California virtually every weekend during April and May of 1964 to speak for and campaign with Rockefeller. Kuchel's goal was to stop the growing influence of Goldwater conservatism in the Republican Party, and he saw passage of the civil rights bill and denying Goldwater the Republican presidential nomination as the two best ways to accomplish this goal.

Another way the Republican presidential nomination fight

213

was effecting the civil rights bill was its alleged effect on President Lyndon Johnson and his level of support for the bill. The logic went like this. Lyndon Johnson was strongly supporting civil rights because, as a Southern Democrat, he wanted to win support among liberal voters in the big cities of the North. If a strong conservative like Barry Goldwater was the Republican nominee, however, President Johnson would get the Northern liberal vote by default. In that case he would not need a strong civil rights bill. In fact, all he would need would be a moderate civil rights bill, just good enough to show civil rights oriented voters that he was a much better choice than Barry Goldwater. As Goldwater would get closer to the nomination, so this theory concluded, Johnson would become ever more willing to compromise the civil rights bill, either with Senate Republican Leader Everett Dirksen or with the Southern Democrats themselves, because a weak bill would serve his political purposes just as well as a strong bill would.

The Johnson forces made no secret of the fact that they hoped Senator Goldwater, and not Governor Rockefeller, would be the Republican nominee. Their view was that a conservative like Goldwater would be an even match for President Johnson in the South, which had traditionally been a conservative section of the nation, but they believed that President Johnson could easily defeat Goldwater in the North, the Midwest, and on the West Coast. Since there were many more voters in the North, the Midwest, and on the West Coast than there were in the South, the Johnson people relished the thought of having Goldwater as their Republican opponent in the November 1964 general election.

If Rockefeller were the Republican nominee, however, it would present real problems to President Johnson's reelection campaign. Rockefeller was a liberal Republican and very popular in large Eastern states like New York and Pennsylvania. Rockefeller would give a Southern Democrat like Johnson a real run for his money in the North, the Midwest, and possibly even on the West Coast. In a race with Rockefeller, Johnson could probably only count on carrying his old homeland of the

American South.

Deputy Attorney General Nicholas Katzenbach made a humorous comment that indicated he and other members of the Johnson administration wanted Goldwater as the Republican nominee. At a civil rights strategy meeting on Capitol Hill in early April, Senator Kuchel announced that he had to play "hooky" the following Saturday and go out and campaign in California in behalf of Nelson Rockefeller. "I have to save the Republican party as well as participate in the civil rights debate," Kuchel remarked. Katzenbach jokingly responded, "Can't you put first things first, Senator?" Katzenbach thereby implied that he and the Johnson forces would much prefer that Kuchel stayed in Washington to work for civil rights and did not go out to California to try and stop Barry Goldwater from getting the Republican nomination. Apparently everyone in the room understood Katzenbach's subtle humor, because his comment was greeted with much hearty laughter from Republicans and Democrats alike.[56]

Senator Goldwater's growing lead in the race for the 1964 Republican presidential nomination presented still more problems to the civil rights forces. As Goldwater, an outspoken critic of key sections of the civil rights bill, won the support of more and more delegates to the Republican convention, this was interpreted by some political commentators as a sign that national support for the civil rights bill, particularly within the Republican Party, was weakening. More worrisome to civil rights forces, however, was thinking about what effect a Goldwater nomination might have on those "crucial 12" conservative Republican senators whose votes were the last ones needed to attain cloture. Most of these men were close friends of Goldwater's and came from the same part of the country as the Arizona senator. Would they want to vote cloture on a civil rights bill which their close friend, perhaps soon to be their political party's presidential nominee, said he strenuously opposed?

As April 1964 turned into May 1964, attention fastened firmly on the 15 May 1964 Oregon Republican presidential primary. If Henry Cabot Lodge won big in Oregon, knocked

Rockefeller out of the race, and thereby guaranteed Barry Goldwater the Republican nomination, the civil rights bill then undergoing a filibuster in the Senate might be in considerable trouble.

THE WALLACE CANDIDACY FOR PRESIDENT

Early in 1964, Alabama Governor George Wallace announced that he was a candidate for the Democratic nomination for president of the United States and that he would run on a platform of all-out opposition to the civil rights bill. Governor Wallace was a formidable candidate running on the anti-civil rights issue. At the time of his inauguration as Governor of Alabama, Wallace took a hard line stand against racial integration. He said:

> From this very Cradle of the Confederacy, this very heart of the great Anglo-Saxon Southland, . . . I draw the line in the dust and toss the gauntlet before the feet of tyranny. And I say: Segregation now! Segregation tomorrow! Segregation forever!

Wallace had gained extensive national publicity when he personally "barred the school house door" at the University of Alabama in his futile attempt to prevent integration of the university by U.S. marshals. Although Wallace had been forced to stand aside and let the university be integrated, he had emerged from the fracas as a Southern segregationist hero and as the national symbol of opposition to school integration and black civil rights.

The Wallace candidacy produced quick action on President Lyndon Johnson's part. Unwilling to permit "open season" on his presidential administration by running against Wallace himself, Johnson set to work recruiting stand-in candidates to run against Wallace in three crucial Democratic presidential primaries -- Wisconsin, Indiana, and Maryland.

216

The Wallace threat to the civil rights bill was serious. Everywhere he went Wallace stated that his presidential candidacy was a referendum on the civil rights bill then being filibustered in the Senate. If Wallace could win only one presidential primary outside the old South, it was feared that the chances of beating the filibuster would be seriously jeopardized. Johnson himself noted that the Wallace campaign "stiffened the Southerners' will to keep on fighting the civil rights measure" in hopes that, following a Wallace primary victory or two, the liberal ranks in the Senate might begin to crumble.[57]

WALLACE IN WISCONSIN

The Wallace campaign began in Wisconsin, where Democratic Governor John W. Reynolds was running as the favorite son front man for President Johnson. When Reynolds learned that Wallace had filed against him in the primary, he canceled a planned trip to Europe and flew instead to Washington to get campaign advice from key Johnson political advisers. Returning home to Wisconsin, he began campaigning strenuously against Wallace.

President Johnson stayed publicly aloof from the Reynolds campaign but did much to help Reynolds from behind the scenes. Johnson sent his postmaster general, John A. Gronouski, a former Wisconsin state official, to campaign for Reynolds in the Polish-American sections of Milwaukee, sections that were close to the black neighborhoods in Milwaukee and regarded as likely to cast a "backlash vote" for Governor Wallace. Gronouski made it clear he did not want the Polish-American neighborhoods of Milwaukee "pointed out the nation over as a center of intolerance and bigotry, because that is not the nature of the Polish people."[58]

President Johnson did take one small opportunity to show the voters of Wisconsin that Reynolds was his man in the presidential primary. At a testimonial dinner for Reynolds only two days before election day, Gronouski read a telegram from President Johnson which praised Reynolds but did not mention either Wallace or the bitterly fought primary election campaign. The presidential telegram described Reynolds as "a patriot and a leader in whom we can all take pride. . . . I salute John Reynolds for his unceasing concern for the well-being of the people in his state."[59]

Unfortunately for civil rights advocates on Capitol Hill, Governor Reynolds made a mistake that would be repeated several times during the Wallace campaign for president. Reynolds seriously underestimated Governor Wallace's appeal and popularity in a Northern state like Wisconsin and therefore made predictions that Wallace would not get very many votes. In fact, Reynolds got specific and said that Wallace would get no more than 100,000 votes in Wisconsin, but even that "would be a catastrophe."[60]

On election day, 7 April 1964, Governor Reynolds easily defeated Wallace, collecting 511,000 votes in the process and guaranteeing all of Wisconsin's delegate votes at the Democratic National Convention to President Johnson. Wallace received 264,000 votes, more than 2 1/2 times the 100,000 votes that Governor Reynolds had said "would be a catastrophe."

The national press reaction to Wallace's unexpectedly high vote totals was one of concern and surprise. Time Magazine labeled it "worse than catastrophe" and went on to make this evaluation:

> The real issue in the primary was civil rights. Wallace had entered the Wisconsin primary to demonstrate that many Northern, as well as Southern, whites are unhappy about current civil rights trends. And he demonstrated just that -- dramatically.[61]

Exactly as civil rights supporters had feared, post election analysis revealed that Wallace had run strongest in normally Democratic urban districts heavily populated by lower middle class, second generation Poles, Italians, and Serbs. These voters, found mainly in southside Milwaukee and in similar city districts

218

in Racine and Kenosha, were said to be apprehensive that the black drive for equality would harm their own economic interests and might produce racial change in their home neighborhoods.[62]

Although he lost the election, Governor Wallace was quick to claim a moral victory. The day after the election he told the press the primary was a major victory in his campaign against the civil rights bill. He explained:

> We won a victory and we know it. We won without winning. . . . Governor Reynolds said if I got 100,000 votes it would be a catastrophe. Well, I guess we've got two catastrophes.[63]

Wallace's unexpectedly strong showing in Wisconsin produced a flurry of statements on Capitol Hill. Senate Democratic Whip Hubert Humphrey tried to minimize the impact of the election results by emphasizing the fact that Wallace had, after all, lost the election. Humphrey mockingly spelled out his viewpoint to reporters:

> I can count. Governor Wallace's effort was a flop, f-l-o-p. His campaign was a fizzle, f-i-z-z-l-e. . . . [In] most Midwest states if you put your name on the party ballot you get 25 percent of the vote, dead or alive.

Senate Republican Leader Everett Dirksen made a somewhat different interpretation, however. He found the size of the Wallace vote in Wisconsin to be "an interesting commentary on the depth of feeling people evidently entertain regarding the civil rights issue." Dirksen also said he thought the Wallace showing would "help amendments of a corrective nature" to the civil rights bill, amendments which, it turned out, Dirksen had ready for presentation in the Senate.

Senate Democratic Leader Mike Mansfield found the Wallace vote in Wisconsin neither bad nor good but simply a sign that the civil rights issue had to be settled and settled in the

Senate. Mansfield said:

> People are, in effect, expressing their views on this
> issue which now confronts us and which we cannot
> avoid or evade any longer. It is an issue which
> the Senate must face up to and decide in its
> wisdom one way or the other . . . ."[64]

WALLACE IN INDIANA

Following his electoral defeat but publicity triumph in
Wisconsin, Governor Wallace turned his attention to the
Democratic presidential primary in Indiana scheduled for 5 May
1964. Indiana looked like it might be a rich hunting ground for
Wallace. Historically the state had been a Northern center of Ku
Klux Klan activities, and populous Lake County, an industrial
suburb of Chicago in Northwestern Indiana, contained many of
the same lower middle class, second generation ethnic voters that
had shown such surprising support for Wallace in Wisconsin.

By now the Wallace campaign was showing the telltale
signs of electoral success and confidence. Wallace was flying to
his various campaign stops in Indiana in a large airliner
decorated with a Confederate flag and the slogan, "Stand Up For
America!" Both directly and indirectly, Wallace let it be known
that a vote for him was a vote against what he called "the civil
wrongs bill." At an airport press conference in Indianapolis,
Wallace said he had come to Indiana "because I want to let the
people have an effective way of opposing some of the trends
going on in Washington."[65]

President Johnson's favorite son stand-in in the Indiana
primary was Democratic Governor Matthew Welsh. Welsh at
one time had· mockingly said to the press: "Who's Wallace?"
As the campaign developed, however, Welsh began to take the
Wallace threat very seriously and began a series of strident
verbal attacks on the Alabama Governor. Welsh charged:

This is the man who tolerated the presence of

220

billboards in his state before the assassination
which demanded, "Kayo the Kennedys." This is
the man who stood by while dogs were set upon
human beings and fire hoses were turned on
groups of peaceful demonstrators. This is the man
who even today is actively denying Negro children
access to the University of Alabama. This is the
man who is trying to destroy the political system
of the United States as we know it, and who seeks
to discredit President Lyndon B. Johnson. This is
the man who flies the Confederate flag over the
Statehouse in Alabama in place of the Stars and
Stripes.[66]

Wallace was quick to demonstrate that he could generate
headlines equally as well as Governor Welsh. Wallace told some
300 applauding students at a campaign rally at Butler University:

I am not a racist. I'm against interracial
marriages. I think the Negro race ought to stay
pure and the white race ought to stay pure. God
intended for white people to stay white, Chinese to
stay yellow and Negroes to stay black. All
mankind is the handiwork of God.[67]

With this much political fur flying, the Wallace campaign
in Indiana received large amounts of newspaper and television
coverage. The actual results on election day were somewhat less
spectacular than the campaign rhetoric, however. Governor
Welsh defeated Wallace, as expected, but Wallace received a
somewhat lower percentage of the vote in Indiana (30 percent)
than he had received in Wisconsin (34 percent). Time
Magazine's coverage of the primary election results highlighted
the fact that Wallace had not done all that well in the vote count
but was continuing to get extensive press coverage for his
efforts:

221

Governor Matthew Welsh, a favorite son stand-in for President Johnson, amassed 368,401 votes. But who got the headlines? Why, none other than Alabama's trouble-hunting Governor George Wallace with 170,146.[68]

As he had done in Wisconsin, Wallace was quick to portray his second place finish as a victory. The Alabama Governor proclaimed:

Our campaign for states rights won. We shook the eyeteeth of those people [liberals in both political parties] in Wisconsin, and the noises you hear now are the teeth falling out in Indiana.[69]

Analysis of the Indiana vote indicated that liberal supporters of civil rights had a good reason to feel "shaken" and possibly "toothless." As expected, Wallace received his strongest support in Northwestern Indiana, mainly in white areas in the working class cities of Gary and East Chicago. The vote analysis led to continued newspaper speculation that there was, indeed, a "white backlash" brewing against civil rights in lower middle class, white, ethnic neighborhoods.[70]

Wallace's twin defeats in Wisconsin and Indiana did not end the Alabama Governor's threat to the civil rights bill. "We are going on to Maryland from here," Wallace said, noting that the Maryland Democratic presidential primary, scheduled for 19 May 1964, would give him one last chance to demonstrate how strong the opposition was to the civil rights bill in the North and the Border States.

CONCLUSIONS

Throughout the month of April and into early May 1964, much of the battle over the civil rights bill shifted away from the Senate floor and was fought in other places and by other means. The pro-civil rights forces concentrated their efforts on creating the impression that there was a wave of public support for the bill. The principal techniques used here were to bring religious leaders supporting the bill to Washington and to have pro-civil rights senators, particularly Hubert Humphrey of Minnesota, give favorable speeches on the bill before enthusiastic audiences of known supporters.

The Southern Democratic fight against the civil rights bill was mainly taken over by Alabama Governor George Wallace in his campaign against President Lyndon Johnson for the 1964 Democratic presidential nomination. The April and May presidential primary elections in Wisconsin and Indiana provided Wallace with a national platform from which to demonstrate that there was considerable opposition to civil rights in the North.

It should be noted that, due to the fact that the Southern Democrats were conducting a filibuster on the floor of the United States Senate, it was logical that national attention would shift away from the Senate floor. After all, the essence of a filibuster is that, by ceaselessly talking and debating, the filibusterers have converted the Senate floor into a forum where no action can possibly take place. It made sense that, under such conditions, national attention and concern about civil rights would shift elsewhere.

It has already been pointed out that legislative strategists must always keep in mind the "total legislative picture" -- the fact that a bill going through Congress is often affected by the progress, or lack of progress, of other bills going through at the same time. To this idea must now be added the concept of the "total political picture" -- the fact that bills going through Congress can be dynamically effected by major political events taking place far away from Capitol Hill.

Perhaps as much as any bill that has ever gone through Congress, the Civil Rights Act of 1964 was subject to the effects of the "total political picture." The changed character of the civil rights demonstrations, the accidental death of Reverend Klunder in Cleveland, the threatened stall-in at the New York World's Fair, the Goldwater campaign for president, and the Wallace campaign for president -- all these events were having a direct effect on the attitudes, feelings, and strategies of the senators debating civil rights on the Senate floor. By mid May 1964 the pressures being created by these external events were getting intense for the senators supporting the civil rights bill.

CHAPTER 11

EVERETT M. DIRKSEN;
THE GREAT AMENDER

There is much evidence to suggest that, from the very beginning of the Senate debate on the bipartisan civil rights bill, President Lyndon Johnson and Senate Democratic Whip Hubert Humphrey realized that Senate Republican Leader Everett Dirksen of Illinois would hold the key to a successful cloture vote on the bill. Thus, as the drone and drawl of the filibuster dragged on throughout the months of April and May 1964, the most important events taking place were Johnson's and Humphrey's attempts to find some way of winning Dirksen's support and getting Dirksen to get his Republican allies in the Senate to vote cloture on civil rights.

A member of the White House staff, Mike Manatos, argued that it was necessary to have Dirksen's support to get cloture, but that it was important to keep in mind that Dirksen was a person who would change his mind about an important national issue. Manatos explained:

> I think that Dirksen is the kind of individual who wants to see progress. And I think that once you persuade Dirksen that he's wrong in a particular area, that he ought to be going in another direction, he can be turned around. There are some things you learn up there [on Capitol Hill]. One of them is that you can't get cloture without Ev Dirksen. So the question is, whether it's on civil rights or anything else, to find out whether

225

you can work out an agreement with Senator Dirksen, maybe take 1/2 loaf or 3/4 of a particular loaf. . . . Senator Dirksen was the kind of individual who could be persuaded on the basis of logic and justice that his course was wrong. He'd do an about-turn.[1]

President Johnson was aware from the moment he became president that the real problem with the civil rights bill would be in the Senate and not the House of Representatives. On 3 December 1963 he told his first congressional leadership breakfast:

Civil rights has been [in the House of Representatives] since May. . . . We all know the real problem will be in the Senate.[2]

President Johnson noted in his memoirs that, shortly after President Kennedy's assassination, he telephoned Dirksen and asked him to convey to his Republican colleagues in the Senate that the time had come to forget partisan politics and get the legislative machinery of the United States moving forward. As Johnson recalled the phone conversation:

There was a long pause on the other end of the line and I could hear him [Dirksen] breathing heavily. When he finally spoke, he expressed obvious disappointment that I would even raise the question of marshaling his party behind the president. "Mr. President," he said, "you know I will."[3]

Turning Senator Dirksen's general statement of support for the president into support for a cloture vote on the civil rights bill would be no small task. The strategy designed by Johnson was to give Dirksen the opportunity to be a "hero in history!" Johnson noted:

I gave to this fight everything I had in prestige, power, and commitment. At the same time, I deliberately tried to tone down my personal involvement in the daily struggle so that my colleagues on the Hill could take tactical responsibility -- and credit so that a hero's niche could be carved out for Senator Dirksen, not me.[4]

Louis Martin, deputy chairman of the Democratic National Committee under President Johnson, argued that Johnson did not "tone down" his personal approach when it came to working personally on Everett Dirksen. He said:

People talk about Johnson's style, but I don't think there's a warmer individual in America on a person-to-person relationship. He needed Dirksen, and he worked on Dirksen, flattered Dirksen, and he gave Dirksen certain privileges.[5]

The major share of the task of winning Everett Dirksen over to the civil rights bill fell to Hubert Humphrey, the Democratic whip in the Senate. Humphrey recalled a telephone call from Johnson just as the civil rights bill was arriving in the Senate. The president told Humphrey:

Now you know that this bill can't pass unless you get Ev Dirksen. You and I are going to get him. You make up your mind now that you've got to spend time with Ev Dirksen. You've got to let him have a piece of the action. He's got to look good all the time.[6]

On 28 February 1964 Humphrey remarked at a meeting of pro-civil rights senators that he had already talked to Dirksen about how the bill could not pass without Dirksen's support. Humphrey said:

I told Dirksen that it is not Hubert H. Humphrey
that can pass this bill. . . . [Ultimately, Ev,] it
boils down to what you do.[7]

By mid March 1964 Humphrey was accelerating his
efforts at nudging Dirksen into that civil rights "hero's niche."
Humphrey recalled that on his first television appearance in
connection with the civil rights bill, a Sunday morning guest spot
on "Meet the Press," he spent most of his time talking about
Senator Dirksen:

I praised Dirksen, telling the nation he would help,
that he would support a good civil rights bill, that
he would put his country above party, that he
would look upon this issue as a moral issue and
not a partisan issue.[8]

Humphrey concluded his television appearance with
soaring personal praise for Dirksen:

Senator Dirksen is not only a great Senator, he is
a great American, and he is going to see the
necessity of this legislation. I predict that before
this bill is through Senator Dirksen will be its
champion.[9]

Apparently Lyndon Johnson watched Humphrey's
performance on "Meet the Press" and believed that Humphrey
had done exactly the right thing. In a subsequent telephone call,
Johnson continued to urge Humphrey on:

Boy, that was right. You're doing just right now.
You just keep at that. Don't you let those bomb
throwers [extremely committed supporters of civil
rights] talk you out of seeing Dirksen. You get in
there to see Dirksen! You drink with Dirksen!
You talk to Dirksen! You listen to Dirksen![10]

Humphrey was careful to point out that his lavish praise for Dirksen was based both on honesty (Humphrey really did admire Dirksen's legislative skills) and on necessity:

> I did so [praised Dirksen] not only because I believed what I said but because we also needed him. I knew that . . . we could not possibly get cloture without Dirksen and his help. Therefore every effort was made to involve him. With few exceptions, I visited with Senator Dirksen every day, encouraging him to take a more prominent role, asking him what changes he wanted to propose [to the bill], urging him to call meetings and discuss his changes.[11]

In looking back on his avid courtship of Everett Dirksen, Humphrey eventually came to use the word "shameless" to describe his behavior and, by implication, Dirksen's:

> I never failed to stroke Ev Dirksen's ego. I don't know whether he realized what I was doing or not, but he liked it. I don't think a day went by when I didn't say, "Everett, we can't pass this bill without you. We need your leadership in this fight, Everett." And I'd say, "This will go down in history, Everett," and that meant, of course, that he would go down in history, which interested him a great deal. Oh, I was shameless. But as I say he liked hearing it all, and I didn't mind saying it.[12]

Humphrey's legislative assistant described the technique which Humphrey was using on Dirksen as "the great man hook." The legislative assistant, who periodically dictated his thoughts on the progress of the civil rights bill through the Senate, outlined the strategy in considerable detail:

> Humphrey has been playing up very strongly the

229

line that this is an opportunity for Dirksen to be the great man of the United States, the man of the hour, the man who saves the civil rights bill. This line has been played up by Humphrey on "Meet the Press," in numerous conversations with journalists. Humphrey instigated Roscoe Drummond's recent article in the Herald Tribune Syndicate pointing up that Dirksen has an opportunity for greatness in the pending civil rights debate. In short, it appears that Dirksen is beginning to swallow the great man hook and, when it is fully digested, we will have ourselves a civil rights bill.[13]

TWO-FACED?

It is important to note that, at the same time President Johnson and Hubert Humphrey were acknowledging privately that they would have to compromise the civil rights bill in order to get Dirksen's support, they were telling the press and the public that they would accept "no compromises" in the House passed bill. There were two reasons for this two-faced procedure in which one view was presented to insiders (we want to compromise with Dirksen) and a completely opposite view was presented to the world (no compromises on the House passed bill). In the first place, once the compromise negotiations with Dirksen finally began, Johnson and Humphrey wanted to sacrifice as little of the House passed bill as possible. The best way to achieve this was to start from a position of "no compromises" and thereby be able to pretend that they were making a big sacrifice to Dirksen just by negotiating compromises with him at all.

The second reason that Johnson and Humphrey took a "no compromises" position was that they were under heavy pressure from the Leadership Conference on Civil Rights. Exactly as they had done in the House of Representatives, Clarence Mitchell, Jr., and Joseph Rauh, Jr., were continuing the strategy that "the best defense is a good offense." By taking the position that no compromises to the House passed bill were acceptable, Mitchell and Rauh hoped to reduce the extent of those compromises once they eventually were negotiated.

Mitchell and Rauh also took a very strong stand against allowing any cloture votes until Humphrey and Kuchel were absolutely certain that they had the necessary 2/3 vote for cloture. The Leadership Conference lobbyists had a good historical reason for taking this position. The 1957 and 1960 civil rights bills had both been compromised to suit the Southerners immediately following unsuccessful cloture votes. Mitchell and Rauh feared that a failed cloture vote in 1964 would have the same devastating effect, i.e., once it had been shown there were not enough votes for cloture, uncommitted senators would demand an immediate agreement with the Southerners that would end the filibuster but leave the civil rights bill, from Mitchell's and Rauh's point of view, emasculated and worthless.

EXTREME MEASURES

In addition to opposing any cloture vote until a successful outcome was guaranteed, Mitchell and Rauh argued that extreme measures should be used to break the filibuster. Mitchell shocked Humphrey and Kuchel by frequently arguing that the Senate's sergeant at arms should arrest the Southern senators and forcefully bring them to the Senate floor when they were needed to help make a quorum call.[14] Rauh repeatedly suggested that a little known Senate rule be used, a rule providing that no senator could make more than two speeches on any given subject.[15] Humphrey and Kuchel repeatedly explained to Mitchell that they thought arresting U.S. senators and dragging them down to the Senate floor for quorum calls was a bad idea. They pointed out that the national and international news coverage that would result from such "arrests" would be very negative and would make the civil rights forces look inept and silly.

Humphrey and Kuchel also carefully pointed out to Rauh

that, once a Southern senator had used up his two speeches under the two speech rule, all he would have to do was introduce a minor amendment to the bill and then he could give two more speeches on the amendment. Then when those two speeches were done, he could introduce another minor amendment, give two more speeches, and thereby go on talking forever. In short, the bipartisan floor managers argued, trying to implement and enforce the two speech rule simply would not work.

Despite Humphrey's and Kuchel's unanimous opposition, Clarence Mitchell, Jr., continued to talk about arresting absent Southern senators and Joseph Rauh kept advocating the two speech rule. Perhaps Mitchell and Rauh intentionally advocated these extreme measures as part of their "strong offense" strategy. Taking such belligerent stands in favor of extreme measures put Humphrey and Kuchel on the defensive and thereby made them less likely to suggest either compromising the bill or moving for cloture before the votes for cloture were definitely in hand.[16]

WARRING WITH THE LEADERSHIP CONFERENCE

By mid April 1964 Hubert Humphrey began hinting at his morning civil rights strategy meetings that, sooner or later, he was going to have to begin negotiating a compromise version of the civil rights bill with Senator Dirksen. These gentle hints on Humphrey's part produced extremely critical reactions from Clarence Mitchell, Jr., and Joseph Rauh, Jr. At a meeting of the pro-civil rights forces on 16 April 1964, Mitchell and Rauh complained bitterly about the fact that there had been a number of newspaper columns speculating that the civil rights bill would be enacted once it had been altered to suit Senator Dirksen. The following discussion, excerpted from notes, illustrated the increasing tension between Hubert Humphrey on the one hand and Clarence Mitchell, Jr., and Joseph Rauh, Jr., on the other:[17]

MITCHELL: There has been an incredible

232

reversal of our agreements. . . . [Is] our side caving in? We are not going to . . . [put the Leadership Conference] in a box and . . . [nail] down the cover. It is unfair to cave in . . . .

RAUH: The Leadership Conference is united in thinking that a cloture discussion is unwise. Cloture means compromise. There should be no cloture until the votes are counted. We had that pledge from Hubert [Humphrey] in this room. We need to hold Dirksen off . . . [with] his amendments. . . .

HUMPHREY: We are going to talk about cloture. We have to think ahead. We have to plan to pass the bill . . . , [if not as it is then as it] might be. We will plan. . . .

MITCHELL: You are shooting your friends if you trade with Dirksen.

HUMPHREY: We don't have . . . [67] votes for cloture. . . .

RAUH: Public discussion of cloture leads to talk of compromise with the Dirksen amendments. Some of the those [the Dirksen amendments] are just as bad as [those proposed by] the Southerners.

HUMPHREY: We have made no deal [with Dirksen]. [But] we have to talk out loud. . . . [Besides that,] we cannot get a quorum this Saturday. All those brave fighters for civil rights are elsewhere. . . . Democratic senators have told me that "if the life of the nation depends on my [being here], . . . then I say to hell with it. . . ."

[MITCHELL and RAUH now press the idea that the civil rights forces should try to exhaust the Southerners with round-the-clock sessions before negotiating a compromise with Senator Dirksen.]

HUMPHREY: Unless we are ready to

move in our clothes and our shavers and turn the
Senate into a dormitory -- which Mansfield won't
have [--] we have to do something else. The
president [Lyndon Johnson] grabbed me by my
shoulder and damn near broke my arm. He said:
"I'd run the show around-the-clock." That was
three weeks ago. I told the president he [was]
grabbing the wrong arm. [Humphrey was implying
the president should have been grabbing
Mansfield's arm.] I have the Senate wives calling
me right now asking, "Why can't the senator be
home now?" They add, "The place [the Senate]
isn't being run intelligently." Sometimes I'm
working for longer hours. [Then] the president
[calls and] says, "What about the pay bill? What
about poverty? What about food stamps?"
Clarence, we aren't going to sell out. If we do, it
will be for a hell of a price. [Bells ring signaling
a quorum call on the Senate floor.] I'd better
answer the quorum. It would be a hell of a thing
if I missed it.

Literally saved by the bell, Humphrey left the meeting
and rushed to the Senate floor for the quorum call. He thereby
was spared from listening to Mitchell's and Rauh's reactions to
his statement that he might "sell out" but for "a hell of a price."

As April turned into May, Humphrey and Kuchel talked
more and more openly about the fact that they would probably
negotiate a compromise bill with Senator Dirksen. At a civil
rights strategy meeting in early May, a pro-civil rights senator
hinted that some "concessions" on the bill might be required.
Joseph Rauh, Jr., described the reaction of Clarence Mitchell, Jr.,
to this suggestion:

Clarence Mitchell, eyes flashing, exploded that the
Negroes of America would never understand
weakening the civil rights bill; he eloquently

portrayed the depth of feeling and the violence that would inevitably flow from any weakening of the bill.

Rauh noted that Hubert Humphrey sought to ease the tension created by Mitchell's vehement statement by looking at Mitchell and saying with a smile, "Clarence, you are three feet off your chair."[18]

Not content with pressuring Humphrey and Kuchel in the civil rights strategy meetings, the Leadership Conference began to put public pressure on the bipartisan floor leaders to not negotiate with Dirksen. On 6 May 1964 Walter Reuther, president of the United Automobile Workers union and a key member of the Leadership Conference, made public a telegram to Humphrey and Kuchel. The telegram said:

> The United Automobile Workers reject as both unwise and unnecessary current suggestions that concessions must be made to Senator Dirksen in order to purchase his vote for cloture. We firmly believe that the compelling urgency of this great moral issue of civil rights will persuade Senator Dirksen to vote for cloture in June whether his proposed amendments are adopted or not.[19]

ABANDONMENT OF THE LEADERSHIP CONFERENCE

What was happening was that Humphrey and Kuchel, in order to get the civil rights bill passed, were about to abandon their previous all-out support of the Leadership Conference and negotiate a final bill that would fall somewhat short of the Leadership Conference's strong demands. Hubert Humphrey's legislative assistant described this process of legislators and lobbyists temporarily parting company:

> In other conversations with Humphrey, it has become increasingly clear that the civil rights

[lobby] groups must be handled with great care and maturity. In short, it is simply impossible to permit the civil rights groups to call all the shots on this legislation. It is also clear that there will come a time when decisions will probably have to be made which the civil rights groups will disagree with. But, as in the House [of Representatives], they will in the end come around and support the bill as it is finally passed and, in fact, claim all the credit for themselves.

In that regard, it is a good object lesson that you must even be willing to go against your strongest supporters when dealing with legislation of such tremendous scope and comprehension as the pending civil rights bill. There [are] enough groups and interests in this nation so that certain accommodations simply have to be made if there is to be a bill. This is a fact which the civil rights groups, looking at the bill from their very narrow perspective, simply cannot comprehend. And, what is even more distressing, is that they immediately interpret any particular change in the legislation as some manner of dastardly sellout. Clarence Mitchell's biweekly eruptions in the leadership meetings only testifies to this fact. . . .

It is easy enough [to] offend your enemies and to attack them openly at the slightest provocation. It is far more difficult and takes far more courage to disagree with your friends, such as the civil rights Leadership Conference, and to have to do things which they oppose. But sometimes these are precisely the actions which will give you the ultimate victory.[20]

THE MAN FROM PEKIN

Who was this man, Senator Everett M. Dirksen of Illinois,

that both President Lyndon Johnson and Democratic Whip Hubert Humphrey would court his favor so directly and so patronizingly? What great power did he hold over the United States Senate that civil rights supporters and Southern Democrats alike saw him as the key to whether or not the bipartisan civil rights bill was passed into law. Was his power really so great that Hubert Humphrey would have to abandon his career long political allies in the Leadership Conference on Civil Rights in order to appease him and thereby get the bill through?

Everett Dirksen grew up in Pekin, Illinois, a small town located on the Illinois River a few miles south of Peoria. As a bustling river town, Pekin had a more diverse economic and social life than that ordinarily associated with the rural Midwestern heartland. As a result, Dirksen was considerably more sophisticated than one might have expected of a small-town Illinois youth.

Pekin had been part of Abraham Lincoln's congressional district when he served in the House of Representatives in the late 1840s. Dirksen often mentioned that he was from Abraham Lincoln's home district, and he constantly quoted Lincoln. Being from Lincoln country and admiring Lincoln as he did must have had some influence on Dirksen -- an influence urging him to work for civil rights in memory of the Great Emancipator from his home state of Illinois.

By the time Dirksen was attending high school in Pekin, he already excelled as an orator and a politician. Upon his return to the United States after serving as a soldier in France during World War I, Dirksen entered politics and, after holding a number of local political offices, was elected to the House of Representatives in 1932. Although a Republican, he strongly supported Democratic President Franklin D. Roosevelt and his New Deal program for ending the Great Depression of the 1930s. Thus, from the very beginning of his long career on Capitol Hill, Dirksen had a record of working with the Democrats in Congress in order to help turn out what he believed to be vital legislation in the national interest.

In 1950 Dirksen ran for and was elected to the United

States Senate. Two years later he was named to the Senate Judiciary Committee, the committee designated to handle civil rights legislation in the Senate. Service on the Judiciary Committee gave Dirksen an intimate knowledge of the nature of civil rights problems in the United States and, more importantly, gave him officiality and stature when speaking out on civil rights issues.

In 1956 Dirksen began his career as a civil rights legislator by introducing an Eisenhower administration civil rights bill in the Senate. The bill went nowhere, but that summer, at the Republican National Convention in San Francisco, Dirksen chaired the party platform subcommittee on civil rights and was the chief exponent of a "forthright" civil rights plank designed to point up the "serpentine weaseling" of the Democratic Party on the civil rights issue.[21]

Following the 1956 elections, Dirksen was named the Republican whip in the Senate. Two years later, when Republican Leader William F. Knowland retired from the Senate to go home to California and run unsuccessfully for governor, Dirksen was elected Republican leader to succeed Knowland. Throughout the 1959-1960 session of Congress, Senate Republican Leader Dirksen worked with Senate Democratic Leader Lyndon Johnson, and one important bill they worked on together was the Civil Rights Act of 1960.

By 1964 Everett Dirksen had established himself as one of the most colorful characters in the United States Senate. His seedy clothes and rumpled hair had become recognizable trademarks. Newspaper reporters wrote physical descriptions of him for their readers. One writer saw Dirksen as possessing a "wavy pompadour, heavy lidded eyes, loose full orator's lips, and (an) imperturbable manner."[22] A second writer described Dirksen's hair as "the kelp of the Sargasso Sea," and a third portrayed him as having "the melancholy mien of a homeless basset hound."[23]

Most of all, however, it was Dirksen's voice while debating on the Senate floor that was distinctive. The Wall Street Journal praised Dirksen for his "mellifluous voice, the archaic hand gestures, the delight in the meandering anecdote."[24]

238

One newspaperman described Dirksen as "the last of the Fourth of July picnic orators."[25]

Because of his speaking ability, Dirksen was known by a series of nicknames referring to the sound of his voice. "Old Silver Throat," "Old Honey Tonsils," "The Wizard of Ooze," and "The Rumpled Magician of Metaphor" were a few of them. A national magazine concluded: "When [Dirksen] rises to speak, senators gather from aisles around to hear." Time Magazine said: "In funereal tones, Dirksen paraphrases the Bible ('Lord, they would stone me. . .') and church bells peal. 'Motherhood,' he whispers, and grown men weep. 'The Flag,' he bugles, and everybody salutes."[26]

Dirksen also was famous for his quick wit when debating on the Senate floor. An example occurred during Dwight D. Eisenhower's presidency when Hubert Humphrey, upset because the Republican budget makers had cut back one of his favorite programs, rose at his Senate desk and accused the Eisenhower administration of suffering from "budgetitis." With barely a half second to think up a reply, Dirksen immediately retorted that Humphrey was suffering from "spenderitis" and "squandermania."[27]

AMENDMENTS AND THE MINORITY PARTY

For most of his long years as a Republican on Capitol Hill, Everett Dirksen found himself functioning as a member of the minority party. Since the committees of Congress are totally dominated by the majority party, Dirksen quickly learned that carefully drawn amendments are the only way a minority party congressman can have an impact on national legislation. Dirksen therefore became an expert at learning the legislative details of major bills going through Congress and then drawing up amendments to them that would have a good chance of receiving a majority vote when the bills came up for final consideration on the Senate floor. Dirksen thus became skilled at using the amendment process to change a bill, sometimes quite considerably, so that it was more to his liking.

239

TO END ALL SEGREGATION

THE GREAT AMENDER

By the early 1960s Dirksen had this "Dirksen Amendment" process down to a well established pattern. Whenever a Democratic president and administration would present a major legislative program to the Congress, Dirksen would promptly announce his opposition, taking the Senate floor to express his "grave doubts" and "considerable concerns." His next step would be to introduce damaging and weakening amendments to the bill in question, but always with an expressed willingness to "negotiate" and "compromise" these amendments with the bill's supporters. The last step was the actual negotiation of the compromise amendment, a process that usually resulted in Dirksen getting much of what he wanted and, simultaneously, considerable credit for getting the particular bill enacted by Congress.

Dirksen had an advantage over other senators when it came down to negotiating the final legal language of Dirksen's amendments. Dirksen was a skilled lawyer who, unlike most senators, loved the details of writing legislation. He prided himself on being a legal draftsman, a professional legislator in the business of writing laws. Furthermore, Dirksen was willing to "do his homework" where learning the legal details of bills was concerned, and many other senators were not willing to work so hard. This often gave Dirksen the ability to argue from a position of great knowledge about the bill under discussion while his opponents had only the barest knowledge of what was going on. In such a situation, Dirksen's fellow senators were often willing, sometimes even glad, to let Dirksen cross the final "t's" and dot the final "i's" of the legislation in question.

The general content of Dirksen's legislative files at the Everett McKinley Dirksen Congressional Leadership Research Center in Pekin, Illinois, bear out this image of Dirksen as a senator mainly concerned with the details of legislation. The files contain an unusually large number of legislative bills, proposed amendments to these bills, and notes and memoranda describing and defending bills and amendments. The general content of the Dirksen files contrasts with the Hubert H. Humphrey Papers at the Minnesota Historical Society in St. Paul, Minnesota. The Humphrey files are more oriented toward memoranda concerning legislative and political strategy rather than the legislative details of the various bills and amendments.

BRINGING THE PARTY ALONG

In addition to being a skilled legal negotiator, Dirksen also had worked very hard, in his role as Senate Republican leader, at getting the Senate Republicans to like him and follow him. When he became Senate Republican leader in 1959, Dirksen carefully saw to it that each Republican senator received at least one choice committee assignment. Twice Dirksen gave up his own seat on a key committee in order to make certain that there would be room to move up a younger Republican colleague. Thus in 1959 he have up his seat on the Senate Appropriations Committee so that Gordon Allott of Colorado could have it, and in 1961 he moved off the Senate Labor Committee to make way for freshman Republican Senator John Tower of Texas. When asked about this magnanimity toward his fellow party members, Dirksen simply replied: "The leader takes what's left."[28]

Dirksen also instituted the technique of having all the Senate Republicans, conservatives and liberals alike, attend a lunch briefing with him every Monday to go over legislation currently pending in the Senate. These luncheons provided the opportunity for a great deal of give-and-take between the Republican leader and his fellow party members in the Senate. Dirksen used these luncheons to tell his fellow Republicans what his thoughts were about various bills before the Senate and to hear back their ideas on what ought to happen. At these luncheons Dirksen worked to find a common ground which the vast majority of Republican members of the Senate could willingly support.

Dirksen also had a good relationship with the national

press. Following his Monday lunches with the Senate Republicans, Dirksen would go up to the Senate press room and, often sitting on the table and bumming cigarettes off the various reporters, brief the press on the latest Republican view of national politics. These briefings soon became institutionalized. Dirksen was joined by House Republican Leader Charles Halleck, and the two of them became well-known on evening television newscasts as "The Ev and Charley Show."

By 1964 Everett Dirksen had demonstrated that he had considerable power over the enactment of legislation in the Senate, even over ordinary bills that required only a majority vote. When the legislation required a 2/3 vote of the Senate, however, such as the approval of a foreign treaty or the voting of cloture, Dirksen's power and control were even more enhanced.

THE NUCLEAR TEST-BAN AGREEMENT

Dirksen's handling of the Kennedy administration's Nuclear Test-Ban Treaty with the Soviet Union was a case study of the typical Dirksen style of operation. In June 1963, immediately after President Kennedy had announced that he was resuming negotiations with the Soviets for a ban on atmospheric testing of nuclear weapons, Dirksen rose in the Senate to question whether this was not "another case of concession and more concession" to the Russians. Carefully reminding everyone that he was a "hard liner" against communism, Dirksen joined with House Republican Leader Charles Halleck to issue a joint statement charging that the proposed treaty might mean the "virtual surrender" of the United States to Soviet duplicity and chicanery.[29]

By August of 1963, American, Russian, and British negotiators had initialed a tentative draft of the treaty. Dirksen's next move was to pass the word that he would not accept an invitation from President Kennedy to fly to Moscow and, as Republican Leader of the Senate, be part of the United States delegation signing the treaty. Dirksen made it clear that he was

242

not participating in the treaty signing because he wished to retain the freedom to criticize the treaty when it came up for the required 2/3 vote of approval in the Senate and, if his judgment were such, vote against the treaty.

Then, right on schedule, the typical Dirksen offer to change and compromise. The Senate Republican leader passed the word to Mike Mansfield, the Democratic leader in the Senate, that he wanted to go down to the White House with Mansfield and discuss his "fears" and "anxieties" with President Kennedy. Dirksen made it clear that what he feared most of all was that the United States might let down its military guard as a result of a false feeling of security that might emerge after the treaty was endorsed by the Senate.

Knowing that his test-ban treaty was in trouble, mainly as a result of opposition from conservative Southern Democrats in the Senate, President Kennedy acquiesced in Dirksen's request for a meeting at the White House. As Dirksen talked at length in the Oval Office, President Kennedy realized that what Dirksen wanted was a letter from the president to Mansfield and Dirksen giving them assurances that the government would not relax its nuclear weapons program if the treaty were approved.

President Kennedy asked Dirksen if he had any notes on which such a letter might be based, and Dirksen replied that he did. Kennedy then asked for the notes, and Dirksen reached into his pocket and pulled out a draft letter for Kennedy to sign. After reading the letter, Kennedy told Dirksen he would sign it.[30]

With the letter as proof that he had exacted important concessions from Kennedy, Dirksen announced his support for the test-ban agreement and turned his oratorical skills to supporting the treaty rather than opposing it. As the Senate approved the treaty by a vote of 81 to 19, Senate Republican Leader Everett M. Dirksen was given the major share of the credit for getting it through.

Dirksen's performance of exacting concessions and then approving the nuclear test-ban treaty occurred in the summer and fall of 1963, exactly at the time when the Kennedy administration's civil rights bill was beginning its long trek through the

House of Representatives. The example of the test-ban agreement could not be ignored by those planning strategy for the civil rights bill. Dirksen would be the key to getting the civil rights bill through the Senate by a 2/3 cloture vote just the way he had been the key to getting the nuclear test ban agreement approved by a 2/3 treaty approval vote.

"DIRKSEN'S BOMBERS"

In line with his reputation as a legislative craftsman, Dirksen began working on the technical language of the bipartisan civil rights bill even while it was still undergoing final passage in the House of Representatives. He carried a copy of the bill with him and devoted many spare moments to studying it and penciling ideas for possible amendments in the margin. He worked on the bill in his Capitol office, at home, and even when he traveled. As he worked, Dirksen made notes in the margin of the bill, and he began to make a list of prospective amendments.[31]

As the ranking Republican on the Senate Judiciary Committee, Dirksen had three lawyers working for him on the staffs of three different subcommittees. Dirksen "borrowed" these three lawyers from their subcommittee posts and put them to work studying the bipartisan civil rights bill and writing the exact legal language of possible amendments. Soon referred to in the press as "Dirksen's Bombers," the three men came to play a crucial role in the drafting of the final bill. Dirksen pointed out that he had to rely on his staff, and that without their help he would flounder.[32]

As early as 17 March 1964 Dirksen's three subcommittee lawyers began making periodic appearances at civil rights strategy meetings. "Where the hell did those three guys come from," privately grumbled Senator Kuchel's legislative assistant following one such appearance.[33]

One of the "Bombers" recalled the event from the Dirksen camp point of view:

Dirksen called the three of us in and said a civil rights bill had been prepared downtown [at the Justice Department]. He wanted us to work with Mansfield's staff to get it in good shape for adoption. Dirksen then said there was a meeting of Democratic staff and would we please attend it. I recall that the three of us walked into a room that was a hubbub of conversation, but the minute the three of us entered, it immediately quieted down. The conversations just stopped. Everyone looked like they were waiting to see what would happen next.[34]

"Dirksen's Bombers" were not trusted by the "insider" pro-civil rights legislative assistants who were completely committed to a strong civil rights bill, and their occasional presence had an inhibiting effect on the customary level of frank and open pro-civil rights discussion. As March turned into April, however, the pro-civil rights legislative aides came to realize more and more with each passing day that it was "Dirksen's Bombers" who were going to have the most to say of any Capitol Hill assistants about the final language of the bill.[35]

THE REPUBLICAN POLICY COMMITTEE LUNCHEONS

On 31 March 1964 Dirksen began presenting the essential details of his proposed amendments to the weekly luncheon meetings of the Republican Policy Committee in the Senate. These lunch meetings were informal and were recognized as the principal power base of the more conservative members of the Republican party in the Senate.[36] As such, they provided an ideal environment in which Dirksen could float out his proposed amendments to his fellow Republicans and, in an atmosphere of brotherly give-and-take, receive their support, opposition, or critical suggestions for his ideas.

Expecting relatively mild amendments from Dirksen, Senators Humphrey and Kuchel were shocked and confused when some of Dirksen's amendment proposals appeared sweeping enough to, in effect, cripple the bill. Humphrey remained silent, however, and left the job of moderating the unacceptable aspects of Dirksen's proposed amendments to liberal Republican senators such as Kuchel, Jacob Javits of New York, and Clifford Case of New Jersey. Dirksen promptly stated that he was still flexible on the final details of his amendments, and he promised to continue his efforts to find legal language that would please liberal and conservative Republicans alike.[37]

THE LONG DELAY

During this period Hubert Humphrey began asking Dirksen if he was ready to begin negotiating the details of his amendments with the Democrats as well as the Republicans. As Humphrey told it:

> I can recall time after time asking him, "Well, Dirk, when do you think we ought to meet and talk over some of your amendments." And he'd say, "Well, give us a couple more days. It isn't time yet." And this went on week after week.[38]

There was much speculation as to exactly why Dirksen delayed the entire month of April without beginning to negotiate a compromise version of the civil rights bill with Hubert Humphrey and the Johnson administration. Some argued it was an attempt to delay what little remained of President Johnson's legislative program for Congress.[39] Others theorized it was to delay a cloture vote until after the Republican presidential primary elections were completed in early June 1964. "Dirksen's Bombers" argued, however, that the fundamental reason for the long delay in beginning final negotiations on the bill was the time it took to produce a draft that would be widely accepted.[40] One of the Dirksen aides gave this explanation of how the process worked:

It took so much time because we were working on the details of the bill as they affected various interest groups. There was a consistent effort to involve all the various groups concerned in the process. We tried to create a spirit of cooperation. We wanted to "take care" of all the various problems with the bill and see that everything was "worked out." We tried to work it so that no big thing was either granted or denied to any particular party. We collected a great deal of input into the final version of the bill, but no one voice prevailed.[41]

The Dirksen aide concluded that Dirksen himself supported the bipartisan civil rights bill from the very beginning and that the Republican leader's changes were only designed to secure the support of other less committed senators.[42]

According to another Dirksen aide, extra time was required to produce an enforceable bill. He explained:

The original Justice Department package would have been difficult to enforce. It relied heavily on subjective intent type language that would have been very hard to interpret and enforce in court. Dirksen wanted the bill to be as self-enforcing as possible, and the Dirksen staff worked to reduce enforcement of the bill to a relatively simple administrative test -- if you were serving one group of people, you had to serve all groups of people.[43]

THE JURY TRIAL AMENDMENTS

With the Senate Republicans discussing how they wanted to amend the civil rights bill to make it more acceptable and, therefore, passable, Senator Richard Russell and the Southern Democrats decided to act. Late on the evening of 21 April 1964, Russell had Senator Herman Talmadge of Georgia introduce and call up an amendment to the civil rights bill to extend the right of trial by jury to persons accused of violating court orders in civil rights cases. By picking the jury trial issue for the first substantive vote on the civil rights bill in the Senate, Russell was strategically playing one of his strongest cards.

The question of jury trials for Southern officials who violated United States court orders was a thorny one. Efforts to desegregate public facilities in the South were usually implemented by court order, but if public officials who failed to obey court orders to desegregate could get a jury trial, a "free, white jury" of their friends and neighbors would find them "not guilty" and the laws requiring desegregation of public facilities would go unenforced. It was the modern version of that traditional Southern institution, "the free, white jury that will never convict."

Civil rights advocates had long supported eliminating the jury trial requirement where criminal contempt for violating court orders in civil rights cases was concerned. They tempered this position somewhat by calling for jury trials in those criminal contempt cases where the fine exceeded $300 or the prison sentence was more than 45 days in jail. Such a jury trial limitation had been written into the public accommodations section of the House passed civil rights bill. The Talmadge amendment would have eliminated this provision and guaranteed a jury trial in all civil rights contempt of court proceedings, no matter how small the fine or how short the jail sentence.

The Talmadge amendment was viewed as a major threat by the civil rights forces in the Senate. The right to "trial by jury" is one of the oldest and best publicized principles of the United States judicial system. The idea had particularly strong appeal to conservative members of the Republican party in the Senate, men who were particularly interested in preserving the traditional values of the American polity. Senators Humphrey and Kuchel "frankly doubted their ability to defeat the Talmadge amendment on a straight up or down vote."[44]

Humphrey and Kuchel were not as worried over the damage the Talmadge amendment would do to the civil rights bill as they were over the psychological lift which adoption of the amendment would give to the filibustering Southerners. Approval of such a weakening amendment would sap the confidence of the civil rights senators, many of whom were beginning to really feel the strain of the long hours and the excessive boredom of the filibuster. If the Talmadge amendment were adopted, the Southerners would propose additional weakening amendments and, if the bandwagon started rolling in their direction, these amendments might also be successful. The introduction of the Talmadge amendment thus required an immediate countermove, and a successful one, on the part of the civil rights forces.

The countermove developed by the civil rights forces was to approach Senator Dirksen and see if he would join them in offering an amendment to the Talmadge amendment that would reduce the number of days a public official could be imprisoned without a jury trial following a contempt of court conviction. The civil rights forces were surprised by Dirksen's readiness to join in cosponsoring such an amendment. Apparently Dirksen, too, "was becoming restless with the lack of action on the Senate floor."[45]

On Thursday, 23 April 1964, a Mansfield-Dirksen substitute jury trial amendment was hammered out by Mansfield, Dirksen, Humphrey, and representatives of the Justice Department. The negotiations and the final compromise were a typical example of this sort of working out of a common position. Dirksen wanted the maximum "no jury trial" penalty to be 10 days in jail. Humphrey argued strenuously in behalf of the 45 day penalty currently in the bill. The final compromise provided that the maximum jail term that could be imposed without a jury trial in criminal contempt of court cases would be 30 days.

In line with the policy of building up Dirksen and letting him take a leadership role in the passage of the civil rights bill, Dirksen was asked to introduce the Mansfield-Dirksen substitute jury trial amendment in the Senate. Dirksen accepted this offer and presented the amendment to the Senate the following day. Dirksen's obvious cooperation gave a real feeling of optimism to the civil right forces, who had been feeling demoralized when the Talmadge amendment was first introduced. "Things are looking great," Hubert Humphrey smiled to the press as he left a key negotiating session with Senator Dirksen. "All last week's stomach aches are gone."[46]

A CLOTURE CONTROVERSY -- AGAIN

Humphrey had spoken too soon. Richard Russell and the Southern Democrats decided against permitting a vote on the Mansfield-Dirksen substitute jury trial amendment and quickly resumed the filibuster. Upset by this action, Senator Dirksen told the news media that he would seek a cloture vote, not on the entire bill, but only on the substitute jury trial amendment. This unilateral decision by Dirksen caused perhaps the worst case of panic to hit the civil rights forces during the entire Senate consideration of the bill. Humphrey and Kuchel fretted, as they had all along, that such an early cloture vote would fail and lead to a crippling of the bill to meet the demands of the Southern Democrats. Senator Mansfield, on the other hand, kept pointing out that Dirksen's support was absolutely essential to final passage of the bill and that he could not antagonize Dirksen by refusing to cosponsor his cloture proposal for the substitute jury trial amendment.

The proposed cloture vote on the jury trial amendment particularly disturbed Senator Humphrey's and Senator Kuchel's legislative staff. When it appeared that legislative staff were going to be excluded from a key strategy meeting between Senator Humphrey and Attorney General Robert Kennedy on the early cloture vote issue, Senator Humphrey's legislative assistant literally "dragged" a pro-civil rights Senate staffer down to the door outside the meeting room and all but shoved him into the meeting as Senator Humphrey entered. "Through this rather preposterous ruse, we managed to get at least one [pro-civil rights] staff person into the meeting."[47]

The argument over whether or not to have a cloture vote on the Mansfield-Dirksen substitute jury trial amendment highlighted one last time the subtle differences between Senator Mansfield on the one hand and Senators Humphrey and Kuchel on the other. Humphrey and Kuchel wanted as strong a bill as possible, but Mansfield was mainly interested in getting some form of the bill passed, and a weak bill would be just as good as a strong one. As Humphrey's legislative assistant noted at this point in the proceedings:

> Mansfield and Dirksen move along in one direction and often do not inform the actual floor managers [Humphrey and Kuchel] of their thinking until the ball has already picked up considerable speed. It is also true that Mansfield seems to follow Dirksen's lead without exception. In other words, Senator Dirksen appears to be acting as the [Senate] majority leader without assuming any of the responsibilities involved. That is not a bad position to be in.[48]

Apparently Hubert Humphrey was so concerned over the possibility that Dirksen would attempt a cloture vote on the substitute jury trial amendment that he endeavored to involve President Johnson in the effort to turn Dirksen off. Humphrey's legislative assistant gave the following account of what happened, based largely on hearsay and rumor:

> Finally, one must not leave out President Johnson. The matter [the civil rights bill] was discussed at some length at the Tuesday morning leadership breakfast [with President Johnson at the White House]. At that point, Mansfield raised the possibility of using cloture on the [substitute jury trial] amendment and the matter was debated at the breakfast but not decided. Subsequently, Humphrey took himself down to the White House to see the president unannounced. He kept [Defense] Secretary [Robert] McNamara and others

251

waiting while he barged into the president's office to lay it on the line. In effect, he told the president that the matter was at the point where victory was in sight but that the law had to be laid down here and now. He set forth the reasons why he opposed cloture on the amendment itself. I do not know what Johnson responded. But it has been said that when Dirksen went to the White House at noon today he found Johnson in a tough and noncompromising mood.[49]

THE MORTON AMENDMENT

For whatever reason, the cloture crisis disappeared. Mansfield and Dirksen stopped talking about a cloture vote on the Mansfield-Dirksen substitute jury trial amendment. At the same time, Republican Senator Thruston Morton of Kentucky met with Senator Richard Russell of Georgia and Sam Ervin of North Carolina and wrote a perfecting amendment to the Talmadge amendment which had the support of all the Southern Democrats and a number of Republicans. Since Russell was willing to allow a vote on this new Morton amendment, Mansfield and Dirksen agreed to let that be the first Senate test of strength on the civil rights bill. The civil rights forces immediately went to work organizing to vote the Morton amendment down and thereby demonstrate that they were in solid control of what was happening on the Senate floor.

What the vote on the Morton amendment demonstrated, however, was that the civil rights forces were barely in control of the Senate floor. Four different votes were required to defeat the Morton amendment, and the civil rights forces won the final vote by only one vote. The narrowness of this victory was made even more disturbing to civil rights supporters by the fact that Senator Dirksen was working with Mansfield and Humphrey and Kuchel to defeat the Morton amendment. At times during the four vote sequence, both Mansfield and Dirksen came close to losing control of their various party forces on the Senate floor.

252

Senator Humphrey's legislative assistant gave the following description of the proceedings:

> Commotion on the floor reached such a pitch that all staff members were ordered into the cloakrooms to reduce the noise level. Accurate surveys of the vote had not been taken in advance and the leadership's apparatus for notifying Senators functioned poorly. [Democrat] Frank Moss [of Utah], for example, missed the first vote entirely because the Democratic cloakroom staff failed to summon him from a phone booth; he then voted against the leadership . . . out of spite. The incident only narrowly avoided becoming a debacle of major dimensions; the party leaders could take scant pride from their ragged performance. . . . On balance, the Southern Democrats in defeat looked better than the civil rights coalition in victory.[50]

After such a sorry performance, Mansfield and Dirksen were anxious to redeem themselves as leaders of the Senate by bringing up and passing the Mansfield-Dirksen substitute jury trial amendment. Mansfield and Dirksen thought they had an agreement with Richard Russell that, following disposal of the Morton amendment, the Mansfield-Dirksen substitute could be voted upon. Suddenly, however, Russell announced that no such understanding existed and that no further votes would be allowed. Knowing they would lose the vote and that the Mansfield-Dirksen substitute would be adopted, the Southern Democrats chose instead to resume their strategy of total obstructionism to the civil rights bill. The filibuster resumed with no prospect of further votes until mid May or perhaps even later.

The civil rights forces were disconsolate when the Southerners refused to allow a vote on the Mansfield-Dirksen substitute. "I would be less than honest if I said I was not unhappy," Hubert Humphrey told the Senate. "This is not what I would call a 'happiness house.' Occasionally it is a quorum of frustration."[51]

In retrospect, however, it appeared that the failure of the Southern Democrats to permit a vote on the Mansfield-Dirksen substitute helped the civil rights forces. Humphrey's legislative assistant put the argument this way:

> Although it could not be fully appreciated at the time, the refusal of the Southern Democrats to permit further votes on the jury trial issue proved to be a major factor in convincing Dirksen to cast his lot with the civil rights forces. . . . As business on the Senate floor in effect ground to a halt due to the inability to continue voting, the battle for the Civil Rights Act of 1964 shifted into the rear of Dirksen's chambers on the second floor of the Capitol.[52]

CHAPTER 12

THE DRIVE FOR CLOTURE;
"AN IDEA WHOSE TIME HAS COME"

On Tuesday, 5 May 1964, negotiations opened in Dirksen's Capitol office to begin writing a version of the civil rights bill acceptable to Dirksen and his small band of Republican supporters in the Senate. An august group turned out for this initial session. Mansfield and Humphrey were there to represent the pro-civil rights Democrats in the Senate. Kuchel came to represent the pro-civil rights Republicans. Attorney General Robert Kennedy was on hand to represent the Johnson administration, along with Deputy Attorney General Nicholas Katzenbach and an assortment of Justice Department lawyers to help write the actual legislative language.

It is important to note that the meeting was held in Dirksen's office. The fact that the attorney general and all the leading pro-civil rights Democrats in the Senate were willing to come and meet on Dirksen's home turf was a clear sign to the political cognoscenti of Dirksen's importance in this situation. Robert Kennedy, Mike Mansfield, and Hubert Humphrey would not have given Dirksen the honor of hosting the meetings if they had not regarded Dirksen as absolutely essential to the successful passage of the bill.

The meetings began with a jarring surprise for the civil rights forces. Dirksen had previously assured Hubert Humphrey that he had no more amendments to the bill other than one small amendment concerning equal access to public accommodations. When the Democratic negotiators walked into Dirksen's office, however, they were startled to receive a heavy sheaf of mimeographed amendments, approximately 70 in all. Whereas Humphrey had previously believed that agreement between Dirksen and the civil rights forces would be relatively easily to achieve, he now had to conclude that the negotiations with Dirksen would be long, difficult, and might result in major and possibly damaging alterations to the bill.

According to Hubert Humphrey's legislative assistant, the sheer number of Dirksen's proposed amendments coupled with the near defeat of the civil rights forces on the Morton amendment brought the bipartisan floor managers yet another period of great discouragement. The legislative assistant noted:

> [This is] a helluva way to run a railroad. For the record, there is a definite lack of urgency and lack of direction to the civil rights forces at present. Humphrey is frustrated and blocked by Mansfield. Kuchel is frustrated and boxed in by Dirksen. . . . I think one must fully appreciate the profound difficulties in getting this bill underway and keeping up a head of steam. Nobody seems concerned except the few committed leaders. The rest seem willing to let the time fritter away. . . . But I will say that it will be somewhat of a major miracle if the pro-civil rights forces can get themselves back in order and push ahead with some degree of resolution and determination. . . . Right now, our [problems] look pretty profound.[1]

Despite the disillusionment of the civil rights forces occasioned by Senator Dirksen's giant pile of amendments, there was nothing for them to do but begin negotiating with Dirksen in good faith and hope that, one way or another, an acceptable package of amendments could be developed. As the meetings proceeded, it soon became apparent that Dirksen and the Justice Department were substantially in agreement on a large number of the amendments. The major point of controversy, it turned out, was on the best way to enforce the various provisions of the bill, particularly the provisions dealing with public accommodations and employment. Dirksen did not want the United States Government meddling in the small details of every minor complaint involving civil rights. The Justice Department contended, however, that without United States Government enforcement much of the South would never comply with the law.

The negotiations went on long enough to become somewhat formalized. Every afternoon a staff level group met consisting of Dirksen's three aides and a group of lawyers from the Justice Department. This group would draft tentative new language for the bill, and then the next morning the new language would be presented to the various senators (primarily Humphrey, Kuchel, and Dirksen). The senators would resolve those issues upon which the staff members could not agree.[2]

One reason the staff negotiations were so successful was that all of the staff members had been told by their respective bosses to produce a bill. As one of Dirksen assistants explained:

> Both the Mansfield people and the Dirksen people had been given a "go" by their leaders to produce a bill. Everyone worked to keep the issue from being more polarized than it might have been. There was no sense that one part of the group was for civil rights and the other part was against it. Everyone was trying to write a good bill. There also was a sense that we were going to breach any impasse, that is, find a solution to any major problem that cropped up during the negotiations. The goal was to write the bill -- find the civil rights policies -- that the entire country would innately want to have.[3]

Apparently the real progress in writing the final version of the bill occurred in the afternoon staff sessions rather than in the morning meetings with the various senators involved. A White House memorandum dated 6 May 1964 strongly hints that it was the staff members rather than the senators who were doing the real work of finishing up the bill:

> Nick Katzenbach [says] that the meetings in Senator Dirksen's office on the package [of] civil rights amendments go much better in the afternoon sessions when the staff technicians and Katzenbach meet. Apparently the morning sessions [with the senators] . . . are meetings which Nick indicates are mostly consumed with educational pursuits [explaining to the senators what is in the bill]. [Nick] indicates it is surprising to note the lack of real understanding of the civil rights bill and the effect amendments proposed would have on it.[4]

"PATTERN OR PRACTICE"

A critical breakthrough in the negotiations occurred when one of "Dirksen's Bombers" proposed that the United States Government be given the authority to initiate enforcement action only where there existed a "pattern or practice" of massive resistance to racial integration.[5] The idea was that the United States would initiate enforcement of the law only in those states where it could be shown that racial discrimination was a widespread and generally accepted practice. The practical effect of this agreement was that, in Northern states where racial discrimination was not widely practiced, the United States Government could not initiate enforcement but would have to wait for aggrieved individuals to file law suits to protect their civil rights. In the Southern states, however, where there was a "pattern or practice" of racial discrimination that could be easily documented, the United States Government could initiate enforcement action without having to wait for the aggrieved individuals to file law suits first.

With some minor refinements, this "pattern or practice" formula broke the impasse with Senator Dirksen that had existed ever since President Kennedy made his initial civil rights proposals to Congress almost a year earlier. One other major concession was made to Dirksen by the civil rights forces. An agreement was reached specifying that an initial period of state jurisdiction over public accommodations and employment cases would be allowed before United States Government enforcement procedures went into effect.

Humphrey later told one of his biographers that he had, on one occasion only, been somewhat devious in his effort to win Dirksen's agreement and support for the pro-civil rights position. Before one of the negotiating sessions in Dirksen's office, Humphrey secretly arranged with Senator Joseph Clark of Pennsylvania for Clark to stage a political "tantrum." At a critical point in the meeting, when Dirksen seemed about to protest that Humphrey was not giving enough on certain key points, Clark stood up, pointed a finger at Humphrey, and shouted, "This is a goddamned sellout." Clark then, exactly as he had prearranged it with Humphrey, stalked out of the room. Humphrey was then able to turn to Dirksen and say, "See what pressures I'm up against? I can't concede any more on this point." Apparently this small ruse worked, because the atmosphere in the room improved immeasurably once Clark had staged his little show and Dirksen quickly reached amicable agreement with Humphrey on the point in question.[6]

THE BIG DEAL WITH SENATOR DIRKSEN

On 13 May 1964 Attorney General Robert Kennedy came back to Dirksen's office to nail down the final points of agreement on the unified package of amendments to the civil rights bill. Around the big mahogany table and under the tinkling chandelier where all the previous negotiations had taken place, the final form of the compromise with Senator Dirksen took shape. As the last minor points were discussed and agreed upon, Dirksen announced that "the amendments would have to be mimeographed, that a [Republican] party conference would have to be called, that he would then attempt to secure agreement with the party, and that [he would] then move directly for cloture."[7]

The goal that President Kennedy, President Johnson, Hubert Humphrey, and Thomas Kuchel had been working for had been achieved. Dirksen was now in favor of the bill, he would himself move for cloture on the bill, and he would work to bring large numbers of Republican senators along with him in supporting both cloture and final passage of the bill.

Dirksen and Humphrey walked out of Dirksen's office and announced their agreement to a small group of waiting newsmen. The two men informed the press that they were now working together to get a cloture vote on the civil rights bill. Humphrey remarked that he felt "like someone going down a ski jump for the first time. Once you pushed off down the slope, you could only hope that somehow you would land on your feet."[8]

As the impromptu press conference broke up, several of the news reporters asked to see the text of the agreed upon amendments. Before he passed his copy of the amendments around, Dirksen said: "The lid is on!" Dirksen thus informed the reporters that the text of the amendments was "off the record" until officially announced and published. As often happens with major political events, leading national newspaper and television reporters saw the details of the Humphrey-Dirksen compromise before anyone else, including most of the United States senators who would have to vote on that compromise.[9]

THE OREGON PRIMARY

Two days after the announcement of the compromise agreement with Senator Dirksen on the civil rights bill, Oregon Republicans went to the polls and gave New York Governor Nelson A. Rockefeller a comfortable victory over Henry Cabot Lodge in that state's G.O.P. presidential primary. Rockefeller's win surprised the pollsters and political observers, most of whom had been predicting a Lodge victory. By taking the Oregon primary, Rockefeller knocked Lodge out of the race and became the only remaining Republican candidate with a chance of defeating Arizona Senator Barry Goldwater for the 1964

G.O.P. presidential nomination. All political eyes were now focussed on the 2 June 1964 California Republican primary. If Rockefeller could defeat Goldwater in California, he would get all of the state's 86 delegate votes, almost enough to give Rockefeller the nomination.

The surprise results of the Oregon primary put added pressure on President Johnson to press for a strong civil rights bill. It now appeared that a Republican liberal, Nelson Rockefeller, rather than a Republican conservative, Barry Goldwater, might win the 1964 Republican presidential nomination. If the liberal Rockefeller won, Johnson would need the strongest civil rights bill possible to win the support of liberal voters in the North, a group with which Rockefeller had proved unusually popular in previous elections.

WALLACE IN MARYLAND

Six days after the announcement of the successful Humphrey-Dirksen negotiations on the civil rights bill, and four days after Rockefeller's victory in the Oregon Republican primary, the Maryland Democratic presidential primary election was held. Still basking in the favorable publicity from his unexpectedly strong showings in Wisconsin and Indiana, Alabama Governor George Wallace was hoping for a victory in Maryland that would demonstrate a significant lack of popular support in the nation for the civil rights bill.

As the Wallace campaign became organized in Maryland, political analysts began speculating that Wallace just might win the Democratic presidential primary contest in Maryland. Although Maryland had not seceded from the Union and joined the Confederacy during the Civil War, it was, after all, a former slave state and south of the Mason-Dixon line. If Wallace could get 30 percent or more of the vote in Northern states like Wisconsin and Indiana, he conceivably could get 50 percent or more in a Border State like Maryland.

Fully aware that Wallace had his best chance at a primary victory in Maryland, President Johnson made a major effort to recruit a strong stand-in candidate and see that he won the election. Johnson's first choice for a stand-in candidate was Maryland Governor J. Millard Tawes, a moderate to conservative political leader who had been overwhelmingly reelected to a second term of office in 1962. Tawes declined to run, however, telling close associates that the race against Wallace was "not a cinch, and not our fight."[10] The Johnson forces then recruited Maryland Senator Daniel B. Brewster, a young (40 years old) freshman senator who, like Tawes, had been elected by a wide margin in the 1962 election.

Brewster later candidly admitted that both principle and self interest convinced him to give in to President Johnson's pleas and make the race against Wallace. Brewster said:

> The eyes of the nation were on Maryland. I liked the idea of being the political leader who would save Maryland from the disgrace of being the only state outside the Old South to give its convention delegate votes to George Wallace. I also believed I would come out of the primary election campaign a national political figure -- the man who had had the courage to stand up and turn back Wallace in his final drive for votes in the North.

Similar to Governor Reynolds in Wisconsin and Governor Welsh in Indiana, Senator Brewster badly underestimated the depth of racist feeling in a Border State like Maryland. He simply had not anticipated the bitterness that would be generated between himself and committed Wallace supporters as the campaign developed. Brewster explained:

> I found that the great popularity I had enjoyed in the 1962 election did not exist in a racial fight. I was called everything from a "Cadillac pink" [wealthy Communist sympathizer] to a "race-mixing socialist." I was booed at a political meeting in Baltimore and cursed, jeered and even

spat upon as I campaigned in place of President Johnson. I had never been razzed before in my political career. The Wallace people actually sent "jeering sections" to follow me around and shout me down. Speaking one time at a meeting in College Park, Maryland, with Senator William Proxmire of Wisconsin, who had come over to Maryland to support me, the catcalls and the jeering were so loud that we could not even talk. Another time Assistant Postmaster General Tyler Abel was trying to help me out, but the two of us were just dwarfed by the pro-Wallace roar.

President Johnson's political advisers at the White House did everything they could to support Brewster short of an outright presidential endorsement. The Democratic National Committee raised a considerable amount of money and funneled it into Maryland on Brewster's behalf. A key White House aide, Clifton Carter, was dispatched to help Brewster in every way possible. The Johnson forces even arranged for a top campaign publicist to come to Maryland and help Brewster with his campaign speeches and press releases. The White House helped Brewster arrange for leading Democrats in the U.S. Senate, including senators Hubert Humphrey and Edward Kennedy, to come into Maryland and help draw crowds to Brewster's campaign rallies. President Johnson himself scheduled a dramatic helicopter flight to inspect "appalachian regional problems" in the Catoctin Mountains of Western Maryland. The president saw to it that Brewster was at his side every minute he was in Maryland.

For his part, Wallace made a major effort to win the Maryland presidential primary. He raised and spent more than $100,000 for radio and television advertising in behalf of his candidacy. Wallace campaigned particularly hard on the Eastern Shore of the Chesapeake Bay, a section of the state that was very Southern in its attitudes and which had been the scene of extended racial demonstrations in the town of Cambridge,

Maryland.

In an act of political defiance, Wallace scheduled a campaign rally in the white sections of Cambridge, dangerously tempting the racially sensitive black community to do something about it. The expected protest against Wallace was not long in coming. Black and white civil rights demonstrators began a march out of the black neighborhoods of Cambridge toward the volunteer firemen's hall where Wallace was speaking.

Ironically, the black-white dividing line in Cambridge was located at Race Street, and it was at Race Street that the civil rights demonstrators were met by 50 Maryland state policemen and 400 National Guardsmen. The confrontation was a bitter and violent one. The civil rights protestors threw rocks and bottles. The National Guardsmen responded with choking clouds of tear gas. For the remainder of the night and three nights after that, "Cambridge's bitter, frustrated Negroes demonstrated with bricks and bottles. And even the town's segregationist whites could wonder if a visit by George Wallace had been worth it."[11]

As election day neared, Maryland voters watched the black demonstrations and rioting in Cambridge on their television sets and read about them in their newspapers. The Wallace campaign had succeeded in creating the violent civil rights protest demonstrations and riots that were Wallace's strongest campaign assets.

According to Congressional Quarterly Weekly Report, the Wallace campaign in Maryland had a direct impact on the Senate filibuster of the civil rights bill, particularly where Southern Democratic strategy making was concerned. The Southerners apparently intentionally waited for the Maryland primary to take place, hoping to pick up votes against cloture after Wallace either won the primary or narrowly missed winning.[12] As the Wallace-Brewster campaign attracted ever more national publicity and the racial bitterness was heightened by the riots in Cambridge, the Southerners became ever more hopeful that a big Wallace victory in Maryland would convince the uncommitted members of the Senate that sentiment for civil rights was weakening across the nation and it would be in their interest not to vote for cloture.

THE MARYLAND PRIMARY OUTCOME

On 19 May 1964 Maryland voters went to the polls to make their choice. Brewster defeated Wallace by a comfortable margin of 57 percent to 42 percent. Since Wallace had done much better than he did in either Wisconsin or Indiana, however, the Alabama governor made his customary claim of winning the election despite coming out on the short end where the votes were concerned. Wallace told a group of his supporters:

> Everyone knows we won a victory tonight. We had against us the national Democratic party, 10 senators at least, and the [Democratic] organization here in your state [Maryland]. Yet, in spite of everyone of those against you and me, you have given me a vote that represents the philosophy of state's rights, local government, and individual liberty.

Later on primary election night in Maryland, Wallace gave his own analysis of the vote to news reporters:

> Look here. If it hadn't been for the nigger bloc vote, we'd have won it all. We have a majority of the white vote.[13]

Wallace was correct in his claim that he had won the white vote in Maryland, but he failed to point out an important fact that was not missed by other observers of the United States political scene. A combination of black votes in Baltimore city coupled with upper income white votes in the Maryland suburbs had produced a clear majority for civil rights. In Northern and Border States where large numbers of blacks had the right to vote, being against civil rights was a losing proposition. Wallace and his anti-civil rights bill campaign had been stopped by a

265

coalition of black and upper income white voters that was a majority in every state north of the Mason-Dixon line.[14]

"There is no substitute for victory," said a jubilant Daniel Brewster on election night. "We will go to Atlantic City [site of the Democratic National Convention in 1964] and Maryland will stand up and cast its votes for President Johnson." Brewster went on to state that Wallace's showing in Maryland would have "no effect on the passage" of the civil rights bill currently being debated in the Senate.[15]

Brewster's comfortable victory in Maryland, despite the claim of victory by Wallace, did end once and for all the Southern Democratic senators' hope that Wallace would win or come close in Maryland and thereby start a national groundswell of opposition to the civil rights bill.[16]

SELLING THE AGREEMENT

Once Dirksen and Humphrey had reached agreement on the final form of the civil rights bill, the package of amendments had to be sold to a variety of individuals and groups -- the Leadership Conference on Civil Rights, the conservative Republicans in the Senate, and the leaders of both political parties in the House of Representatives (where the new Senate version of the bill would have to be repassed without amendment).

SELLING THE LEADERSHIP CONFERENCE

Immediately following the announcement of his agreement with Senator Dirksen, Hubert Humphrey scheduled a meeting with Clarence Mitchell, Jr., and Joseph Rauh, Jr., of the Leadership Conference on Civil Rights. At this meeting, the general form of the agreement was outlined to Mitchell and Rauh, who were not particularly happy following this brief description but agreed to withhold final judgment until they had an opportunity to examine the language first hand. Joseph Rauh, Jr., described what happened next:

266

The next morning the Leadership Conference representatives received the still unpublished text of the tentative agreement. Reading the changes with trepidation, it soon became evident that Humphrey's patience, good humor and courage had won the day.

True, under the Humphrey-Dirksen package those discriminated against in public accommodations and employment must first seek their remedy before the appropriate state agency, but there are no such state agencies in the South and Senator Russell was not far from right when he suggested that Senator Dirksen had thus aimed the bill more directly at the South. True, under the Humphrey-Dirksen package the attorney general cannot bring suit on behalf of aggrieved individuals, but he can intervene in such a suit by an individual and, even more important, he can sue wherever there is a 'pattern or practice' of discrimination against any person or group of persons. True, concessions had been made to Senator Dirksen in language and on occasion in substance, but the basic structure of the House passed bill remained intact.[17]

Despite Mitchell's and Rauh's frequent statements that any compromise with Dirksen would be a sellout, Rauh was elated when he read the legal text of the proposed amendments. "I was reading the new language with a lawyer from the AFL-CIO," Rauh said, "and he and I looked at each other and said, 'We've won!'"[18]

As usual, however, the Leadership Conference on Civil Rights did not want to let the press and public know that they were so enthusiastic about the latest version of the civil rights bill. Rauh described the dilemma:

Everyone quickly recognized that at long last here

267

was an agreed upon strong bill. The quandary on what to do was this: If civil rights advocates claimed victory, this would undoubtedly lead Senator Dirksen to ask for new concessions and might also weaken the cloture efforts. If, on the other hand, civil rights advocates charged that the bill had been weakened, such a charge would dismay civil rights forces throughout the country and intensify racial tensions. The resulting statement issued by the Leadership Conference that afternoon was a masterpiece of saying both and neither at the same time.[19]

Thus, exactly as they did with President Kennedy's negotiated compromise when the civil rights bill was before the House Judiciary Committee, Mitchell and Rauh pretended, for political strategy reasons, to be unimpressed with a bill which, in reality, they liked a great deal. Hubert Humphrey's legislative assistant gave an insider's analysis of the Leadership Conference position:

> The Leadership Conference has had a number of meetings with Humphrey and Justice Department officials. They have a variety of specific concerns, but they do not have any basic objections to what has been done. In other words, they are not saying that the roof is falling in, that the bill has been sold out, that there are unacceptable amendments in the Dirksen package. [In fact,] Joe Rauh has told Humphrey privately that if this bill passes, it will be a great victory for the cause of civil rights.[20]

SELLING THE CONSERVATIVE REPUBLICANS

Senator Dirksen also had the task of selling the Humphrey-Dirksen compromise to the conservative Republicans

268

in the Senate. In typical Dirksen fashion, he began by making the amendments the subject for discussion at the next weekly meeting of the Republican Policy Committee. Dirksen encountered stiff resistance, mainly from Midwest and Far West Republicans who remained instinctively hostile to invoking cloture, but by the close of the meeting he sensed that he was making gains. Talking to the press immediately after the Policy Committee meeting, Dirksen noted that members of the Senate were talking about cloture who, previously, were not willing to discuss it. There is a moment when the time calls for action, Dirksen said, and that time had come in the United States Senate.[21]

By the following week, Dirksen was being described as having "the bit in his teeth and running full steam ahead for cloture." Dirksen told his weekly news conference that he was a student of history and that he found great truth in a line he recalled from the diary of Victor Hugo: "Stronger than an army is an idea whose time has come." Dirksen then pointed out that this sweeping legislative attempt to guarantee the rights of black Americans was clearly an idea whose time had come. Later he recited a list of similar events in American history -- civil service reform, the popular election of U.S. senators, the women's suffrage movement, the pure food act, the child labor law. Dirksen pointed out that these events could not be stopped, and that no one was going to stop the compromise civil rights bill.[22]

As Dirksen worked to win support for the civil rights bill, his efforts were being recorded by a growing number of news reporters. With few exceptions, Dirksen was being given the major share of the credit for advancing the civil rights bill in the Senate. One newsmagazine writer later explained:

> Dirksen had done an extraordinary thing. On this most painful of domestic issues, with great skill and energy, Dirksen had simply imposed himself as the arbiter of the Senate. On him alone now depended whether the civil rights bill would

become law, and everyone in Congress knew it.[23]

All over Washington, government observers were now referring to the civil rights bill as "the Dirksen package" or "the Dirksen formula." On Tuesday, 26 May 1964, Dirksen was given the honor of introducing the results of the Humphrey-Dirksen negotiations in the Senate. Now officially known as the Mansfield-Dirksen substitute amendment, the new legislative language would be adopted in a single vote just as soon as cloture had been invoked and the filibuster was ended.

But the battle was not over yet. In order to win the support of wavering Republicans as well as meet some of the minor objections raised by the Leadership Conference on Civil Rights, Humphrey and Dirksen continued to make minor amendments to their package. Two political goals were accomplished by this process of continuing negotiation and amendment. It permitted individual senators to recognize their handiwork in the bill, and it continued to build the widest cross section of support for the bill by accommodating as many interests as possible. "This process of marginal accommodation and adjustment was to continue until the last day before the cloture vote."[24]

SELLING THE HOUSE OF REPRESENTATIVES

Deputy Attorney General Nicholas Katzenbach took on the job of seeing that the bipartisan leaders of the House of Representatives approved of the Humphrey-Dirksen compromise package of amendments. Katzenbach had built up an unusually cordial relationship with the various House leaders when the civil rights bill was under consideration in the House. In clearing the proposed Senate amendments with the House, he worked mainly with Democrat Emanuel Celler, the Chairman of the House Judiciary Committee, and William McCulloch, the ranking Republican on the committee.

Representative McCulloch worked particularly hard at seeing to it that none of the Senate alterations to the civil rights bill would generate opposition when these amendments came back to the House for final adoption. He had his staff publish an article by article comparison of the House passed bill and the amended bill proposed to be passed in the Senate.[25] This comparison of the two versions of the bill was widely circulated by McCulloch in the House so that any objections could be reported to Humphrey and Dirksen and appropriate amendments added to the bill before it finally passed in the Senate. As a result of this high level of coordination between the House and the Senate on the final version of the Senate bill, the civil rights forces were confidant that the Senate version of the bill would sail to swift final passage in the House of Representatives.

SETTING THE DATE

On 27 May 1964 Senate Democratic Leader Mike Mansfield spoke with a group of Capitol Hill reporters. Mansfield said:

> I think, by and large, the senators have just about had enough. They're tired of all this. You have to hit bedrock sometime and have a showdown.[26]

On 1 June 1964 Mansfield and Dirksen jointly announced that the cloture vote would be on Tuesday, 9 June 1964. That date had been selected very carefully. It was after the California Republican presidential primary (scheduled for 2 June 1964) but soon enough that the civil rights bill could clear both the Senate and the House of Representatives prior to Congress adjourning for the Republican National Convention in San Francisco in July.

Dirksen had a special reason for postponing the cloture vote until after the California Republican primary. Senator Barry Goldwater, who was pitted against Nelson Rockefeller, had privately told Dirksen that it was his intention to vote against cloture on the civil rights bill. Dirksen feared that if Goldwater was forced to cast his negative vote on cloture prior to the California primary, his close Republican friends in the Senate

271

would feel obligated to vote against cloture with Goldwater in an effort to bolster Goldwater's standing with the California Republican electorate. By postponing the cloture vote until after the California voting, Goldwater's friends in the Senate could vote for cloture without fear of hurting Goldwater's drive for the Republican presidential nomination. It was another example of the fact that Senate leaders have to take into account the "total political picture" when endeavoring to get legislation enacted by the U.S. Congress.

As it turned out, it was very important that Dirksen made the cloture vote wait until after the California primary. The battle between the conservative Goldwater and the liberal Rockefeller had turned into a hard fought ideological contest. On election day, Goldwater defeated Rockefeller by only 1 percent of the popular vote, but under California's winner take all primary election rules, Goldwater received all of California's 86 convention delegates, enough to give Goldwater the nomination. Goldwater's friends in the Senate thus were freed to vote for cloture without any qualms that they might unintentionally deny Goldwater the 1964 G.O.P. presidential nomination.

THE COUNTERFILIBUSTER

As might have been expected, Senator Richard Russell of Georgia was not going to let Mansfield and Dirksen march toward cloture without pulling a few tricks of his own. On 2 June 1964 Russell suddenly announced that the Southern Democrats were ready to halt the filibuster temporarily and permit some more votes on jury trial amendments. Russell had thereby activated his famous "tidbit" tactic, a maneuver designed to "decelerate the momentum for cloture by permitting a vote or two without, however, making any commitments [for a vote] on the entire bill."[27] In short, Russell was offering the civil rights forces a "tidbit" in the form of allowing a few votes on amendments but had no intention of ever voluntarily giving a "full meal" in the form of a vote on the bill itself.

272

By this time, the pro-civil rights forces were not interested in tidbits. Allowing votes at this late point in the proceedings would only dissipate the accelerating momentum building toward a cloture vote. With what aides described as a broad grin on his face, Mansfield made the kind of speech in the Senate that is customarily made by senators staging a filibuster. Mansfield told his fellow senators:

> Beginning this afternoon there will be some speeches on the question of the pending jury trial amendment, and beginning tomorrow a number of senators . . . have indicated their intention to speak on the Mansfield-Dirksen substitute.[28]

What the pro-civil rights forces were doing was to stage a counterfilibuster of their own to make certain that there would be no intervening votes until the ultimate showdown vote on cloture. Exactly as the Southerners had done so many times before, the civil rights senators dusted off unused speeches and consumed several days of Senate debating time with no great difficulty. When the cloture vote came it would, in effect, be on the civil rights forces counterfilibuster rather than on the Southern filibuster itself. The civil rights forces would, in short, be cloturing themselves. To have this long fight end in this manner was ironic, but that was what was happening.

THE HICKENLOOPER REVOLT

Just at the moment when everything appeared to be in order for a successful cloture vote, a new obstacle suddenly appeared. Republican Senator Bourke B. Hickenlooper of Iowa, who apparently resented the publicity and the big play in the press that Dirksen was getting, started to balk openly and publicly at voting for cloture. Hickenlooper had long been jealous of Dirksen's leadership in the Republican party in the Senate, and he had walked out of several of the negotiating sessions with Hubert Humphrey and the Justice Department,

273

claiming that Dirksen was giving "too much" to the Democrats and stating that he would not be bound by the results of Dirksen's negotiations.

On Tuesday, 2 June 1964, Dirksen became ill and could not come into the Senate to work. This gave Hickenlooper the opportunity to make his move. He began holding a series of meetings with Midwestern and Western Republicans like himself who had some questions about the Humphrey-Dirksen compromise. With Dirksen absent, Hickenlooper began picking up strength and soon had five or six conservative Republican senators supporting him, enough to cause the cloture vote to fail if these five or six should decide to vote against it.

On Friday, 5 June 1964, Hickenlooper took the Senate floor and asked unanimous consent that three amendments be acted upon prior to the cloture vote. One amendment was a jury trial amendment that would make it somewhat easier for Southern officials to get jury trials in civil rights oriented contempt of court cases. The second amendment would have somewhat weakened the equal employment opportunity section of the bill, and the third would have eliminated United States Government financial aid to school systems in the process of racially desegregating.

Hickenlooper's request created yet another dilemma for the civil rights forces. If Humphrey and Dirksen refused Hickenlooper the chance to vote on his amendments, the Iowa Senator probably could withdraw enough votes to prevent cloture. If Humphrey and Dirksen agreed to a vote on the amendments, however, the jury trial amendment, and one or both of the others, might very well pass, mainly because many Senators might feel this was the price of Hickenlooper's vote for cloture. After a day of checking and rechecking his Republican supporters, a recently recovered Everett Dirksen told Humphrey and Kuchel they had better grant Hickenlooper the privilege of a vote on his amendments. The reason was that Dirksen simply did not have enough votes for cloture without the support of Hickenlooper and his small band of followers.

The decision was made to vote on Hickenlooper's three

274

amendments, and the cloture vote was delayed one more day until Wednesday, 10 June 1964. As the civil rights forces had feared, the amendment giving Southern officials greater access to trial by jury was narrowly adopted. The other two amendments were easily defeated. The end result was important, however. In return for being given the right to vote, even though only one of those three votes was successful, Senator Hickenlooper and his group committed themselves to vote for cloture.

The Hickenlooper revolt illustrated several things about the United States Senate. Since Humphrey and Dirksen barely had the 67 votes required for cloture, it illustrated the fact that, under such tight conditions, any small group of senators could have demanded certain amendments to the bill in return for their votes for cloture. Out of necessity, Humphrey and Dirksen would have had to give them their amendments (or at least a vote on their amendments). It also illustrated that legislative leaders must always be careful to give their followers an important role to play and must not take all the credit for themselves. As one of Hickenlooper's renegade senators confided in a personal conversation with Hubert Humphrey: "All we really wanted was the chance to show that Dirksen wasn't the only Republican on the Senate floor."[29]

Perhaps the most important thing the Hickenlooper revolt demonstrated was how essential Everett Dirksen was to getting the required Republican votes for cloture. It was Dirksen's temporary illness and absence from the Senate that gave Hickenlooper the opportunity to get his revolt organized. If there had been any doubts in civil rights supporters' minds that they absolutely needed Dirksen, those doubts were thoroughly dispelled when they saw what happened the few days Dirksen was sick.

It is interesting to note that the civil rights forces, on the last day before the cloture vote, allowed the Hickenlooper Republicans to vote on amendments but would not let the Southern Democrats do so. Hubert Humphrey particularly remembered discussing the subject with Richard Russell. Humphrey said:

I can recall Senator Russell complaining quite bitterly that we hadn't cooperated with him when he wanted to vote, and I said to him, somewhat in jest, but also in truth, "Well, Dick, you haven't any votes to give us for cloture, and these fellows do." That was the sum and substance of it.[30]

A BAD ENVIRONMENT

The civil rights forces were badly shaken by the unusual series of events that occurred the week before the cloture vote. Every day seemed to bring a new emergency situation that had to be "handled." Humphrey's legislative assistant ably summarized the mood of the week:

The Southerners' decision to stop talking and to [call for] votes on jury trial amendments [thus necessitating the counterfilibuster], Goldwater's victory [over Rockefeller] in California, and Dirksen's illness [which made the Hickenlooper revolt possible] -- all served to create a bad environment for the cloture vote.[31]

THE FINAL DRIVE

As the drive for cloture came down to the final days, there appears to have been some, but not very much, influence exerted on wavering senators by President Johnson. Hubert Humphrey recalled:

We did not bother the president very much. The president was not put on the spot. He was not enlisted in the battle particularly. I understand he did contact some of the senators, but not at our insistence.[32]

One theory for President Johnson's uncharacteristic lack

of direct involvement was that he did not want to antagonize the Southern Democrats unnecessarily and, as always, would need to have their votes on other issues on other days.[33]

It was the view of Clarence Mitchell, Jr., Washington Director of the NAACP, that President Johnson was very much involved behind the scenes in lining up Senate votes for cloture on the civil rights bill. Mitchell recalled that he gave President Johnson a list of senators who needed direct persuasion from the president in order to win their support for the civil rights bill. According to Mitchell, the president agreed to take the list and work with it. Mitchell's exact words were:

> This picture over here on my wall showing that little piece of paper beside the president is an illustration of it [the way Mitchell and Johnson would work together counting votes]. On that piece of paper are the names of the senators that I felt Mr. Johnson had to get. I told him all those that I had gotten. And he agreed to take that list and did produce on it.[34]

President Johnson's low public profile when it came to lobbying Senate votes for cloture produced a critical political column in a Washington newspaper. The columnist wrote:

> The civil rights bill is not moving according to plan and senators favoring it are beginning to ask each other: "Where's Lyndon?" As majority leader, the president was all muscle and scant conversation. In the present impasse, the criticism is freely heard that the reverse is true. . . . Reporters covering the civil rights story in detail agree that they have seen no traces of the old brooding and impatient Johnson presence that they learned to know so well during the Eisenhower years.[35]

On Tuesday evening, 9 June 1964, Humphrey made his

277

final vote calculations in his Capitol office and could count only 65 sure votes, two short of the 67 needed for cloture. Then the news teletypes in the Capitol press room carried the story of Senator Hickenlooper's official announcement that he was going to vote for cloture. That made 66 sure votes. The telephone rang and Humphrey answered it. It was President Johnson, calling to ask about the prospects for the cloture vote. "I think we have enough," Humphrey replied. The president responded to this weak statement in a harsh tone of voice: "I don't want to know what you think. What's the vote going to be? How many do you have?" Subdued and nervous as a result of the president's impatient manner, Humphrey admitted that he was still one vote short. The search for votes would have to continue into the night.[36]

Humphrey decided to work on three last Democratic holdouts -- Edmondson of Oklahoma, Yarborough of Texas, and Cannon of Nevada. None would give him a definite answer. At 1 A.M., when it was too late for any more telephone calls, Humphrey ceased his last minute efforts and paid a brief visit to the Senate floor. There he had a friendly exchange with Senator Robert Byrd of West Virginia, who was getting some national and home state publicity by giving an all-night speech against the principle of ending a filibuster with a cloture vote. Humphrey then went home, fairly certain he had the votes for cloture but keeping in the back of his mind one final thought: "You can never be sure about anything in the Senate."[37]

CONCLUSIONS

The civil rights forces in the Senate got themselves to a cloture vote on the civil rights bill by being willing to negotiate a compromise version of the bill with Everett M. Dirksen of Illinois, the Republican leader in the Senate. Although the "no amendments" strategy had made for a strong original bargaining position, it was the willingness of the civil rights strategists to meet with Dirksen and amend the bill more to his liking that made the cloture vote possible.

The Humphrey-Dirksen negotiations in Dirksen's Capitol office were the most interesting and unusual part of this process. Because of the obstructionism of Senator Eastland, there had been no Senate Judiciary Committee markup of the civil rights bill. In other words, there had been no point in the Senate legislative process where a standing committee of the Senate marked up the bill, i.e., voted on the provisions of the bill section by section before recommending it to the Senate floor.

In retrospect, it is clear that the meetings in Dirksen's office became an informal substitute for committee consideration and markup of the civil rights bill. Instead of a duly constituted committee of the United States Senate marking up the bill, it was done by an ad hoc group consisting of Senator Dirksen and his "Bombers" on the one hand and Senator Humphrey and a staff of lawyers from the Justice Department on the other. As Senator Humphrey's legislative assistant asked at the time: "When has an ad hoc group such as this come up with such important legislation?"[38]

There were crucial differences, however, between the Humphrey-Dirksen negotiations and a routine committee markup session. Humphrey's legislative assistant explained the differences this way:

> The Dirksen negotiations were convened under the sponsorship and control of the elected leaders of both parties. They were designed expressly to serve the leaders' interests in finding a formula that could pass the bill. The sessions provided an informal, ad hoc forum to arrive at the kind of compromises which could not have been secured in public debate on the Senate floor. . . . Consistent with the general notion of party leaders being ill equipped to handle complex substantive questions on the floor or in committee, the leadership found Dirksen's back room more to their liking. True give-and-take was possible, decisions were neither public nor final, and the

279

need to sustain one's public posture on certain
issues was greatly reduced. In this environment,
the party leaders could explore the content of
. . . [various senators' proposals] without risking a
loss of leadership control.[39]

At the level of legislative theory, it can be argued that the
Humphrey-Dirksen negotiations suggest a different and, perhaps,
more effective way of organizing a legislature. Instead of having
legislation reviewed by standing committees, over which the
various party leaders have reduced political control, why not have
each major bill reviewed by an ad hoc committee appointed by
the various party leaders to consider that one piece of legislation. This means that all major pieces of legislation would be
reviewed by specially appointed legislators who would tailor the
legislation to the direct political needs of the Democratic and
Republican leaders. Such a system would, as was the case with
the Humphrey-Dirksen negotiations, produce more sophisticated
legislation which, at the end of the negotiating and compromising
process, both party leaders could support enthusiastically. This
idea should particularly recommend itself to those legislative
reformers who would like to see more power in the hands of the
party leadership and less power in the hands of the various
committee chairmen.

One of the most noticeable things about the
Humphrey-Dirksen negotiations was the prominent role played by
the Justice Department, principally Deputy Attorney General
Nicholas Katzenbach. In fact, the negotiations were really
between Dirksen and the Justice Department with Humphrey
mainly playing the role of convincing strong civil rights
supporters to accept the Dirksen compromises.

The fact that the Justice Department was a major party to
the Humphrey-Dirksen negotiations permitted President Johnson's
interests to be furthered without Johnson himself having to
become publicly involved in the Senate's internal business.[40]
Nicholas Katzenbach and the Justice Department staff were
essentially negotiating the president's interests, thereby leaving

Johnson free to stand apart from the conflict and do little more than repeatedly call for the Senate to pass the bill. This also explains why there is no public record of President Johnson personally lobbying the various provisions of the bill. Katzenbach did much of his work for him in the Humphrey-Dirksen negotiations.

If it can be argued that the Humphrey-Dirksen negotiations became the committee markup session on the civil rights bill, then it also can be argued that clearing all the proposed Senate amendments with representatives Emanuel Celler and William McCulloch became the House-Senate conference committee on the bill. As has been previously noted, the civil rights bill did not go to a House-Senate conference committee because the conference report would have had to come back to the Senate for final passage and thus would have been subject to a second filibuster. To make certain the Senate version of the bill would be repassed in the House without amendment, Nicholas Katzenbach carried all the proposed Senate amendments to Celler and McCulloch and made sure they had no objections. In essence, therefore, Katzenbach became the Senate conferee on the bill and Celler and McCulloch became the House conferees. Here again, Southern Democratic control over a key point in the legislative process (the ability to filibuster at length a House-Senate conference report) forced civil rights supporters to use unusual and unorthodox means to get their bill enacted into law.

THE VOTE ON CLOTURE

Cloture day, 10 June 1964, dawned sunny, warm and humid, with a pleasant breeze blowing. By 10:00 A.M. the public galleries of the Senate had been filled for hours. In order to prevent crowded conditions on the Senate floor, all senatorial aides, most of whom ordinarily have the privilege to go on the Senate floor to work with their senators, were banned from the Senate chamber. Staff members, even those who had worked hard for and against the civil rights bill, had to squeeze into the crowded public galleries.

Some legislative aides stepped out on the Capitol lawn to watch television newsman Roger Mudd, then working for <u>CBS</u> television news, as he waited to receive a verbal report of each vote by telephone from the press gallery and then record it on a large cloture scoreboard.[41] (Senate rules in 1964 forbade live television coverage of debates and roll call votes on the floor of the Senate.) With television cameras pointed at Mudd and his scoreboard, the cloture vote was going to be one of the few votes in the history of the United States Senate, if not the only vote in the history of the United States Senate, to be reported live, vote by vote, on national television.

On the Senate floor Hubert Humphrey was in a confident and ebullient mood. Follow-up telephone calls that morning had produced verbal commitments from Democrats Edmondson, Yarborough, and Cannon that they would, indeed, vote for cloture. Just before the scheduled vote, Humphrey passed a note to Senator Philip Hart of Michigan, a staunch civil rights supporter, predicting they had 69 to 70 sure votes, at least 2 more than the 67 required.

A number of senators were delivering their final statements prior to the vote. The occasion called for high toned rhetoric and grandiose phraseology, and many senators proved equal to the occasion. Democratic Leader Mike Mansfield, consistent to the end, arranged the schedule so that Republican Leader Everett Dirksen could give the final speech. It was Dirksen's general policy to speak extemporaneously in the Senate, but he considered this occasion so important that, for one of the few times in his long Senate career, he wrote the speech out ahead of time.[42]

It was one of Dirksen's better oratorical efforts, and he built the speech around the famous phrase of Victor Hugo's that he had first used at an earlier press conference. Dirksen said:

Stronger than all the armies is an idea whose time has come.

The time has come for equality of

opportunity . . . in government, in education and in employment. It will not be stayed or denied. It is here. . . .

America grows. America changes. And on the civil rights issue we must rise with the occasion. . . .

[This issue] is essentially moral in character. It must be resolved. It will not go away. Its time has come. . . .

I appeal to all senators. . . . Today let us not be found wanting in whatever it takes by way of moral and spiritual substance to face up to the issue and to vote cloture.[43]

At 11:10 A.M. the bells and buzzers rang throughout the Senate side of the Capitol to signal the cloture vote. It was exactly one year to the day since President Kennedy had first announced the details of his civil rights bill to Congress. Humphrey sat at his desk in the front row on the Democratic side of the aisle, between Democratic Leader Mike Mansfield at the first desk and Harry Byrd of Virginia, one of the filibustering Southerners, at the third. Two rows behind, at his desk on the aisle, sat Richard Russell of Georgia, leaning forward to hear every word as the roll call vote proceeded. Across the aisle from Mansfield, in the number one desk on the Republican side, sat Everett Dirksen, the one man more than any other who had made the day's proceedings possible. Next to him sat Thomas Kuchel, the most powerful liberal Republican voice in the Senate.

In almost total silence, the clerk of the Senate began to call the roll. Each of the party leaders, including Senator Russell, held a tally sheet in his hand on which to mark the votes of the various senators as their names were called in alphabetical order. Mansfield, Humphrey, Dirksen, and Kuchel were looking to see if any of their pledged votes might "jump ship" at the last minute and vote against cloture. Richard Russell was waiting, not with very much hope, for enough "surprise switches" to make the cloture vote fail.

283

All 100 senators were present and responded as the clerk called their names. Senator Clair Engle of California, critically stricken with cancer, was brought into the Senate chamber on a wheelchair. So paralyzed he could not utter the single syllable, "Aye," Engle indicated his affirmative vote by pointing to his eye. "Dirksen's voice, as usual, was mellow and breathy as he called 'Aye.' Humphrey answered his name softly, almost shyly. 'Aye,' he said, lingering on the word, affectionately stretching out the sound for an extra second. Russell almost shouted his terse 'No.'"[44]

Senator Lee Metcalf, a Democrat from Montana, was the acting president of the Senate for this historic occasion. When the voting was completed and the clerk had tallied the results, Metcalf announced there were 71 yeas and 29 nays. "Two-thirds of the Senators present having voted in the affirmative," Metcalf said, "the motion is agreed to."[45] Cloture had been achieved with four votes more than necessary.

As if to highlight the fact that the civil rights forces had cloture votes to spare, Senator Carl Hayden, a Democrat from Arizona, did not answer the roll call vote the first time his name was called. Apparently Hayden had promised his old friend, Lyndon Johnson, that he would stay away if necessary, thereby reducing by one the number of votes needed for cloture. When the roll call was completed and it was clear that the civil rights forces had votes to spare, Senator Hayden walked onto the Senate floor and voted "No." Hayden was anxious to vote against cloture because of the historical fact that a filibuster had been required to win statehood for Arizona back in 1912.

A memorandum to President Johnson from Secretary of the Interior Stewart L. Udall suggested there was something more than friendship involved in Senator Hayden's willingness to not vote if the civil rights forces only had 66 votes for cloture. Hayden had long been interested in a major U.S. Government water project for Arizona known as the Hayden-Brown proposal, and the memorandum suggested that verbal commitments were made to expedite that project in return for Hayden's cooperation on the cloture vote. The memorandum read in part:

The reports I get from Senator Hayden's staff indicate that your gambit on cloture with the senator at our Tuesday meeting was very persuasive. From a tactical standpoint, I think it would be wise for you to defer your final decision on the Hayden-Brown proposal until after the vote on cloture. . . . You are, of course, fully aware of the effect which a Hayden vote for cloture would have; some of the senators tell me that he will carry several other votes with him -- such as the two Nevada senators.[46]

Mike Manatos, a White House staff member, provided this summary of the negotiations with Senator Hayden:

You recall the spade work that has gone into our attempts to work out an arrangement with Senator Hayden and the Central Arizona Project contingent upon the promise of a cloture vote by Hayden on Civil Rights. . . . After last week's leadership breakfast the president saw Hayden, and this was a ten strike because it provided clear evidence of the president's personal interest. . . . I am convinced this can be worked out to Hayden's satisfaction, . . . thus gaining one cloture vote . . . .[47]

Following the cloture vote, Senator Richard Russell stood up to begin his last series of arguments against the bill. His voice was angry. In a statement that civil rights supporters regarded as highly ironic, Russell complained that he was "confronted with the spirit of not only the mob, but of a lynch mob in the Senate of the United States."[48]

Up in the Senate public galleries and out on the Capitol lawn, the various senatorial aides and pro-civil rights lobbyists celebrated their victory. Exclamations of joy, exuberant pats on the back, and heartfelt handshakes were shared by the less well-known persons who had worked for the bill along with the senators.

Wednesday, 10 June 1964, was the 75th day of Senate debate on the House passed bill. For the first time in the history of the United States Senate, cloture had been invoked on a civil rights bill. To civil rights supporters, final passage of the bipartisan administration civil rights bill now appeared to be assured.

CHAPTER 13

"TO DIE ON THE BARRICADES;"
TO EARN "A PLACE OF HONOR"

If the civil rights leaders had thought they were going to sit around the Senate floor for a few hours and enjoy the fact that cloture had been invoked on the civil rights bill, they were mistaken. Immediately after cloture and following a brief exchange of congratulations, Senator Sam Ervin of North Carolina rose at his desk and offered an amendment which, if accepted, probably would have greatly weakened the bill.

The amendment appeared acceptable at first glance. It provided that government officials who violate civil rights laws could not be tried by both the state government and the United States Government for the same violation. Not until several minutes after the amendment was presented did the civil rights forces realize that Southern states could use the amendment to punish civil rights violators with light or nonexistent state penalties and thereby protect the violators from prosecution and heavy fines and jail sentences in U.S. courts.

To the amazement of the civil rights forces, Senator Ervin's amendment looked so good at first glance that it was adopted by a vote of 49 to 48. Only a procedural misstep on Ervin's part saved the newly clotured civil rights bill from what civil rights supporters would have considered disaster. In his eagerness to present the amendment, Ervin had offered it to a previous Southern amendment rather than to the Mansfield-Dirksen substitute amendment which had been produced by the Humphrey-Dirksen negotiations. Ervin's amendment, although officially passed by the Senate, died when the original Southern amendment to which it was attached failed to be adopted.

It soon developed that events on the Senate floor immediately following cloture were extremely disorganized. Part of this was the great emotional letdown that occurred following such an historic legislative victory. More important, however, was the fact that the Senate leadership had concentrated so heavily on getting cloture that practically no attention whatsoever had been given to the problem of how to handle the Southern Democrats during the postcloture period. No basic organizational plans had been developed to deal with Southern amendments, and no one had done any extensive research and planning on just what the parliamentary situation would be on the Senate floor once cloture was enacted. Going from a precloture to a postcloture Senate turned out to be, in the words of a pro-civil rights Senate aide, like "going from the frying pan right into the blooming fire."[1]

LIFE UNDER CLOTURE

Once cloture is invoked in the United States Senate, each senator may speak for only one more hour on the bill itself or any pending amendments. Only those amendments which had been introduced prior to the cloture vote could be called up, and therein lay the real "kicker" for the civil rights forces. If the Southern Democrats were to get one of their amendments (introduced prior to the cloture vote) added to the bill, the civil rights forces could not introduce an amendment of their own to get the Southern amendment out of the bill. In effect, any Southern amendment adopted in the tumultuous days immediately following cloture was going to be a permanent part of the bill, and there would not be anything the civil rights forces could do about it. "Under these conditions, the bipartisan [floor managers] could ill afford any miscalculations in the numerous roll call votes which lay ahead."[2]

During the first two days immediately following the cloture vote, the civil rights forces held several meetings to try and develop a policy for handling the expected spate of Southern amendments to the bill (over 300 had been introduced prior to the cloture vote). A disagreement promptly broke out between Humphrey and the Leadership Conference lobbyists over how the situation could best be handled. The Leadership Conference and the strongly pro-civil rights senators urged the outright rejection of all amendments and to push the Mansfield-Dirksen compromise to final passage as quickly as possible. Humphrey, on the other hand, wanted to be more accommodating and work with the Southerners in those few cases where their amendments would improve the bill and could get the approval of the staff lawyers from the Justice Department.

Humphrey's legislative assistant sought to explain why Humphrey was taking such a conciliatory attitude toward the Southerners under a parliamentary situation where any amendment adopted would be a permanent part of the bill with no opportunity for future changes or corrections. He noted:

> Humphrey seemed to be quite distraught and not really in command of the situation. The push for cloture had been a deeply demanding one, and he seemed to let up and relax after the vote had been taken in a way which could not be helpful under the demanding nature of the new circumstances which confronted everyone.[3]

It soon became obvious, however, that the Southern Democrats were not interested in perfecting the bill but mainly wanted to present amendments that would "gut" the bill completely. Humphrey's legislative assistant summed up the situation:

> The Southerners appeared more interested in compiling a record of total hostility to the legislation rather than resolving specific substantive problems through the good offices of the party leadership.[4]

Under these conditions, a policy slowly developed on the part of the civil rights leaders to systematically vote down any and all amendments that were presented by the Southern Democrats. A small number of amendments were accepted by Humphrey and Mansfield, always after consulting with Everett Dirksen, but most Southern amendments were rejected across-the-board with a minimum of debate or analysis by the bipartisan forces supporting the bill.

THE POSTCLOTURE FILIBUSTER

Without quite realizing what they were doing at first, the Southerners were discovering a way to extend the filibuster even after having lost the cloture vote. When a senator calls up and debates a proposed amendment, the time is charged against his 1 hour of speaking time allowed under cloture. The time for the quorum call and the roll call vote to approve or defeat the amendment is not charged to the senator, however, and a quorum call and roll call of all 100 senators can take anywhere from 20 minutes to 1 hour, depending on how long it takes to get a sizable number of senators on to the floor.

Soon the various Southerners had learned to call up a particular amendment, use anywhere from 30 seconds to 2 minutes to explain the amendment, and then settle back and watch 20 minutes to 1 hour of Senate time be used up for the quorum call and the roll call vote. If a senator averaged 1 minute for each amendment he presented, he could introduce 60 amendments in the course of his 1 hour of postcloture speaking time and, at an average rate of 30 minutes per quorum call and roll call, delay the Senate a total of 30 hours while it was voting down his amendments. Once civil rights leaders multiplied 30 potential hours of delay per senator times the 18 filibustering Southerners, the magnitude of the potential for delay became obvious.

This technique for delay which the Southerners had discovered came to be known as the postcloture filibuster.[5] Suddenly the Senate floor, which had been a quiet and boring

290

place during the long days of the filibuster, became a place of action and tumult. The Southern Democrats presented amendment after amendment, thus requiring the pro-civil rights forces to answer a quorum call and a roll call vote every 1/2 hour. Having a vote on an amendment every 30 minutes seemed to be almost as grim a fate as the previous torture of going 2 months without any meaningful votes at all.[6]

Soon the major question for civil rights supporters was how long would the Southern Democrats persist in calling up amendments and thereby extend their postcloture filibuster. On Monday, 15 June 1964, Richard Russell acknowledged the futility of prolonging the struggle further and informed Mansfield and Humphrey that he was ready to conclude the debate as soon as possible.[7] Senator Russell did this despite the fact that he could have easily prolonged the postcloture filibuster for a month or two more. As it turned out, however, Russell was unable to get the more dedicated Southerners to join him in bringing a stop to the debate. Sam Ervin of North Carolina, Russell Long of Louisiana, and Strom Thurmond of South Carolina appeared determined to continue. Thurmond announced he was going to offer all his amendments, and Ervin said he would offer amendments as long as Thurmond did. Humphrey's legislative assistant came to the following conclusion:

> It was . . . clear during this period that Russell was having trouble controlling his own troops. . . . Russell clearly was not able to exercise any control over these actions by Thurmond and Ervin.[8]

Although he was their official leader, Richard Russell could not dictate orders to the Southern Democratic senators any more than Mansfield and Humphrey could dictate orders to the Democratic senators or Dirksen and Kuchel could dictate orders to the Republican senators.

When Senate Democratic Leader Mike Mansfield realized that the Southerners were not going to stop their postcloture filibuster, he decided to bear down hard and have the Senate work late into the night. On Tuesday, 16 June 1964, the Senate went into session at 10:00 A.M. and did not quit until midnight. Over 33 Southern amendments were brought up, briefly debated, and defeated by roll call vote. It set the all-time Senate record for the largest number of roll call votes in one calendar day.

PAST THE BREAKING POINT
ON THE SENATE FLOOR

The pressure of having to vote down all the Southern amendments began to take its toll on the civil rights forces:

> As the day wore on into evening on that Tuesday, senators began to get rather well oiled by frequent visits to their respective hideaways around the Capitol. There were some amusing incidents which took place because of this, principally Dirksen's outburst against Russell Long. [Dirksen and Mansfield] had accepted several of Long's minor amendments to the bill, and it was implicitly assumed that the acceptance of the amendments would limit the number of other amendments Long would be offering, but it did not seem to work this way. At one point Long offered an amendment and Dirksen, obviously a little under the weather, jumped to his feet and ran back to Senator Long, gesticulating wildly, and said something to the effect of, "Goddam you, you've broken our agreement. Why, you've welched on our deal." Long looked absolutely horrified at the specter of Dirksen running up the center aisle of the Senate and there were a few moments of some concern if not high comedy. Dirksen calmed down and soon he and Long were striding about the Senate floor, arm in arm.[9]

292

The Senate is regarded as the world's most exclusive private club, and, on those few occasions where Senators lose their decorum and behave in an unfriendly manner towards each other, they quickly come to their senses and publicly show the world that friendship and good manners are still the order of the day.

This long day in the Senate was not over, however. Later in the evening Senator James Eastland of Mississippi made a motion to adjourn, a procedural motion reserved strictly for the Democratic leader (when the Democrats are in the majority). This was a challenge to the principle of party leadership in the Senate which neither Mansfield nor Dirksen could ignore. They lined up every non-Southern Democratic vote available, Democrats and Republicans alike, to try to crush this minor rebellion. Then, in a totally unexpected slap at Dirksen in his role as Republican leader in the Senate, Republicans Peter Dominick of Colorado and Edwin Mechem of New Mexico voted in favor of adjournment.

Outraged at Dominick's and Mechem's actions, Dirksen "hit the roof" and dispatched a covey of Senate pages to locate the errant senators and bring them back to the Senate chamber. When Dominick returned, Dirksen "dashed wildly about the chamber and made Dominick change his vote." When Mechem returned, he "was protesting quite visibly and Dirksen was also quite visibly telling him he had to change his vote." Finally, Dirksen grabbed Mechem by the arm, marched him into the well of the Senate, looked him squarely in the eye and commanded, "Okay, now vote!" Mechem quietly responded, "Nay," and thereby voted against adjourning. The motion to adjourn was rejected by a vote of 73-18, and Mansfield's and Dirksen's authority as party leaders in the Senate remained unthreatened.[10]

All of this quite remarkable and unsenatorial behavior was too much for Mike Mansfield. The Democratic leader decided it was foolish to continue any longer and adjourned the Senate at the midnight hour.

CONTRASTS ON A JUNE NIGHT

It was during this period of repeated Southern amendments and the requisite roll call votes that a legislative aide to Senator Thomas Kuchel of California decided to take a needed break from the tumult on the Senate floor and stepped out on the front portico of the Senate wing of the Capitol. Standing between the marble pillars and enjoying the pleasant cool of a June evening in Washington, he gazed over at the marble steps leading up to the center section of the Capitol building, the section midway between the Senate wing and the House of Representatives wing which contains the Capitol dome. On these steps sat a large racially integrated audience, about half white and half black, listening to a concert band playing on the sidewalk below. These public band concerts on the main Capitol steps were held frequently during the summertime. At the particular moment the legislative aide looked over, it was the "sing along" portion of the band's evening program and the audience was singing "America the Beautiful."

The legislative aide was struck by the contrast between the two separate worlds he was observing that evening. Inside the Capitol, on the Senate floor, was the tumult and anger of the forces of Southern racial segregation making their final stand against inevitable change. Out on the Capitol steps, however, a completely integrated audience was peacefully singing about "brotherhood from sea to shining sea." The two groups were completely oblivious to each other. The senators were unaware of the band concert less than 100 yards from their intense legislative battleground. The relaxed concertgoers had no idea that just behind them and to the left the "brotherhood" about which they were singing was striving to take a giant step forward.[11]

ACCEPTING THE INEVITABLE

On Wednesday, 17 June 1964, Mansfield and Humphrey

entered into negotiations with Southern Democrats Thurmond and Ervin to end the postcloture filibuster and permit the Senate to get on with its work. Even these two committed Southerners could see that the wearing process of voting down amendment after amendment was pushing the Senate majority to the breaking point. Thurmond and Ervin agreed to introduce only a certain number of additional amendments, and these were disposed of by late in the afternoon on that same day. The bill received its third reading that evening, which closed it to further amendment, and the Senate adjourned. Final speeches on the civil rights bill were scheduled for all day Thursday and all day Friday with the final vote anticipated at the close of business on Friday, 19 June 1964.

THE FINAL SOUTHERN BARRAGE

The two days set aside for final speeches gave Richard Russell and the Southern Democrats one last chance to sum up their arguments against the bipartisan civil right bill. Even as modified by the negotiations with Senator Dirksen, the Southerners charged, the bill was unconstitutional. The Southerners hit hard on the point that the major effect of the Dirksen negotiations, amending the bill so it applied only where there was a "pattern and practice" of racial discrimination, guaranteed that the new law would mainly effect the South and have little or no effect in the North and the West.

Senator Richard Russell's final speech, given just prior to the final vote on the bill, ably summed up the Southern position on civil rights and revealed the fact that the Southerners were as committed to their cause as the pro-civil rights senators were to theirs. Russell said:

> The central issue at stake in this debate has been
> the preservation of the dual system of divided
> powers [between the national government and the
> states] that has been the hallmark of the genius of
> the Founding Fathers.

I am proud to have been a member of that small group of determined senators that since the 9th of March has given . . . the last iota of physical strength in the effort to hold back the overwhelming combination of forces supporting this bill until its manifold evils could be laid bare before the people of the country.

The depth of our conviction is evidenced by the intensity of our opposition. There is little room for honorable men to compromise where the inalienable rights of future generations are at stake. . . .

Mr. President, the people of the South are citizens of this Republic. They are entitled to some consideration. It seems to me that fair men should recognize that the people of the South, too, have some rights which should be respected. And though, Mr. President, we have failed in this fight to protect them from a burgeoning bureaucracy that is already planning and organizing invasion after invasion of the South, . . . our failure cannot be ascribed to lack of effort. Our ranks were too thin, our resources too scanty, but we did our best. I say to my comrades in arms in this long fight that there will never come a time when it will be necessary for any one of us to apologize for his conduct or his courage.[12]

Similar to Hubert Humphrey and the civil rights senators, the Southerners were proud of the fact that the debate on the civil rights bill was carried out on a high level and was, for the most part, free of racial jokes and racial epithets. An aide to Senator Lister Hill of Alabama (one of the filibustering Southern Democrats) explained:

The fight had to be made. There were strong legal arguments against the bill. We were proud of the fact that the Southerners argued the bill on the basis of its constitutional aspects. The racial aspect was not emphasized. There was good unity among the Southerners in the effort made, and we honestly believed we were upholding the ideals of Thomas Jefferson and James Madison in pointing out the unconstitutional nature of the bill. The Southern side of the debate was prepared in a careful and scholarly manner. The arguments that were made against the bill were good ones. They are still good. I have no problem defending those arguments.[13]

THE FAILURE OF SOUTHERN STRATEGY

In the days immediately following the successful cloture vote on the civil rights bill, there was much speculation in the press as to why the Southern Democrats, who previously had never been defeated in their attempts to stop a strong civil rights bill with a filibuster, had been defeated this time around. In a newspaper interview, Senator Russell acknowledged that he had been thinking a great deal about his tactics and had not found one thing he would have done differently. Russell explained:

> The cards were stacked from the beginning. The odds were insuperable, overwhelming. We carried the fight for about 80 days, and this was a remarkable legislative achievement. . . .
> This time we had the public stirred up by the clergy, the moralists, the faculties of the colleges, the demonstrations. Nearly every day someone raised the claim that, unless we passed this bill, there would be more riots in the streets this summer.[14]

Many observers felt that Russell and the Southern

Democrats made a major strategy mistake when they did not offer to bargain with Mansfield and Humphrey and thereby gain for themselves the kind of concessions that were won by Senator Dirksen. According to <u>Congressional Quarterly Weekly Report</u>:

> Northern sources say that had Russell come to them at the outset of the filibuster and tried to make a bargain, it is likely that he could have extracted some teeth from the bill. It is also likely that had Southerners allowed more voting on amendments before cloture, especially before Dirksen and other Republicans were committed to the bill, several [pro-Southern] amendments would have carried. "They could have caused us fits," one Northern source said, "but their strategy was surprisingly unimaginative." Russell never approached the leadership for bargaining purposes, and allowed voting only on jury trial amendments, a side issue.[15]

Hubert Humphrey shared this view that the Southern Democrats made a mistake by not letting the Senate vote on amendments to the civil rights bill:

> Frankly, I was rather surprised at the Southerners' tactics. I never could quite understand why they didn't let us vote more often. . . . If they had done so, they could have insisted that the legislative process was working, that amendments were being voted upon. Instead of that, they just kept talking and talking. It seemed to me that they lost their sense of direction and really had little or no plan other than what they used to have when filibusters [always] succeeded.[16]

Humphrey's legislative assistant also believed the Southerners could have made real gains by allowing votes on amendments. He noted that the civil rights forces became disorganized and had great difficulty holding their shaky alliance together when the Southerners allowed votes on jury trail amendments:

> We [the civil rights forces] were really quite disorganized and unhinged at that point and only escaped through mistakes of the opponents and a certain amount of good luck for ourselves. [It was] one helluva way to pass a civil rights bill.[17]

Although Richard Russell was the acknowledged leader of the Southern bloc, Congressional Quarterly Weekly Report pointed out that he could not be charged with total responsibility for the failure of Southern strategy. In accord with their "Confederate" tradition, the Southern Democrats operated under a rule of unanimity, and it only took the objection of one Southern senator to prevent voting on Senate amendments to the civil rights bill. Several of the Southerners were known to be considerably more intransigent than others, and these senators possibly prevented Russell from following a more flexible strategy which might, in turn, have been more successful.[18]

The Southerners missed another opportunity to amend (and thereby weaken) the bill in the pandemonium that occurred following the successful cloture vote. Hubert Humphrey remarked privately to an aide that a carefully prepared strategy by the Southern Democrats for proposing amendments immediately following cloture might have produced some real reverses for the civil rights forces.[19] The aide elaborated on Humphrey's thinking on this point:

> It was . . . evident that the Southerners really had given very little thought to their strategy after cloture. Their amendments were not called up in any particular order, which was a mistake. Had they plotted out precisely which amendments would be called up, they could have scored, perhaps,

some impressive victories early in the debate after
cloture and thereby opened up the danger of bad
amendments being adopted to the bill . . . .[20]

The Southerners could claim partial victory on one point,
however. The extended filibuster did put Mansfield and
Humphrey in a position where they had to compromise with
Senator Dirksen, and Dirksen's amendments to the bill did
somewhat check the ability of the United States Government to
interfere with state and local governments on civil rights
matters. An aide to Alabama Senator Lister Hill explained:

It was a partial victory in that deals had to be
struck to get the bill through. If nothing else, the
filibuster forced the other side to compromise.[21]

THE REALITIES OF SOUTHERN POLITICS

When arguing that the Southern Democrats should have
allowed more voting on amendments and should have been more
willing to compromise with the Northerners, one must never
forget the realities of Southern politics in the early 1960s.
Because of various white stratagems for keeping Southern blacks
from being able to vote, most Southern senators had few black
voters among their voting constituents. The white majority vote
that ruled the South politically at that time was strongly opposed
to racial integration of any kind or degree. Even the slightest
hint of being willing to accept integration in the American South
would have put the Southern Democratic senators in deep
political trouble when they came up for reelection.

It thus was clear that, on the issue of civil rights in 1964,
no accommodation or compromise was possible on the part of
the Southern Democrats:

Any legislation which would satisfy the demands
of the Negro community and those committed to
civil rights could not be acceptable to the

South. . . . The final speeches by many members of the Southern bloc . . . clearly illustrated that there [was] no satisfactory compromise [possible] between the South and supporters of civil rights legislation. Under these circumstances it [was] not surprising to find absolute opposition [on the part of the Southerners]. . . . Regardless of personal feelings, political realities demanded that the Southern senators "die on the barricades" in their effort to defeat the bill.[22]

SENATOR GOLDWATER'S VOTE

The two days set aside for final Senate speeches on the civil rights bill set the stage for Senator Barry Goldwater to make public his final position on the bill. As a result of Goldwater's victory over Nelson Rockefeller in the California Republican primary, most observers were convinced that Goldwater would be the 1964 Republican nominee for president. Although Goldwater had voted against cloture, there was considerable speculation in the newspapers that he might "work both sides of the street" by voting for the civil rights bill on final passage.[23]

Everett Dirksen worked particularly hard to get Senator Goldwater to support the bill, particularly in view of the fact that the G.O.P. nominating convention was less than a month away. "You just can't do it," Dirksen said when Goldwater told him he was going to vote against the bill as well as against cloture. "You can't do it [to] the party," Dirksen went on. "The idea has come!" But Goldwater refused Dirksen's earnest entreaties to vote for the bill on final passage. Dirksen had imposed his will on the Senate, but not on the likely presidential nominee of his own Republican party. For Dirksen, Goldwater's negative vote took away part of the savor of his great legislative triumph with the civil rights bill.[24]

On Thursday, 18 June 1964, Goldwater took the Senate floor to announce his vote against the civil rights bill on final passage and to give his reasons. While explicitly recognizing the responsibility of the United States Government in the area of civil rights, Goldwater asserted that there was absolutely no constitutional basis for either the public accommodations or equal employment sections of the bill. Goldwater also took the position that enforcement of the various provisions of the bill would be very difficult, requiring a U.S. Government police force and a national network of spies and informers.[25]

THE LAST WORDS

Friday, 19 June 1964, found the principal architects of the Senate version of the civil rights bill praising both themselves and the ability of the Senate to legislate successfully on such a complicated and emotionally charged issue. Senator Winston Prouty, a Republican from Vermont, compared Everett Dirksen's efforts on behalf of the civil rights bill to Abraham Lincoln's efforts during the Civil War. Prouty told the Senate:

> Mr. President, 103 years ago -- when the House of this Nation was divided -- to serve the cause of freedom and make our people one, a man came out of Illinois.
> One hundred and three years later, to open the doors of our National House and to serve the cause of freedom, another man has come out of Illinois.
> True it may be that no one man was responsible for the abolition of slavery. True it may be that no one man is responsible for our statute to prohibit discrimination. But, without Lincoln there would have been no Emancipation Proclamation, and without Dirksen there would have been no civil rights bill.[26]

Hubert Humphrey decided to base his final words on Benjamin Franklin's closing statement to the Constitutional

Convention held at Philadelphia in 1787. Humphrey told the Senate he would "consent to this measure because I expect no better and because I am not sure it is not the best."[27]

In line with his goals throughout the entire filibuster, Democratic Leader Mike Mansfield praised the Senate for being able to make a decision over such a controversial and divisive issue as civil rights. The fact that there was a final vote, Mansfield concluded, was of even greater significance than the outcome of the vote itself. Mansfield told the Senate:

> It [the vote on the civil rights bill] underscores, once again, the basic premise of our government -- that a people of great diversity can resolve even its most profound differences, under the Constitution, through the processes of responsible, restrained, and reciprocal understanding.[28]

As on the cloture vote, Mansfield again recognized Senator Dirksen's role in Senate passage of the bill and allowed him to deliver the last speech before the vote. Dirksen used this opportunity to further develop his theme that irresistible forces of change and progress were guiding the civil rights bill toward final adoption in the Senate. Dirksen said:

> Mr. President, . . . in the history of mankind there is an inexorable moral force that carries us forward. No matter what statements may be made on the [Senate] floor, no matter how tart the editorials in every section of the country, no matter what the resistance of people who do not wish to change, it will not be denied. Mankind ever forward goes. There have been fulminations to impede, but they have never stopped that thrust....
>
> In line with the sentiment offered by the poet, "Any man's death diminishes me, because I am involved in mankind," so every denial of

303

freedom, every denial of equal opportunity for a livelihood, for an education, for a right to participate in representative government diminishes me.

[That] is the moral basis for our case.

It has been long and tedious, but the mills [of change] will continue to grind, and, whatever we do here tonight as we stand on the threshold of a historic roll call, those mills will not stop grinding.

So, Mr. President, I commend this bill to the Senate, and in its wisdom I trust that in bountiful measure [this bill] will prevail.[29]

Moments after Dirksen finished speaking, the final Senate roll call on the Civil Rights Act of 1964 began. Once again all 100 senators were present, and once again ailing Senator Clair Engle of California was brought in in a wheel chair and voted in the affirmative by pointing to his eye. For this final vote the administrative assistants and legislative aides to the various senators were allowed on the Senate floor, and they crowded the limited space at the back and the sides of the Senate chamber. The bipartisan civil rights bill passed the Senate by a vote of 73 to 27, and upon the official announcement of the vote by the chair, there was spontaneous clapping and cheering from the packed Senate galleries. The junior Democrat in the chair, Lee Metcalf of Montana, quickly pounded the gavel and called for silence, but not too quickly. It seemed the customary decorum and quiet of the Senate might be suspended for this one historic occasion, at least for 10 seconds or so.[30]

And then, almost as if the filibuster, the historic cloture vote, and the vote on final passage had never occurred, Democratic Leader Mike Mansfield rose at his desk and announced the Senate's debate and voting schedule for the next few days. Mansfield said:

Mr. President, for the information of the

304

Senate, it is anticipated that on Monday the Senate will start consideration of the Interior appropriations bill, to be followed, although not necessarily in this order, by the Treasury and Post Office appropriation bill, the atomic energy authorization bill, [and] the National Aeronautics and Space authorization bill.[31]

And so the Senate moved on. It moved from the greatly consequential to the comparatively inconsequential, the rhythm that had been broken by the long filibuster instantly restored as if nothing that important had taken place. The filibuster of the Civil Rights Act of 1964 had been successfully overcome. The Senate of the United States of America turned its attention to other business.

THE CELEBRATION ON THE CAPITOL LAWN

Shortly after the roll call vote on final passage of the Senate version of the civil rights bill, Humphrey and Dirksen and other key supporters of the bill gathered for a round of hand shaking, press statements, and photographs. An aide reported to Humphrey that a crowd of several thousand persons had ringed the approaches to the Senate wing of the Capitol, waiting to congratulate and applaud the senators who had led the successful fight. Responding to the natural instinct to acknowledge the cheers of joyous supporters, Humphrey left the press conference and hurried down the long marble steps leading toward the crowd. One of Humphrey's biographers described the scene:

The people recognized him and applauded. Many were Negroes. Humphrey shook hands, gazed into their faces, and said, "Isn't this fine? You're happy, aren't you?" Some of the people shouted "Freedom" as he walked among them. Others called, "God bless you." One woman whispered, "I hope you get picked to be Vice-President." An

305

old man said, "I'm from Georgia, and I want you to know a lot of us are with you." A student said, "You gave us justice, Senator. Thank you." Others cried, "Good job -- you did a good job."[32]

Fully three hours later, when Senator Humphrey and several key legislative aides started out for a celebratory dinner at a downtown Washington restaurant, they were astounded to find several hundred persons still milling around the Senate end of the Capitol grounds and continuing to celebrate Senate passage of the bill. "Their enthusiasm appeared boundless. In his 15 years in the Senate, [Hubert Humphrey] could recall no similar outpouring of public sentiment over a bill's passage."[33]

BITTERSWEET

But the sense of total elation which Hubert Humphrey and the other bipartisan Senate leaders should have felt over the passage of the bill was denied to them. In Humphrey's case, he had been informed two days earlier that his eldest son had a lymph node in his neck which, when removed, turned out to be malignant. Although the youth recovered completely in the coming weeks, Humphrey was, quite naturally, deeply disturbed by this great family concern.

Then, as Humphrey and his aides were enjoying their victory dinner at Paul Young's Restaurant in Washington, the news was brought to them that Senator Edward Kennedy of Massachusetts and Senator Birch Bayh of Indiana, who had left Washington after the final vote in a private plane to fly to Boston, had crashed. First reports of the airplane accident claimed that Ted Kennedy had been killed, although it later turned out he had only sustained a serious and painful back injury. The combination of Humphrey's ailing son and Kennedy's and Bayh's plane crash turned the victory dinner into a "drag."[34]

HOUSE CONSIDERATION OF
THE SENATE VERSION OF THE BILL

Due to the close contact which Deputy Attorney General Nicholas Katzenbach had maintained with the bipartisan leaders in the House of Representatives, the Senate amendments to the civil rights bill had been fully accepted by the House leadership even before the bill passed the Senate. The only obstacle that lay in the path of routine and overwhelming approval of the Senate version of the bill in the House was Representative Howard Smith and his House Rules Committee.

Howard Smith at least was honest and above board about his continued opposition to the civil rights bill. He had pointedly warned the speaker of the house, Democrat John W. McCormack of Massachusetts, of his "enthusiastic and complete lack of cooperation" on moving the bill.[35] It was clear that Smith would not call the Rules Committee together to recommend the Senate version of the bill to the House floor unless he was forced to do so.

The White House staff anticipated strong opposition from Rules Committee Chairman Smith and began formulating plans for getting the civil rights bill out from under Smith's control before the bill passed the Senate. A memorandum from Lawrence F. O'Brien to President Johnson dated 18 June 1984 reviewed various strategies for wresting control of the Rules Committee away from Smith. It also described Smith's probable strategy:

> We must assume that Howard Smith will delay as long as possible on granting a rule, and that he can parade witnesses through for several weeks unless we move to cut him off.[36]

Under the leadership of Democratic Representative Ray J. Madden of Indiana, a bipartisan coalition was formed to wrest control of the Rules Committee from Chairman Smith and move the bill to the House floor as quickly as possible. The first step in the process was to file a formal request with Smith asking for a meeting of the committee, a request which Smith granted only because, if he had refused, the bipartisan committee members could have called the meeting themselves. The meeting date was set for 30 June 1964.

Once the meeting of the Rules Committee began, Chairman Smith was administered rebuff after rebuff by the committee majority. Smith had planned to filibuster the bill in the Rules Committee, hoping to drag out committee consideration of the Senate version of the bill for several days, but the bipartisan coalition now running the committee voted to hold a final vote to report out the bill at 5 P.M. that day. When the appointed hour of 5 P.M. arrived, the Rules Committee moved the civil rights bill to the House floor by a vote of 10 to 5.

But the bipartisan committee majority had even more public embarrassment in store for Chairman Smith. Although Smith had accepted the fact that the Rules Committee would send the bill to the House floor, he had at least expected to be in charge of presenting the bill to the House. That would have allowed him, under House rules, to have delayed the bill a full ten days, thereby putting the critical House vote off until just before the Republican National Convention, when Republican members of the House would be anxious to get away. In order to avoid such a conflict, President Lyndon Johnson was pressuring the House leadership to have the bill on his desk for his signature before July 4.

In "the unkindest cut of all," the bipartisan coalition, now fully in charge of the Rules Committee, voted to have Representative Madden rather than Chairman Smith present the bill to the House. Madden, of course, made the bill immediately available for House action. "Smith may have been hurt by this insult, but no remedy was available to him." His public embarrassment and humiliation were complete.[37]

On 2 July 1964 the House of Representatives, by a vote of 289 to 126, adopted a resolution to approve the civil rights bill as amended by the Senate. The bipartisan administration civil rights bill was now an Act of Congress. It lacked only

President Johnson's signature to make it the law of the land.

ABANDONING "ANOTHER LOST CAUSE"

At the time of House approval of the Senate amendments to the civil rights bill, considerable press attention was given to Representative Charles L. Weltner, a Democrat from Atlanta, Georgia, who had voted against the civil rights bill when it first came up for passage in the House. In a surprise development, Representative Weltner switched his position and voted for the House resolution accepting the Senate amendments. He was the only Southern Democrat to make such a switch.

Weltner had first attracted attention as an unusually progressive Southerner when he voted to continue the work of the Civil Rights Commission in October 1963. At that time he made reference to the song "Dixieland," the historic theme song of the Confederacy and the regional anthem of the American South. The last line of the song, Weltner noted, is, "Look away, look away, look away -- Dixieland." Weltner then said:

> Like all Southerners I grew up to the tune of "Dixieland." But we in Dixieland cannot "look away" forever -- nor can the rest of the nation [fail to acknowledge] its own paradox of prejudice.

Weltner went on to wonder just how much longer the South would continue to "look away" from the reality of the civil rights demonstrations and the continuing pleas of a significant segment of the Southern population for equal rights.[38]

Weltner's speech to the House at the time he voted for the Senate version of the civil rights bill was equally emotional. Weltner said:

> Change, swift and certain, is upon us, and we in the South face some difficult decisions. We can offer resistance and defiance, with their harvest of strife and tumult. We can suffer continued

309

demonstrations, with their wake of violence and disorder. Or we can acknowledge this measure as the law of the land. We can accept the verdict of the nation.

I will add my voice to those who seek reasoned and conciliatory adjustment to a new reality, and, finally, I would urge that we at home now move on to the unfinished task of building a new South. We must not remain forever bound to another lost cause.[39]

THE LAW OF THE LAND

President Lyndon Johnson wasted no time affixing his signature to the Civil Rights Act of 1964. Within hours of House of Representatives approval of the Senate amendments, Johnson had one of the largest bill signing ceremonies in United States history arranged at the White House. Ordinarily the president signs bills in the Oval Office, but in order to accommodate as large a crowd of onlookers as possible, President Johnson arranged this particular signing ceremony in the East Room of the White House with more than 100 notables in attendance. The guests included key members of the House and Senate, several cabinet members, important foreign ambassadors, and the major leaders of the civil rights movement.

The ceremony was carried live on national television at 6:45 P.M., Eastern Daylight Time, on 2 July 1964. Most of the newsmen covering the signing noted that it was 101 years to the day since Abraham Lincoln had announced his intention to issue his Emancipation Proclamation freeing the slaves during the Civil War. The president, who had spoken out strongly urging the House and the Senate to pass the civil rights bill, had a few last words to say to the nation:

We believe all men have certain inalienable rights, yet many Americans do not enjoy those rights. We believe all men are entitled to the

310

blessings of liberty. Yet millions are being deprived of those blessings -- not because of their own failures, but because of the color of their skin.

The reasons are deeply imbedded in history and tradition and the nature of man. We can understand -- without rancor or hatred -- how this happened, but it cannot continue. . . . Our Constitution, the foundation of our republic, forbids it. The principles of our freedom forbid it. Morality forbids it. And the law I will sign tonight forbids it.[40]

In line with maintaining his image as an action oriented chief executive, President Johnson used the signing ceremony to announce that he would nominate former governor Leroy Collins of Florida, a Southern Democrat, to be director of the Community Relations Service established by the bill. The president also told the television audience that at a cabinet meeting that afternoon he had directed all pertinent government agencies and government officials to begin implementing and enforcing the new law, and he promised that he would ask Congress for supplemental appropriations of money to pay the costs of implementing the new law.

The actual request for funds was transmitted to the House of Representatives on 20 July 20 1964 and totaled $13,088,000. In his letter of transmittal, President Johnson noted that passage of the Civil Rights Act of 1964 would earn "a place of honor" for the 88th Congress. The letter continued:

By enacting this charter, the Congress has assured that we shall achieve ultimate victory in the long struggle to guarantee the fundamental rights of every American . . . . The more promptly we are able to make effective the act's protections, the sooner justice will be provided to all our citizens in the manner prescribed by the Constitution. To delay that justice would be to deny it.[41]

311

As the civil rights bill was nearing final passage in the Senate, there was considerable concern within the Johnson administration that there would be widespread noncompliance with the equal accommodations section and that the result would be civil rights protest demonstrations. In mid May 1964 Attorney General Robert Kennedy sent President Johnson a five page memorandum reviewing such possible developments:

> At a meeting on May 15 [1964], I am informed that the SCLC [Southern Christian Leadership Conference] leaders decided to cooperate with any compliance demonstration program which could be achieved in Birmingham. This would involve the testing of facilities which had in advance agreed to comply with the Civil Rights Act [of 1964]. On the other hand, if there is no compliance with the Civil Rights Act by hotels, theaters, and restaurants in Birmingham, there is wide anticipation of new, large scale demonstrations. The SCLC organizer in Alabama is Reverend James Bevel, who believes in direct action and street demonstrations of a provocative type. . . . The chances of disturbances . . . will probably turn on whether there is compliance with the provisions of the public accommodations title of the Civil Rights Act, when it becomes effective, and on the occurrence of unpredictable events. In this connection it should again be noted that there are white extremist groups, such as the Klan, which are active. . . . If there is noncompliance on a large scale, there are bound to be a great many protests, and the federal government is bound to become involved since federal rights will be asserted.[42]

President Johnson took direct action to head off concerns such as those expressed in the memo from Attorney General Robert Kennedy. Following the signing ceremony for the Civil

312

Rights Act of 1964, President Johnson held a brief meeting at the White House with the prominent black political leaders who attended the signing ceremony. The president emphasized the twin themes that there was no longer any need for protest demonstrations and that any court tests of the new civil rights law should be carefully chosen. A White House staff member's memo to the files summarized the meeting:

> The president indicated . . . how essential it was that there be an understanding of the fact that the rights Negroes possessed could now be secured by law, making demonstrations unnecessary and possibly self-defeating. He made clear how important it was that the court tests be carefully selected to guard against any initial decisions ruling the Act unconstitutional (regardless of the fact that ultimately the Supreme Court would find it to be constitutional).[43]

At the time he signed the Civil Rights Act of 1964, Lyndon Baines Johnson had been president of the United States for only seven months. In his memoirs, Johnson pointed out that he had thrown his total support behind the civil rights bill, even though some of his most trusted staff members and advisers did not think the bill could be passed.

"Mr. President," one of the advisers had said, "you should not lay the prestige of the presidency on the line."

"What's it for if it's not to be laid on the line?" the president replied.[44]

In deciding to put the full prestige of his office and his political career behind the civil rights bill, President Johnson was following the advice of an old politician who also happened to be a good poker player. The man had told Johnson that there comes a time in every president's career when he has to throw caution to the winds and bet his entire stack of chips. Johnson had studied the political tumult surrounding the civil rights bill and "decided to shove in all my stack on this vital measure."

313

The president gambled, and the final result was the Civil Rights Act of 1964.[45]

In his memoirs, Johnson revealed what he was thinking about at the moment he signed the bill:

> I signed the bill in the East Room of the White House. My thoughts went back to the . . . day I first realized the sad truth: that to the extent Negroes were imprisoned, so was I. On this day, July 2, 1964, I knew the positive side of that same truth: that to the extent Negroes were free, really free, so was I. And so was my country.[46]

CHAPTER 14

CONCLUSIONS

In his speech closing the Senate debate on the Civil Rights Act of 1964, Senator Everett Dirksen of Illinois used the terms "tedious" and "inexorable." These two words provided an apt description of the legislative history of the Civil Rights Act of 1964, from the moment when President Kennedy presented the civil rights bill to the Congress in June 1963 until the signing of the bill into law by President Johnson in July 1964. Throughout the entire period of congressional consideration of the bill, the Southerners made the process tedious through their many attempts at delay and dilution. On the other hand, supporters of the bill were able to keep the bill moving (even though at times that movement seemed almost imperceptible) toward inexorable final passage.[1]

The Senate filibuster was the ultimate example of the tedium created as the bill moved toward enactment. The Senate debate set many records which lasted into the 1990s and which, because of subsequent changes in Senate rules of procedure, could possibly stand forever.[2] The Senate debate lasted a total of 83 days. It consumed more than 6,300 pages in the Congressional Record. One estimate held that over 10 million words were spoken, with at least 1 million more words spoken during the earlier House debate on the bill. The 4 months Senate debate also set a record of 166 quorum calls and 121 roll call votes.[3]

It is important to note that not all senators were equally involved in the extended Senate debate on the Civil Rights Act of 1964. Eleven of the 100 Senators never bothered to speak on the civil rights bill. Another 42 spoke only 10 or fewer times. Combining these 2 groups, a total of 53 senators, or a slight majority of the Senate, were not involved in the civil rights debate to a great extent.

At the other extreme 5 senators spoke more than 100 times during the debate, 2 of them Northerners speaking for the bill and 3 of them Southern Democrats speaking against. The two Northerners were Hubert Humphrey of Minnesota and Jacob Javits of New York. The three Southern Democrats were Sam Ervin of North Carolina, Russell Long of Louisiana, and John Stennis of Mississippi.

Ironically, the senator who gave the most speeches during the filibuster of the Civil Rights Act of 1964 was Hubert Humphrey, who rose at his desk and orated on the bill a grand total of 153 times.[4] Although Humphrey could not claim to be the greatest filibusterer of all time, in terms of number of speeches given he could claim to be the greatest "speaker during a filibuster" of all time.

The Senate debate on the Civil Rights Act of 1964 was not a true debate in the sense that discussion of proposed legislation was guiding a body of rational individuals toward an enlightened decision. The debate was conducted haphazardly, with the various parts of the bill being discussed out of order and most of the main arguments being repeated several times over. In reality, the Senate filibuster was an elaborate marking of time by both the Northerners and the Southern Democrats during which Hubert Humphrey and Thomas Kuchel were struggling to find the necessary votes for cloture. That struggle led them inevitably to Everett Dirksen.

DIRKSEN THE KEY

The fact that Everett Dirksen was the key to the cloture vote and final passage of the civil rights bill is perhaps the major conclusion to be drawn from any study of the Civil Rights Act of 1964. As early as 29 June 1963, less than three weeks after

President Kennedy had sent the administration civil rights bill to Congress, Deputy Attorney General Nicholas Katzenbach wrote a memo to Attorney General Robert Kennedy pointing out that "we have to work out some tentative strategy" designed to get Dirksen to support the bill. Katzenbach went on to say that the Kennedy administration could not hope to get the bill through the House of Representatives until they could convince House members they had a reasonable chance of getting Dirksen's support in the Senate. Although the memo did not say it specifically, the implication was that the House members all knew that Dirksen was the key to Senate passage of the bill and would not support civil rights in the House until they were reasonably convinced Dirksen could be persuaded to support the bill in the Senate.[5]

By 8 July 1963, less than a month after the introduction of the Kennedy civil rights bill, the Kennedy Justice Department had already identified a "Dirksen Group" of Republicans in the United States Senate and noted that their votes for cloture "could well depend on the opinion of Dirksen. . . ."[6] Prophetically, the memo also noted that Republican Senator Bourke Hickenlooper of Iowa might also be critical in the effort to get the "Dirksen Group" to vote cloture on civil rights.

Dirksen's principal biographer, Neil McNeil, argued that the Kennedy Administration considered Dirksen so crucial to passage of the bill that they purposefully gave House Republicans a large role to play in the House passage of the bill as a way of putting additional pressure on Dirksen to support the bill when it came over to the Senate. McNeil wrote:

> By having the House of Representatives act first, the administration had the opportunity to carry Dirksen further in civil rights legislation than the senator intended to go. The president's men hoped to find a way to persuade Dirksen to agree to some kind of federal protection for Negroes to use public accommodations. They hoped it could be done by bringing the Republicans in the House

317

massively behind the whole bill. . . .

The plan of the president's men was to persuade [Representative William] McCulloch [of Ohio] to support the whole Kennedy bill in substance, and then through McCulloch to win the mass of the Republicans in the House, including the Republican floor leader, Charles Halleck. By so doing, the administration's strategists calculated to put Dirksen in such a position with his party that he would have to go along with at least some kind of public accommodations guarantees.[7]

Thus it appears that Dirksen was the ultimate target of the pro-civil right forces from the very moment President Kennedy sent his civil rights bill to Congress. Even the emergency meetings at the White House in October 1963, ostensibly designed to win the support of McCulloch and Halleck in the House of Representatives, were aimed, through McCulloch and Halleck, at Dirksen. Can one man have so much power over the legislative process in a large nation that his vote and support have to be sought from the very beginning of the legislative process? That is apparently what happened with Everett M. Dirksen and the Civil Rights Act of 1964.

HOW MUCH DID DIRKSEN CHANGE THE BILL?

Although there is general agreement that Senator Dirksen's support was crucial to getting the bill through the Senate, there is considerable disagreement over whether Dirksen's "amendments" changed the bill very much. Although he strenuously opposed Dirksen's amendments at the time they were being considered for inclusion in the bill, Joseph Rauh, Jr., of the Leadership Conference on Civil Rights, later took the position that Dirksen really did not change very much at all. In fact, Rauh contended, Hubert Humphrey received much more from Dirksen than Dirksen needed to give. Rauh said:

318

What a genius Hubert Humphrey was in letting
Dirksen think he was writing the final draft of the
bill. Dirksen was only switching "ands" and
"buts." Humphrey pulled the greatest charade of
all time. Dirksen sold out cheap. We would have
paid a higher price if Dirksen had really demanded
it. Humphrey talked Dirksen out of it. Dirksen
wanted the credit; Humphrey wanted the bill.[8]

As would be expected, Dirksen's aides do not agree with
the view that Dirksen was "trapped" or "tricked" into permitting
a stronger civil rights bill than he might otherwise have wanted.
When told that the Democrats (primarily Humphrey and his staff)
had a grand strategy for "hooking" Dirksen, one of Dirksen's
"Bombers" commented:

Dirksen approached the 1964 civil rights bill
no differently from any other bill. Dirksen was
what I like to call an "activist at the middle." His
goal was a bill that would satisfy the vast majority
of Americans, most of whom are somewhere in the
middle on most political issues. If some people
thought they were going to trap Dirksen into
supporting the civil rights bill, they were
mistaken. Dirksen would have done what he did
whether they tried to lay a trap for him or not.
No one needed to set him up to be part of it and
to do his share in it.
While others were concocting elaborate
plots to get the civil rights bill through the Senate,
Dirksen and his "Bombers" played it straight, and
that confused the plotters. Dirksen always said
that if you were telling the truth and the other
guys weren't, it would "confuse the hell out of
them." Dirksen stated exactly where he stood --
in the middle -- and he made sure the bill would
fit the needs of the entire country. It was those

319

who were concocting the devious plots who were
out-maneuvered.

The Dirksen aide then repeated the idea that Dirksen's
major contribution to the Civil Rights Act of 1964 was
amendments that made the new law easier to enforce:

> Dirksen and his people worked at finding a
> self-enforcing way of requiring access to public
> accommodations. It was an emotional issue, but
> we worked to diffuse the issue. By the time
> Dirksen was finished with the bill, violations could
> easily be proved (you either served minority
> citizens the same as others or you did not). As a
> result the public accepted it. More legislation
> should be as self-enforcing.[9]

The argument over who "hooked" whom comes down to
this. The Democrats, from the very beginning, had an elaborate
series of strategies for getting Dirksen to support the bill.
Because Dirksen eventually did support the bill, they naturally
claim that these strategies worked. The Dirksen people, on the
other hand, argue that Dirksen had a standard way of amending
legislation as it moved through the Senate, and he would have
amended and then supported the bill no matter what the
Democrats might have done.

WHO WAS THE HERO?

Who was the hero in the successful passage of the Civil
Rights Act of 1964? Was it Martin Luther King, Jr., who
completely changed the atmosphere on Capitol Hill where civil
rights was concerned with his nonviolent demonstrations in
Birmingham? Was it Nicholas Katzenbach, the deputy attorney
general who served as top legislative strategist for both the
Kennedy and Johnson administrations and who, from the very
beginning, orchestrated every move of the bill so as to eventually

end up with Dirksen's support? Was it Clarence Mitchell, Jr., and Joseph Rauh, Jr., the lobbyists for the Leadership Conference on Civil Rights who, for more than a year, put unrelenting pressure on all concerned for as strong a civil rights bill as possible? Was it William McCulloch of Ohio, the House Republican who pressed both Everett Dirksen and the Senate Democratic leadership to make sure that the strong House passed civil rights bill was not significantly weakened in the Senate? Was it Hubert Humphrey, the Democratic whip in the Senate, who did the final persuading and negotiating with Dirksen and, with his "great man hook," tried to catch Dirksen and haul him into the civil rights boat? Or was the hero Everett M. Dirksen himself, the man who had carefully and effectively organized his small band of Republican supporters in the Senate so that, at key moments in the legislative process, he had the final say on exactly what did and did not become law?

No matter which of these men is cast as the ultimate hero, one fact remains clear. Everett Dirksen was so powerful that he had a choice in the matter, but King, Katzenbach, McCulloch, and Humphrey had little choice but to do what Dirksen wanted. Dirksen could have decided to support the civil rights bill, and it would have passed, or he could have decided not to support the civil rights bill, and it would have failed. No such all-powerful choices existed for King, Katzenbach, Mitchell and Rauh, McCulloch, and Humphrey. They wanted the bill passed, and therefore their only choice was to get Dirksen's support and, in the end, give him whatever he demanded in return for his support. King, Katzenbach, Mitchell and Rauh, McCulloch, and Humphrey were fortunate that, in the end, Dirksen did not demand as much as he might have for delivering the key votes for cloture.

WHO COULD HAVE ACHIEVED A
STRONGER BILL - KENNEDY OR JOHNSON?

Many persons involved with the successful passage of the Civil Rights Act of 1964 commented on the question of whether

President Kennedy, had he not been assassinated, could have delivered as strong a civil rights bill as President Johnson did. One of Lyndon Johnson's biographers put the point this way:

> The greatest difference between the 1964 civil rights bill as it would probably have been passed in that year under Lyndon was that Lyndon made sure he got everything he asked for. Kennedy, faced with inevitable Senate opposition, would almost surely have compromised somewhere, traded the deletion of one section, say, for the passage of the rest. Lyndon refused to delete, refused to compromise, anywhere.[10]

Robert C. Weaver, a leading black official in the Johnson administration, saw Johnson as both more committed and more skillful than Kennedy in getting a civil rights bill through Congress. Weaver said:

> I think Kennedy had an intellectual commitment for civil rights and a broad view of social legislation. Johnson had a gut commitment for changing the entire social fabric of this country. . . . I don't think we would ever have got the civil rights legislation we did without Johnson. I don't think Kennedy could have done it. He would have gone for it, but he was a lot more cautious than Johnson.[11]

Clarence Mitchell, Jr., of the NAACP, argued that Kennedy could not have won as strong a bill as Johnson did but believed the key difference was in the ability of the two men to lobby Congress. Mitchell explained:

> Unhappily it may have been true no bill could have passed without the assassination of President Kennedy. It certainly would have been more

322

difficult if Kennedy had remained as president. Lyndon Johnson just had powers for getting Congress to act that John Kennedy lacked.[12]

A similar view was expressed by Roy Wilkins of the NAACP:

> John Fitzgerald Kennedy had a complete comprehension and an identity with the goals of the civil rights movement. Intellectually he was for it. . . . But, I think that precisely the qualities that Lyndon Johnson later exhibited, and which only Lyndon Johnson could have, by reason of his experience and his study and the use of materials of government -- precisely that lack in President Kennedy forced him to hesitate and weigh and consider what he should do in the civil rights field. I don't think it was from any inner nonconviction. I think he was convinced that this ought to be done. He just did not know how to manipulate the government to bring it about.[13]

Apparently Georgia Senator Richard Russell, the leader of the filibustering Southerners, was another person who saw the rise of Lyndon Johnson to the presidency as critical to the passage of such a strong civil rights bill. Clarence Mitchell, Jr., told a pro-civil rights Senate aide that he had a "frank discussion" with Senator Russell. The aide put Mitchell's report in his notes:

> As Mitchell reports this discussion, Russell also knows the jig is just about up. The main distinction which Russell drew between the situation now and the situation when President Kennedy was alive was that they [the Southerners] have absolutely no hope of ultimately defeating President Johnson on the bill itself or even gaining

any major compromises or capitulations from President Johnson. Interestingly enough, Senator Russell stated that he felt they could have gained major compromises from Kennedy.[14]

The general consensus seemed to be that President Kennedy probably would have obtained some sort of civil rights bill from Congress in 1964, but that it would not have been anywhere near as strong a bill as Lyndon Johnson obtained. It is sad to have to say it, but a large number of those involved with the Civil Rights Act of 1964 believed that the tragic assassination of President Kennedy helped the final passage of the bill by putting Lyndon Johnson in the White House.

In retrospect, therefore, John F. Kennedy and Lyndon B. Johnson appear to have had something of a symbiotic political relationship (in the sense that each needed something important from the other). With his great speaking ability and his talent for inspiring political followers, John F. Kennedy convinced many Americans of the great need to pass civil rights legislation. Kennedy apparently lacked, however, the ability to get Congress to pass such legislation in a strong enough form to please strong civil rights supporters. Lyndon Johnson, on the other hand, lacked Kennedy's speaking ability and inspirational quality, but he had great talents for getting definite action on Capitol Hill. It might be said of the two men that, in terms of civil rights, President Lyndon Johnson was able to deliver on the exciting goals and promises so inspirationally presented by President John F. Kennedy.

NO COMPROMISE POSSIBLE

One view of the United States Congress is the idea that most pieces of legislation are based upon compromise. Traditionally these compromises are worked out in such a way that they accommodate the vital interests of all major ethnic, economic, and regional segments of the society. Above all compromise is traditionally applied to those persons and groups who are directly affected by the proposed law under consideration. In line with this tradition, the two previous civil rights acts to come out of the Congress prior to 1964 had been compromised -- compromised in such a way that small gains were given to black Americans but no fundamental change was made in the ability of Southern whites to practice racial segregation.

On the question of civil rights in 1964 no such compromise was possible. Any new law which would have satisfied the demands of black Americans and their committed white allies could not have been remotely acceptable to Southern whites. The demands of civil rights supporters in the past had been muted, but by 1963 and 1964 these demands were well articulated, highly dramatized, and had significant national political support. As the expectations of American blacks rose and were supported by the courts, the old solution, the satisfaction of only the minutest part of black demands, was no longer possible. At the same time, however, the Southern white commitment to a racially segregated way of life was so great that giving in to only a small portion of black civil rights demands was regarded as totally out of the question. It was these circumstances which generated the absolute Southern white opposition which made the legislative process so long and difficult. Since no compromise was possible, a fight to the finish was the only possible outcome for the Civil Rights Act of 1964, and such a fight to the finish was what occurred.[15]

THE GETTYSBURG OF THE SECOND CIVIL WAR

Throughout the debate on the Civil Rights Act of 1964, the Southern Democrats made many references to the Civil War and the fact that, in their opinion, the civil rights bill literally called for a "reinvasion" of the South by U.S. Government officials and a new period of vindictive "Reconstruction."[16] Although the comparison runs the risk of being overdrawn, the civil rights movement of the early 1960s can be described somewhat aptly as a second Civil War. The white violence against black demonstrators at Birmingham was the equivalent of the Southern attack on Fort Sumter. The "Irrepressible Conflict" of the 1860s had, by 1963, become the "Irrepressible Debate."

Clearly the Civil Rights Act of 1964 was the Gettysburg of this second Civil War. The entire structure of Southern segregation was based on keeping the United States Government from interfering in the "Southern way of life," and the key to keeping the United States Government out of the South had always been the filibuster weapon in the United States Senate. As a result, final passage of the Civil Rights Act of 1964 was nowhere near as important as the breaching of the filibuster citadel by the successful cloture vote. The cloture vote freed the Senate to act on civil rights, which in turn freed the entire Congress to act on civil rights, which in turn freed the United States Government to enter the South and put an end to most legal and governmental forms of racial segregation.

Southern public segregation patterns thus were as thoroughly destroyed by the cloture vote on the Civil Rights Act of 1964 as General Robert E. Lee's Confederate Army was destroyed (in terms of winning the final victory) at Gettysburg. In fact, to carry the simile to its final conclusion, the final speeches of the Southern Democratic Senators just prior to the cloture vote were the "Pickett's Charge" of this second Gettysburg, a final, desperate, foredoomed attempt to stop the North from enforcing its political and governmental ideas about relationships between the races on the South.

Just as Gettysburg was the "turning point" in the first Civil War, the passage of the Civil Rights Act of 1964 was the "turning point" in the second Civil War. Up until this point in the conflict, the South had always won congressional battles over civil rights. After the successful cloture vote on 10 June 1964, however, the South never won another one. The second Civil War continued through the successful passage of the Voting Rights Act of 1965 and the Housing Rights Act of 1968, but in both cases the Southern filibuster was overcome by a cloture vote made much easier by the precedent of the victorious cloture vote of 1964.

CONCLUSIONS

FIGHTING THE RULES

As much as they were fighting the Southern Democrats, however, the pro-civil rights forces were fighting the rules of the Senate and the House of Representatives as they went about the task of enacting the Civil Rights Act of 1964. The inordinate power of the House Rules Committee in the House of Representatives and the total control of Committee Chairman James Eastland over the Senate Judiciary Committee were the first two "rules" problems encountered, but even these two great legislative roadblocks paled when compared with the filibuster and cloture rules of the Senate. As one researcher noted:

These rules, designed to balance the rights of the majority on the one hand and the protection of the minority on the other, were of critical importance in shaping both the debate and its outcome. From the time H.R. 7152 was sent to the Senate from the House until it was passed by the Senate these rules were the chief weapon in the hands of the [Southern] opposition who used them to prevent or at least delay action. The actions of the [pro-civil rights forces] supporting the bill were governed by both the rules and the rule based tactics of the opposition. The significance of the rules is clearly demonstrated when one formulates a picture of what the Senate debate would have been if the rules had been the same as those in the House of Representatives. The attempt to prevent passage of the bill would have to have been made in committee, and the issue would have been clearly decided prior to a relatively brief floor debate.[17]

One of the major lessons to be learned from the Civil Rights Act of 1964 is the fact that procedural rules have substantive effects. In this case, the rule requiring a 2/3 vote for cloture in the Senate forced the Democratic leadership to bid for the support of a considerable number of Republican senators. To get those Republican senators to support the bill, substantive changes had to made in the bill, changes that would not have been required if the bill could have been passed by a simple majority in the Senate. The end result of the 2/3 vote for cloture rule, therefore, was that the Senate Republicans were able to leave their substantive mark on the bill and take much of the credit for passing the bill.

To put this idea another way, one of the substantive effects of the procedural rule requiring a 2/3 vote for cloture was to give power to minority party legislators who, under ordinary circumstances, would not have had such power. If the civil rights bill could have passed the Senate with a simple majority, the Democratic leadership would have needed only the votes of a relatively small number of liberal and moderate Republicans. They would have not needed Everett Dirksen, nor would they have had to make substantive concessions to Dirksen in the language of the bill.

Dire effects might have resulted if the pro-civil rights forces in the U.S. Senate had been unable to come up with a 2/3 vote for cloture and the 1964 civil rights bill had not been enacted. In such a situation, it would have been clear that procedural rules were denying a substantive change in the laws of the nation supported by both a majority of the national legislature as well as a majority of the population at large. To put the proposition another way, suppose the rules of procedure had proven stronger than the ability of the Senate leadership to meet a national need for substantive change. In the spring of 1964, many observers thought, and some feared, that this would be the likely outcome. Some even wondered if the Senate, as an institution, could survive such an outcome.

STRATEGY MAKING

Rather than there being a single strategy for getting the 1963-1964 civil rights bill through Congress, there were several strategies. One of the reasons there were so many different strategies was that, among strong civil rights supporters, there were frequent and heated arguments over what was the best strategy to pursue. The fight within the civil rights camp over choosing the right strategy at times eclipsed the battle with the filibustering Southern Democrats that was taking place on the Senate floor.

There were seven major groups making and pursuing strategy where the 1963-1964 civil rights bill was concerned:

1. Clarence Mitchell, Jr., and Joseph Rauh, Jr., of the Leadership Conference on Civil Rights. They were pressing for as strong a bill as possible, arguing strenuously against any major compromises, even those required to get Senator Dirksen's support.

2. Hubert Humphrey. He was mainly attempting to get Dirksen's support for the bill but trying at the same time to compromise the bill as little as possible (mainly because he was under so much pressure from Mitchell and Rauh).

3. William McCulloch. His major goal was to stop both the Democratic leadership in the Senate and Senator Dirksen from watering down the House passed bill to please the Southern Democrats in the Senate.

4. The Kennedy-Johnson administrations. Their major goal was to get Dirksen's support for the bill, but they appeared somewhat more willing than Humphrey to support a more moderate bill, particularly if that was what was required to keep the support of William McCulloch and the House Republicans.

5. Senate Majority Leader Mike Mansfield. He appears to have been mainly interested in getting the Senate to pass a civil rights bill, but he apparently was much readier to compromise with either Dirksen or the Southern Democrats in order to achieve that goal.

6. Everett Dirksen. According to his staff assistants, his goal was to write a more moderate, more easily enforceable bill which Republicans could support and for which Republicans could take a major portion of the credit.

7. Southern Democrats. They used the filibuster to delay action as long as possible in hopes that events external to the

Senate would cause a widespread public reaction against the civil rights bill.

One impression that emerges clearly about strategy making for the 1963-1964 civil rights bill is the fact that, for all concerned, there was no clear and obvious "correct" strategy. What to do next was often unclear and, as a result, strenuously debated. There also was much trial and error. There was little sense that these men were legislative masters who always knew what to do and always had a surefire plan for keeping the bill moving. The correct legislative choices were not always obvious. Day after day all concerned searched for strategies, debated and critiqued these strategies, and struggled to solve the puzzle. At times, chance and luck seemed to have more to do with what happened than the legislative skills of the various participants involved.

IMPACT

Despite the frequent claims by the Southern Democrats that the public accommodations section of the civil rights bill was unconstitutional, equal access to public accommodations and every other major section of the bill were quickly declared constitutional when tested in court and appealed to the United States Supreme Court. Within five months of final passage of the Civil Rights Act of 1964, the Supreme Court ruled in Heart of Atlanta Motel v. United States that the commerce clause of the Constitution gave the Congress all the power it needed to integrate public accommodations, even when the wrong being corrected was "moral and social" rather than "economic." In something of a surprise move, the high court applied the law not only to restaurants and motels whose customers came mainly from out of state but also to restaurants and motels that received a substantial portion of their food and supplies from out of state.[18]

Once the constitutional issue had been disposed of by the Supreme Court, the implementation of equal access to public accommodations throughout the American South went very smoothly. As pro-civil rights supporters had argued all along, racial integration of restaurants and motels was easily implemented by "voluntary compliance" once it was the law of the land and no restauranteur or motel owner had to fear losing customers to a competitor who was still segregated. The primary impact of the successful passage of the Civil Rights Act of 1964, therefore, was that virtually overnight black Americans could and did receive services in innumerable places of public accommodation that had previously been unavailable to them. The South's "peculiar institution" of racial segregation in public places disappeared almost immediately once the filibuster weapon was bested and Congress was free to end the "peculiar institution."

After equal access to public accommodations, clearly the most important part of the Civil Rights Act of 1964 was the provision calling for the cutting off of U.S. Government funds to state and local governments and institutions that practiced racial discrimination. As predicted, the desire for (if not the dependence on) U.S. Government dollars led all but the most reactionary governments and institutions to rapidly desegregate their facilities and the administration of their services. Congress subsequently became quite enamored of the funds "cutoff" as a tool for enforcing compliance with Congressional law, including it in several subsequent pieces of legislation (such as laws guaranteeing access to public facilities for the physically handicapped).

The equal employment opportunity provision of the law that was so strongly supported by the AFL-CIO had a significant impact on hiring practices in the United States and on the composition of the American work force. The law was used to gain wider access to equal employment opportunity for all minority groups, not just blacks, and was particularly effective in gaining greater employment opportunities for women. When combined with the funds "cutoff" provision, the EEOC caused an immediate, dramatic, and visible increase in the number of minority and women workers in United States factories and offices.

By giving the United States Government strong powers to enforce school desegregation in the United States, the Civil Rights Act of 1964 brought about the quick demise of all forms of legal (de jure) school segregation. The law did not, however, bring an end to racially segregated schools caused by the existence of all black and all white neighborhoods (de facto segregation). The Congress attempted to further address this problem of segregated neighborhoods producing segregated schools in the Housing Rights Act of 1968, but the problem of de facto segregation continued to be a controversial one, particularly when United States courts began ordering the busing of students to schools in different neighborhoods in order to achieve integration.

Whether the voting rights provisions of the Civil Rights Act of 1964 were effective or not is a moot point. Within little more than one year after the passage of the 1964 act, Congress passed the Voting Rights Act of 1965 and included in it virtually all of the strong provisions which were suggested for the 1964 act but failed to be enacted. Clearly, the precedent of breaking a filibuster with a successful cloture vote was the great contribution of the Civil Rights Act of 1964 to voting rights. The major improvements in black voting participation in the American South that occurred in the late 1960s and early 1970s were the direct result of the 1965 act, not the 1964 act.

POLITICAL IMPACT

At the Republican National Convention held in San Francisco in July of 1964, Senator Barry Goldwater of Arizona received the Republican nomination for president on the first ballot. Throughout the fall election campaign against Democratic incumbent Lyndon Johnson, Goldwater continued to argue that he was a supporter of civil rights but that he voted against the Civil Rights Act of 1964 because it represented too great an expansion of U.S. Government power.

The 1964 presidential election campaign went badly for the Arizona Senator. In addition to exploiting Goldwater's ambivalent position on civil rights, President Johnson succeeded in portraying Goldwater as a "trigger-happy" person who would be much more likely than Johnson to use nuclear weapons in time of war. On election day in November 1964, Johnson defeated Goldwater by one of the largest margins in United States electoral history.

Largely as a result of his votes against the civil rights bill, Goldwater carried the five "Deep South" states of Louisiana, Mississippi, Alabama, Georgia, and South Carolina. However, he lost every other state in the Union except for his home state of Arizona.

Lyndon Johnson carried the upper South, all of the West except for Arizona, and the entire Midwest and Northeast sections of the nation. His strong stand in favor of the civil rights bill won him almost unanimous support from black voters, Johnson's percentage of the vote in some urban black precincts in the North exceeding 95 percent. In some cases this exceeded by almost 20 percent the percentage vote John F. Kennedy had received from blacks in the 1960 presidential election.

This movement of black voters out of the Republican party and into the Democratic party continued throughout the late 1960s and the 1970s. The passage of the Voting Rights Act of 1965 and the Housing Rights Act of 1968, both of which occurred while Johnson was still president and the Democrats were still in control of both houses of Congress, further cemented the allegiance of most black Americans to the Democratic party. Although the Republican leader of the United States Senate, Everett M. Dirksen of Illinois, was instrumental in the passage of all three of these major civil rights bills, black voters did not repay Dirksen by going to the voting booth and voting Republican.

As a result of his highly successful pro-civil rights legislative record, President Johnson earned both the friendship and respect of key black political leaders. According to Roy Wilkins of the NAACP:

Mr. Johnson will go down in our history as the

man who, when he got in the most powerful spot
in the nation, . . . committed the White House
and the administration to the involvement of
government in getting rid of the inequalities
between people solely on the basis of race. And
he did this to a greater extent than any other
president in our history. It will take many, many
presidents to match what Lyndon Johnson
did. . . . When the chips were down he used the
great powers of the presidency on the side of the
people who were deprived. And you can't take
that away from him.[19]

Whitney Young, Jr., of the National Urban League,
credited Lyndon Johnson with "the greatest leadership job in civil
rights done by any president." Young concluded:

The moment he was placed in the position of
being president of all the people, I don't know
anybody who exhibited a greater respect for the
Constitution and the Bill of Rights as far as black
people are concerned than did President Johnson.[20]

Equally strong praise came from Thurgood Marshall, who
was appointed solicitor general and then named to the Supreme
Court by President Johnson. Marshall said:

[When it comes to] minorities, civil rights, people
in general, the inherent dignity of the individual
human being -- I don't believe there has ever been
a president to equal Lyndon Johnson -- bar none![21]

Clarence Mitchell, Jr., Washington director of the
NAACP, compared Lyndon Johnson to Lincoln, Roosevelt, and
Kennedy. He concluded:

President Johnson made a greater contribution to

334

giving a dignified and hopeful status to Negroes in the United States than any other president, including Lincoln, Roosevelt, and Kennedy.[22]

LEGITIMATING PROTEST DEMONSTRATIONS

There is no question that successful passage of the Civil Rights Act of 1964 legitimated the nonviolent protest demonstrations of Martin Luther King, Jr., as an effective and acceptable technique for bringing about political change in the United States. Virtually all participants in the titanic struggle over the Civil Rights Act of 1964 agreed that it was the Birmingham demonstrations that created the national drive that put the law on the books.

Passage of the Civil Rights Act of 1964, however, tended to delegitimate many subsequent protest demonstrations, particularly those that were not carefully kept nonviolent and which took place in areas where legal remedies to problems had been created by the 1964 act itself. The result was that racial disturbances continued to be a part of the American political scene, but the public reaction to many of these demonstrations was highly negative in view of the fact that a strong law now was on the books to provide redress of minority grievances.

The White House staff became increasingly concerned during July and August 1964 about racial protest demonstrations and their possible connection to a "backlash" among white voters. A staff memorandum to President Johnson, dated 17 July 1964, summed up the problem this way:

I am disturbed about the continued demonstrations and what I see on radio and TV. I am convinced that a great deal of the Negro leadership simply does not understand the political facts of life, and think that they are advancing their cause by uttering threats in the newspapers and on TV. They are not sophisticated enough to understand the theory of the backlash unless they are told

335

about it. . . . We have not done with the Negro leaders what we did with the business community and with Southern public officials -- i.e., make a major and organized effort to direct their thinking along a proper course, but I believe this is possible and that demonstrations and picketing can be avoided through personal contact and explanations of the seriousness of the problem.[23]

Five days later a magazine article was circulated among President Johnson's staff that further revealed White House concern over the possibility of "white backlash." The article, by David Danzig, was entitled, "Rightists, Racists, and Separatists: A White Bloc In The Making?"[24] Less than two weeks later a White House staff member received a memorandum from Senator Hubert Humphrey expressing Humphrey's and Clarence Mitchell, Jr.'s, concern over the way the television networks and the news services were playing up the possibility of black protest demonstrations and riots.[25]

Apparently an attempt to reach out to black leaders and quiet the demonstrations was successfully undertaken. In mid October of 1964 a memorandum from a White House staff member to President Johnson summarized both the program and its success:

Lee White and I had a series of meetings with Negro federal officials. . . . They have established regular lines of contact and through them we have eliminated major sources of frictions in St. Louis, Chicago, and Seattle. . . . The development of these procedures has served to correct many misunderstandings and led to substantial changes in the pronouncements and activities of local civil rights leaders. There is less belligerence and more constructive activity. . . . There has been no more rioting and all of the activist leaders I talk to agree that no more is to be anticipated.[26]

336

Any discussion of protest demonstrations and the Civil Rights Act of 1964 raises uneasy questions, however, about why black Americans had to organize nonviolent protests in order to gain rights that were theoretically guaranteed to them by the United States Constitution. Political scientist Daniel M. Berman pointed out:

> It is a sad commentary on the American system of government that the Negro had to go into the streets before anything even approximating serious attention was paid to his legitimate grievances. Those who glorify the [American] system [of government] in terms of its responsiveness to the long range public interest will not find it easy to explain why it required street demonstrations and the imminence of chaos to awaken presidents and congressmen to their responsibilities.[27]

A TRIUMPH - OR MUCH TOO LATE?

The American system of government "oscillates fecklessly between deadlock and a rush of action," one prominent political scientist has noted.[28] Clearly passage of the Civil Rights Act of 1964 was a great "rush of action" following a "deadlock" over civil rights for black Americans that had lasted for almost 100 years. The Civil Rights Act of 1964 therefore proved that, when the crisis is great and the need is clear, Congress does have the power to act to solve the problems of the nation. The extensive "checks and balances" built into the American system of government can frustrate the national will only so long. In fact, it was those famous "checks and balances," by frustrating early action on civil rights problems in the 1940s and the 1950s, which created the need for that great burst of long delayed reform that was the Civil Rights Act of 1964.

Was the passage of the Civil Rights Act of 1964 a triumph, or simply a late surge of reform necessitated by decades of neglect and failure to act? A reasonable conclusion might be

337

that both propositions were true. Passage of the law was a triumph, but part of what made that triumph so glittering and important was that the reforms included in the legislation were so long overdue.

CALLS FOR SOUTHERN COMPLIANCE

Tribute was paid to many Southern senators for the manner in which they called on their constituents to comply with the new law. "There is no alternative but compliance," said Senator Herman Talmadge of Georgia. Violence "could leave scars for a long time to come. . . . I would hope now that all the American people would exercise restraint, wisdom, and good judgement [in following] the law of the land."

Senator Allen J. Ellender of Louisiana warned in a Fourth of July statement that violent disobedience of the new law would be "foolhardy and indefensible." The new civil rights law, he said, must be tested "within the framework of the orderly processes established by law." If laws are defied, he concluded "then respect for all law will be diminished."[29]

Thus it was that voices that had filled the Senate chamber with denunciations of the civil rights bill called for compliance and acceptance once the bill had become law.

The Johnson White House had sought to stimulate such speeches by Southern senators. In a memorandum dated 21 May 1964, Attorney General Robert F. Kennedy proposed to President Johnson that he encourage Southern senators who had opposed the civil rights bill to give speeches calling for compliance with the new law.[30] On 23 July 1964 President Johnson sent thank you letters (written by Lee C. White) to the first three Southern senators who gave such speeches.[31]

LESSONS FOR OTHER PEOPLES

The events leading to the introduction and passage of the Civil Rights Act of 1964 do provide some lessons for other peoples facing similar racial problems. One obvious lesson is the necessity for civil rights demonstrators to keep their protests defiant but <u>nonviolent</u>. As long as civil rights protests remained orderly and nonviolent, they built national support for the civil rights bill in Congress. When various protest groups turned to more violent demonstrations, some of them bordering on riots, support for civil rights reform was harmed rather than strengthened.

Another lesson is the necessity for groups protesting racial discrimination to present a unified front in their drive for civil rights reforms. One of the most important factors in the successful passage of the Civil Rights Act of 1964 was the key role played by the Leadership Conference on Civil Rights in unifying the various civil rights groups and lobbying Congress with a single voice. The lobbying influence of Clarence Mitchell, Jr., and Joseph Rauh, Jr., was greatly enhanced by the fact that they were representing virtually all of the established groups supporting the civil rights bill.

To be effective, nonviolent protest demonstrations must be covered extensively by the news media. Demonstrations that do not receive widespread news coverage have little or no effect. Birmingham was absolutely crucial in building public support, through the news media, for the civil rights bill. It thus must always be kept in mind that the target of civil rights demonstrations is not the immediate government officials involved but national or international public opinion to be reached through the news media.

Perhaps the most important lesson to be learned is the difficulty, in a democracy, of trying to exclude any major group from participating in the political process. Despite the great extent of racial segregation in the American South and the procedural barriers to reform established in the Congress, civil rights supporters still were able to harness the machinery of a representative democracy and enact a major civil rights bill. Once a society has extended democratic freedoms to one group of citizens, it can be argued it is only a matter of time until those democratic freedoms have to be extended to <u>all</u> citizens.

"TO ELIMINATE THE LAST VESTIGES OF INJUSTICE"

In his speech at the time of the final signing of the Civil Rights Act of 1964, President Lyndon Johnson had particularly emphasized the theme of complying with the new law, and he paid unacknowledged tribute to Everett Dirksen by pointing out that the law provided for local and state action prior to U.S. Government action. The president said:

> Most Americans are law-abiding citizens who want to do what is right. That is why the Civil Rights Act relies first on voluntary compliance, then on the efforts of local communities and states to secure the rights of citizens. It provides for the national authority to step in only when others cannot or will not do the job.[32]

Toward the end of his bill signing address, President Johnson called on the American people to go beyond the strict legal requirements of the new law and eliminate racial discrimination everywhere it occurred in the United States. The president said:

> This Civil Rights Act is a challenge to all of us to go to work in our communities and our states, in our homes and in our hearts, to eliminate the last vestiges of injustice in our beloved America.

340

NOTES

CHAPTER 2

1. Congressional Quarterly Weekly Report, 8 March 1963, 303.

2. CQ Weekly Report, 5 April 1963, 527.

3. CQ Weekly Report, 8 March 1963, 293.

4. Joseph Rauh, Jr., unpublished manuscript (magazine article) on the role of the Leadership Conference on Civil Rights in the civil rights struggle of 1963-1964, 1. Rauh was legal adviser to the Leadership Conference on Civil Rights.

5. In 1975 the Senate amended its rules to provide that only a 3/5 vote of the Senate (60 votes if all senators are present and voting) is required for cloture.

6. Clarence Mitchell, Jr., interview, 30 April 1969, Tape 1, 2-3, Oral History Collection, LBJ Library, Austin, Texas

7. Theodore C. Sorensen, Kennedy (New York: Harper and Row, 1965), 476.

8. Sorensen, Kennedy, 476. See also Public Papers of the Presidents, 1961, 8 March 1961, 157

9. Rauh manuscript, 2.

10. Michael Dorman, We Shall Overcome (New York: Dial Press, 1964), 143.

11. Congressional Quarterly Almanac - 1963, 336.

12. Dorman, We Shall Overcome, 171.

13. Washington Evening Star, 14 May 1963.

14. Washington Post, 28 May 1963.

15. Stephen Kurzman, minority counsel, Senate Committee on Education and Labor, 20 April 1966, quoted in Peter E. Kane, The Senate Debate on the 1964 Civil Rights Act (Ph.D. dissertation, Purdue University, 1967), 30.

16. Rauh manuscript, 5.

17. Sorensen, Kennedy, 489.

18. CQ Weekly Report, 14 June 1963, 971.

CHAPTER 3

1. CQ Weekly Report, 15 September 1961, 1582-1585. For a summary of the entire five volume Civil Rights Commission Report of 1961, see CQ Almanac - 1961, 394-398.
2. CQ Weekly Report, 29 September 1961, 1669-70.
3. CQ Weekly Report, 16 October 1961, 1722.
4. CQ Weekly Report, 17 November 1961, 1860.
5. CQ Weekly Report, 17 November 1961, 1861.
6. Rauh manuscript, 3-4. See also James L. Sundquist, Politics and Policy: The Eisenhower, Kennedy, and Johnson Years (Washington: Brookings, 1968), 263.
7. Sundquist, Politics and Policy, 263.
8. Rauh manuscript, 5.
9. Rauh manuscript, 5.
10. Whitney Young, Jr., interview, 18 June 1969, 4-5, Oral History Collection, LBJ Library.

CHAPTER 4

1. There were 67 Democrats and 33 Republicans in the 1963-1964 session of the Senate. See CQ Weekly Report, 11 January 1963, 30.
2. Memo for John S. from Senator, 12 March 1963, Hubert H. Humphrey Private Papers on Civil Rights, Minnesota Historical Society, St. Paul, Minnesota. John S. is Humphrey's legislative assistant, John G. Stewart. See also Humbert H. Humphrey from Senator Joseph S. Clark, 14 March 1963.
3. CQ Weekly Report, 5 April 1963, 527.
4. Personal recollection of the author. The aide was Stephen Horn.
5. Nicholas Katzenbach, interview, 12 November 1968, 14-15, Oral History Collection, LBJ Library.
6. Memorandum to the attorney general from Norbert A. Schlei, assistant attorney general, 4 June 1963, 2, Robert F. Kennedy General Correspondence, John F. Kennedy Library, Boston.
7. Memorandum marked John S/FYI, 18 June 1963, Hubert H. Humphrey Private Papers on Civil Rights, Minnesota Historical Society.
8. Memorandum to the attorney general from Nicholas Katzenbach, deputy attorney general, 29 June 1963, 1, Robert F. Kennedy General Correspondence, John F. Kennedy Library. Katzenbach's assumption that House Republican Leader Charles Halleck of Indiana would not support the strengthened Kennedy civil rights bill later turned out to be incorrect.
9. Nicholas Katzenbach, interview, 12 November 1968, 18, Oral History Collection, LBJ Library.
10. CQ Weekly Report, 26 July 1963, 1318.
11. CQ Weekly Report, 26 July 1963, 1318.

12. Newsweek, 19 August 1963, 20.

13. Memorandum to the attorney general from Nicholas Katzenbach, deputy attorney general, 19 August 1963, 3, Robert F. Kennedy General Correspondence, John F. Kennedy Library.

14. Personal recollection of the author.

15. Sundquist, Politics and Policy, 264-265.

16. CQ Weekly Report, 28 June 1963, 1068.

17. CQ Weekly Report, 26 July 1963, 1319

18. CQ Weekly Report, 26 July 1963, 1319, and 2 August 1963, 1374.

19. Sundquist, Politics and Policy, 259.

20. Statement on Civil Rights, 8 May 1963, 1-2, Papers of Representative William McCulloch, Ohio Northern University, Ada, Ohio.

21. CQ Weekly Report, 12 July 1963, 1131.

22. CQ Weekly Report, 12 July 1963, 1131.

23. CQ Weekly Report, 12 July 1963, 1131.

24. CQ Weekly Report, 12 July 1963, 1131.

25. The Leadership Conference on Civil Rights, a coalition of lobby groups supporting the civil rights bill, devoted the major portion of its first newsletter to its member groups to the question of whether equal access to public accommodations should be guaranteed by the commerce clause or the 14th Amendment. Joseph Rauh, Jr., a lobbyist for the Leadership Conference, wrote a legal brief on the "Commerce Clause-14th Amendment Controversy" which was distributed with the newsletter. See Memorandum #1, 25 July 1963, Series D, Box 4, Leadership Conference on Civil Rights Collection, Library of Congress, Washington.

26. CQ Weekly Report, 21 June 1963, 1000.

27. Memorandum to the attorney general from Nicholas Katzenbach, deputy attorney general, 19 August 1963, 3, Robert F. Kennedy General Correspondence, John F. Kennedy Library.

28. Kane, The Senate Debate, 48.

29. Kane, The Senate Debate, 130.

30. CQ Weekly Report, 2 August 1963, 1374.

31. Rauh manuscript, 10.

32. CQ Weekly Report, 2 August 1963, 1374.

33. CQ Weekly Report, 2 August 1963, 1374.

34. CQ Weekly Report, 25 October 1963, 1863.

35. Rauh manuscript, 6.

36. Rauh manuscript, 6.

37. Rauh manuscript, 7.

38. Memorandum #1, 25 July 1963, Series D, Box 4, Leadership Conference on Civil Rights Collection, Library of Congress.

39. Memorandum #2, 5 August 1963, and in succeeding memoranda, Series D, Box 4, Leadership Conference on Civil Rights Collection, Library of Congress.

40. Clarence Mitchell, Jr., interview by the author, 17 August 1983, Baltimore.

41. Joseph Rauh, Jr., interview by the author, 15 August 1983, Washington.

42. Joseph Rauh, Jr., interview by the author, 15 August 1983.

43. Clarence Mitchell, Jr., interview by the author, 17 August 1983.

44. Clarence Mitchell, Jr., interview, 30 April 1969, Tape 1, 27, Oral History Collection, LBJ Library.

45. CQ Almanac - 1963, 347.

46. Memorandum, Lee C. White to President Johnson, Subject: Civil Rights Program, 11 March 1964, 2, Legislative Background CR 64, Box 1, LBJ Library.

47. New York Times, 29 August 1963, 1.

48. CQ Weekly Report, 20 September 1963, 1632.

49. CQ Weekly Report, 20 September 1963, 1632.

50. CQ Weekly Report, 20 September 1963, 1632-1633.

51. CQ Weekly Report, 20 September 1963, 1633.

52. Nicholas Katzenbach, interview, 12 November 1968, 16, Oral History Collection, LBJ Library.

53. Personal recollection of the author.

54. Rauh manuscript, 12.

55. CQ Weekly Report, 11 October 1963, 1749.

56. Nicholas Katzenbach, interview, 11 November 1968, 18, Oral History Collection, LBJ Library.

57. Kane, The Senate Debate, 51.

58. CQ Weekly Report, 18 October 1963, 1814.

59. CQ Weekly Report, 18 October 1963, 1814.

60. CQ Weekly Report, 18 October 1963, 1814.

61. Joseph Rauh, Jr., interview by the author, 15 August 1983.

62. CQ Weekly Report, 18 October 1963, 1814.

63. CQ Weekly Report, 1 November 1963, 1879.

64. Sorensen, Kennedy, 501.

65. CQ Weekly Report, 1 November 1963, 1875.

66. Nicholas Katzenbach, interview, 12 November 1968, 17, Oral History Collection, LBJ Library.

67. CQ Weekly Report, 1 November 1963, 1875.

68. CQ Weekly Report, 1 November 1963, 1875.

69. CQ Weekly Report, 29 November 1963, 2105.

70. CQ Weekly Report, 1 November 1963, 1875-1876

71. Rauh manuscript, 13.

72. CQ Weekly Report, 1 November 1963, 1876.

73. CQ Weekly Report, 29 November 1963, 2105.

74. Rauh manuscript, 14.

75. CQ Weekly Report, 29 November 1963, 2105.

76. Sundquist, Politics and Policy, 263.

77. William B. Welsh, administrative assistant to Senator Philip A. Hart (Democrat, Michigan), 21 April 1966, quoted in Kane, The Senate Debate, 37.
78. Sorensen, Kennedy, 470.
79. Sorensen, Kennedy, 475-476.
80. Sorensen, Kennedy, 501. Sorensen's reference is to Arthur Vandenberg, a Republican senator from Michigan who, immediately following World War II, turned away from partisan politics and worked out a bipartisan foreign policy with Democratic President Harry Truman. A "Vandenberg" thus was a politician who put national needs ahead of partisan advantage and getting reelected.
81. Memorandum to the attorney general from Nicholas Katzenbach, deputy attorney general, 19 August 1963, 1-4, Robert F. Kennedy General Correspondence, John F. Kennedy Library.
82. Memorandum to the attorney general from Nicholas Katzenbach, deputy attorney general, 19 August 1963, 1, Robert F. Kennedy General Correspondence, John F. Kennedy Library.
83. Memorandum to the attorney general from Nicholas Katzenbach, deputy attorney general, 29 June 1963, 3, Robert F. Kennedy General Correspondence, John F. Kennedy Library.
84. Sorensen, Kennedy, 500.

CHAPTER 5

1. Clarence Mitchell, Jr., interview, 30 April 1969, Tape 1, 29-30, Oral History Collection, LBJ Library.
2. Louis Martin, interview, 14 April 1969, 22, Oral History Collection, LBJ Library.
3. Nicholas Katzenbach, interview, 12 November 1968, 5-6, Oral History Collection, LBJ Library.
4. CQ Weekly Report, 29 November 1963, 2089.
5. Memorandum to the attorney general from Norbert A. Schlei, assistant attorney general, 4 June 1963, VI, Robert F. Kennedy General Correspondence, John F. Kennedy Library.
6. Lyndon Baines Johnson, The Vantage Point (New York: Popular Library, 1971), 29.
7. Whitney Young, Jr., interview, 18 June 1969, 9, Oral History Collection, LBJ Library.
8. Roy Wilkins, interview, 1 April 1969, 5, Oral History Collection, LBJ Library.
9. Clarence Mitchell, Jr., interview, 30 April 1969, Tape 1, 4, Oral History Collection, LBJ Library.
10. Memorandum, Lee C. White to President Johnson, Suggested Items for Discussion with Roy Wilkins, 29 November 1963, 1, Appointment File (Diary Back-up), Box 1, LBJ Library. See also Memorandum, Lee C.

White to President Johnson, Possible Items for Discussion with Martin Luther King, 3 December 1963, and Memorandum, Lee C. White to President Johnson, Suggested Items for Discussion with Mr. James Farmer [national director of CORE, the Congress of Racial Equality, a civil rights group], 4 December 1963, EX/HU2, Box 2, LBJ Library.

11. Memorandum, Lee C. White to President Johnson, 4 December 1963, Appointment File (Diary Back-up), Box 2, LBJ Library.

12. Memorandum, Lee C. White to President Johnson, Civil Rights Activities During the First 100 Days, 15 April 1964, 1, EX/HU2, LBJ Library.

13. Johnson, The Vantage Point, 29.

14. Clarence Mitchell, Jr., interview, 30 April 1969, Tape 1, 29, Oral History Collection, LBJ Library.

15. Rowland Evans and Robert Novak, Lyndon B. Johnson: The Exercise of Power (New York: New American Library, 1966), 162.

16. Off the Record Remarks to Governors, 25 November 1963, 4, Appointment File (Diary Back-up), Box 1, LBJ Library.

17. CQ Weekly Report, 6 December 1963, 2130.

18. CQ Weekly Report, 6 December 1963, 2118.

19. Off The Record Remarks to Governors, 25 November 1963, 4, Appointment File (Diary Back-up), Box 1, LBJ Library.

20. CQ Weekly Report, 6 December 1963, 2129.

21. Daniel M. Berman, A Bill Becomes a Law: Congress Enacts Civil Rights Legislation, 2nd ed. (New York: Macmillan, 1966), 95.

22. Memorandum, Lee C. White to President Johnson, Subject: Assistance of Businessmen on the Discharge Petition, 9 December 1963, EX LE/HU2, Box 65, LBJ Library.

23. CQ Weekly Report, 6 December 1963, 2118.

24. Rauh manuscript, 15.

25. CQ Weekly Report, 6 December 1963, 2118.

26. Memorandum, Lawrence F. O'Brien to the President, 29 November 1963, EX LE/HU2, WHCF, Box 65, LBJ Library.

27. Notes on the First Congressional Leadership Breakfast Held by the President on 3 December 1963, 3, 8, Appointment File (Diary Back-up), Box 2, LBJ Library.

28. CQ Weekly Report, 13 December 1963, 2150.

29. CQ Weekly Report, 13 December 1963, 2150.

30. CQ Weekly Report, 13 December 1963, 2218.

31. CQ Weekly Report, 10 January 1964, 48.

32. For an analysis of subsequent refinements in the Rules Committee's role of providing a "dress rehearsal" for the subsequent debate on the House floor, see Bruce I. Oppenheimer, "The Rules Committee: New Arm of Leadership in a Decentralized House," Lawrence C. Dodd and Bruce I. Oppenheimer, Congress Reconsidered, 1st ed. (New York: Praeger, 1977), 105-113.

33. These and subsequent quotes from the House Rules Committee

hearings are from CQ Weekly Report, 24 January 1964, 157.
    34. CQ Weekly Report, 24 January 1964, 157.
    35. Rauh manuscript, 15.
    36. For a fuller discussion of this Rules Committee rule, see Berman, A Bill Becomes A Law, 2nd ed., 96.
    37. Berman, A Bill Becomes A Law, 2nd ed., 95.
    38. Rauh manuscript, 15.
    39. Berman, A Bill Becomes A Law, 2nd ed., 96-97.
    40. CQ Weekly Report, 10 February 1964, 250.
    41. CQ Weekly Report, 7 February 1964, 250.
    42. CQ Weekly Report, 7 February 1964, 250.
    43. Time, 17 January 1964, 12.
    44. CQ Weekly Report, 7 February 1964, 250.

CHAPTER 6

    1. CQ Weekly Report, 7 February 1964, 281.
    2. CQ Weekly Report, 7 February 1964, 281.
    3. Rauh manuscript, 16.
    4. This and subsequent quotes from the opening day debate are from CQ Weekly Report, 7 February 1964, 250.
    5. CQ Weekly Report, 14 February 1964, 296.
    6. CQ Weekly Report, 14 February 1964, 293.
    7. CQ Weekly Report, 7 Feburary 1964, 250.
    8. Rauh manuscript, 17.
    9. Clarence Mitchell, Jr., interview, 30 April 1969, Tape 1, 28, Oral History Collection, LBJ Library.
    10. This description of the gallery watcher-office visitor system is taken from "How Supporters 'Got out the vote' on Key Amendments," CQ Weekly Report, 21 February 1964, 365.
    11. Clarence mitchell, Jr., interview, 30 April 1969, Tape 2, 1-2, Oral History Collection, LBJ Library.
    12. Rauh manuscript, 17.
    13. Clarence Mitchell, Jr., interview by the author, 17 August 1983.
    14. Rauh manuscript, 18.
    15. Congressional Record 110, Pt. 2 (7 February 1964) 2503. See also Sundquist, Politics and Policy, 266, and Rauh manuscript, 19-20.
    16. CQ Weekly Report, 21 February 1964, 365.
    17. CQ Weekly Report, 21 February 1964, 365-366.
    18. Nicholas Katzenbach, interview, 12 November 1968, 19-20, Oral History Collection, LBJ Library.
    19. Kane, The Senate Debate, 155-156.
    20. Rauh manuscript, 18.
    21. CQ Weekly Report, 14 February 1964, 293.
    22. CQ Weekly Report, 14 February 1964, 293-294.

23. CQ Weekly Report, 14 February 1964, 293-294.

24. Congressional Record 110, Pt. 2 (8 February 1964) 2577. See also CQ Weekly Report, 14 February 1964, 296, and Time, 21 February 1964, 22.

25. Congressional Record 110, Pt. 2 (8 February 1964) 2578-2580. See also CQ Weekly Report, 14 February 1964, 296.

26. Congressional Record 110, Pt. 2 (8 February 1964) 2581. See also CQ Weekly Report, 14 February 1964, 296, and Time, 21 February 1964, 22.

27. Congressional Record 110, Pt. 2 (8 February 1964) 2581. See also CQ Weekly Report, 14 February 1964, 296-297, and Time, 21 February 1964, 22.

28. Time, 21 February 1964, 22.

29. Congressional Record 110, Pt. 2 (8 February 1964) 2578. See also Kane, The Senate Debate, 56-57.

30. Jo Freeman, The Politics of Women's Liberation (New York: Longman, 1975), 53-54. See also Congressional Record 110, Pt. 2 (8 February 1964) 2581-2582.

31. Memorandum, George E. Reedy to the Vice-President, 7 June 1963, Office Files of George Reedy, Civil Rights 1963, WDT Box 434(22), Folder 1, LBJ Library. See also Ramsey Clark, interview, 21 March 1969, Tape 1, 14, and 11 February 1969, Tape 1, 11, Oral History Collection, LBJ Library.

32. Rauh manuscript, 19.

33. CQ Weekly Report, 14 February 1964, 293.

34. Sundquist, Politics and Policy, 266-267.

35. Senator Richard Russell of Georgia, Congressional Record 110, Pt. 4 (9 March 1964) 4743. See also Sundquist, Politics and Policy, 266.

36. Berman, A Bill Becomes A Law, 2nd ed., 114.

37. Papers of Lee C. White, Box 1, Civil Rights Bill, 1963-1964, LBJ Library.

38. CQ Weekly Report, 14 February 1964, 294.

39. Personal recollection of the author.

40. Time, 14 February 1964, 13.

41. Burke Marshall, interview, 28 October 1968, 27, Oral History Collection, LBJ Library.

42. Time, 14 February 1964, 13.

43. Merle Miller, Lyndon: An Oral Biography (New York: G. P. Putnam's Sons, 1980), 367. Reprinted by permission of the Putnam Publishing Group. See also Rauh manuscript, 19, and Clarence Mitchell, Jr., interview, 30 April 1969, Tape 1, 30-31, Oral History Collection, LBJ Library.

CHAPTER 7

1. Bruce I. Oppenheimer, "Changing Time Constraints on Congress:

Historical Perspectives on the Use of Cloture," in Lawrence C. Dodd and Bruce I. Oppenheimer, Congress Reconsidered, 3rd ed. (Washington: Congressional Quarterly, 1985), pp. 393-413.

2. Berman, A Bill Becomes A Law, 2nd ed., 64.

3. The views of Professor Rogers on the filibuster and those of other prominent scholars are summarized in Berman, A Bill Becomes A Law, 2nd ed., 64-65.

4. John G. Stewart, Independence and Control: The Challenge of Senatorial Party Leadership (Ph.D dissertation, University of Chicago, 1968), 139. Stewart was the legislative assistant to Senator Hubert H. Humphrey at the time the civil rights bill was debated in the Senate.

5. Stewart, Independence and Control, 137.

6. Berman, A Bill Becomes A Law, 2nd ed., 67.

7. Stewart, Independence and Control, 137.

8. Stewart, Independence and Control, 137. For a fuller discussion of the impact of procedures on policy outcomes, see Walter J. Oleszck, "Functions of Rules and Procedures," David C. Kozak and John D. McCartney, Congress and Public Policy (Homewood, Illinois: Dorsey Press, 1982), 214-217.

9. Stewart, Independence and Control, 180.

10. Hubert H. Humphrey, Memorandum on Senate Consideration of the Civil Rights Act of 1964, summer 1964, 1, Hubert H. Humphrey Papers, Minnesota Historical Society, St. Paul, Minnesota.

11. Humphrey memorandum, 2-3.

12. Humphrey memorandum, 5.

13. Memorandum, Mike Manatos to Larry O'Brien, 11 May 1964, EX/HU2, Box 2, LBJ Library.

14. Clarence Mitchell, Jr., interview by the author, 17 August 1983.

15. Clarence Mitchell, Jr., interview, 30 April 1969, Tape 1, 35, Oral History Collection, LBJ Library.

16. Humphrey memorandum, 12-13.

17. Stewart, Independence and Control, 183.

18. Stewart, Independence and Control, 184.

19. The plan of action is summarized from Stewart, Independence and Control, 185-186.

20. Humphrey memorandum, 9-10.

21. Clarence Mitchell, Jr., interview by the author, 17 August 1983.

22. Stewart, Independence and Control, 186.

23. Rauh manuscript, 21.

24. Stephen Horn, Periodic Log Maintained During the Discussions Concerning the Passage of the Civil Rights Act of 1964, unpublished, 24. Horn was legislative assistant to Senator Kuchel.

25. Memorandum, Mike Manatos to Larry O'Brien, 15 February 1964, EX LE/HU2, Box 65, LBJ Library.

26. Humphrey memorandum, 209.

27. Congressional Record 110, Pt. 3 (27 February 1964) 3850-3854.
28. Washington Post and Times Herald, 24 February 1964, 1A.
29. These and subsequent quotes from Mansfield's speech are from Congressional Record 110, Pt. 3 (17 February 1964) 2882-2884. See also Kane, The Senate Debate, 68-69.

CHAPTER 8

1. Letter, Richard Russell to Eugene Talmadge, 9 December 1935, Series IV, Box Number B24, Russell Papers, Richard B. Russell Memorial Library, University of Georgia, Athens, Georgia.
2. Atlanta Constitution, 24 July 1936, 11, and 9 August 1936, 10.
3. David Daniel Potenziani, Look to the Past: Richard B. Russell and the Defense of Southern White Supremacy (Ph.D. disseration, University of Georgia, 1981), 18.
4. Potenziani, Look to the Past, 100-111.
5. Miller, Lyndon, 228.
6. Potenziani, Look to the Past, 5-6.
7. Potenziani, Look to the Past, 39-40
8. Congressional Record 92, Pt. 1 (25 January 1946) 380.
9. Potenziani, Look to the Past, 194.
10. Kane, The Senate Debate, 49, 110, 130.
11. Kane, The Senate Debate, 108-110, 140.
12. Kane, The Senate Debate, 131.
13. Kane, The Senate Debate, 106-108.
14. Congressional Record 110, Pt. 4 (9 March 1964) 4746.
15. Kane, The Senate Debate, 107, 198.
16. Washington Post and Times Herald, 6 March 1964, A6.
17. Letter, Russell to Mary Ann Clarke, 29 October 1963, Series X, Box 148, Russell Papers.
18. Letter, Russell to Mrs. Robert E. Dobkins, 13 March 1964, Series X, Box 184, Russell Papers.
19. Congressional Record 110, Pt. 4 (9 March 1964) 4744-4746.
20. Strom Thurmond, Statement (TV) In Opposition to the Civil Rights Package, 6 June 1963, Speeches, Box 19, Thurmond Collection, Special Collections, Robert Muldrow Cooper Library, Clemson University.
21. Strom Thurmond Reports To The People, Volume X, No. 11, 30 March 1964, 1, Speeches, Box 22, Thurmond Collection.
22. Albert Lachicotte, Rebel Senator (New York: Devin-Adair, 1967), 217.
23. Strom Thurmond, Statement (Radio) In Opposition to Proposed Statute Which Would Make Businessmen Sell and Serve to Negroes, recorded 6 June 1963, Speeches, Box 19, Thurmond Collection.
24. Stewart, Independence and Control, 201.

CHAPTER 9

1. Time, 28 February 1964, 22.
2. Congressional Record 110, Pt. 3 (17 February 1964) 2882.
3. Congressional Record 110, Pt. 5 (26 March 1964) 6419.
4. Congressional Record 110, Pt. 5 (26 March 1964) 6419.
5. Congressional Record 110, Pt. 5 (26 March 1964) 6431.
6. Horn log, 23.
7. CQ Weekly Report, 27 March 1964, 597.
8. Horn log, 24.
9 Congresssional Record 110, Pt. 3 (26 February 1964) 3719.
10. Stewart, Independence and Control, 10. Also see Horn log, 23. Horn reported that political columnist Robert Novak called him (and presumably other pro-civil rights senators' aides) to find out if Mansfield's motion had come as a surprise.
11. Congressional Record 110, Pt. 3 (27 February 1964) 3830.
12. Stewart, Independence and Control, 212.
13. Congressional Record 110, Pt. 4 (9 March 1964) 4741-4754.
14. Congressional Record 110, Pt. 4 (9 March 1964) 4754.
15. Kane, The Senate Debate, 68.
16. Stewart, Independence and Control, 214.
17. Stephen Horn, legislative assistant to Senator Thomas H. Kuchel, 20 April 1966, quoted in Kane, The Senate Debate, 81.
18. Congressional Record 110, Pt. 4 (11 March 1964) 4999-5000.
19. Personal recollection of the author.
20. Humphrey, Kuchel, and Mitchell quotes from Horn log, 24.
21. Stewart, Independence and Control, 216.
22. Stewart, Independence and Control, 217.
23. Horn log, 51.
24. The assistant was Stephen Horn. See Horn log, 51.
25. Congressional Record 110, Pt. 4 (12 March 1964) 5042, 5046, 5079.
26. Stewart, Independence and Control, 215.
27. Stewart, Independence and Control, 216-217.
28. Stewart, Independence and Control, 217-218.
29. Stewart, Independence and Control, 218.
30. Congressional Record 110, Pt. 5 (26 March 1964) 6417.
31. Congressional Record 110, Pt. 5 (26 March 1964) 6455.
32. Congressional Record 110, Pt. 5 (26 March 1964) 6445-6451. See also CQ Weekly Report, 27 March 1964, 596-597.
33. Congressional Record 110, Pt 5 (26 March 1964) 6446-6451.
34. New York Times, 22 March 1964, 41.
35. Congressional Record 110, Pt. 5 (26 March 1964) 6455.

CHAPTER 10

1. Humphrey memorandum, 8-9.
2. Time, 10 April 1964, 22.
3. Congressional Record 110, Pt. 5 (30 March 1964) 6532.
4. Congressional Record 110, Pt. 5 (30 March 1964) 6542.
5. Time, 10 April 1964, 22. See also CQ Weekly Report, 3 April 1964, 654.
6. Horn log, 79.
7. Congressional Record 110, Pt. 6 (9 April 1964) 7380.
8. Theodore H. White, The Making of the President 1964, (New York: Atheneum, 1965), 162-163.
9. Personal recollection of the author.
10. Time, 17 April 1964, 35-36.
11. Congressional Record 110, Pt. 5 (4 April 1964) 6863.
12. Rauh manuscript, 24.
13. Stewart, Independence and Control, 223.
14. Stewart, Independence and Control, 224.
15. The Democratic staff member was Kenneth Teasdale, assistant counsel, Senate Democratic Policy Committee. The Republican staff member was J. Mark Trice, secretary for the Senate Minority (Republicans). See Horn log, 77.
16. Time, 24 April 1964, 18.
17. CQ Weekly Report, 17 April 1964, 717.
18. CQ Weekly Report, 28 February 1964, 385.
19. CQ Weekly Report, 6 March 1964, 477.
20. CQ Weekly Report, 13 March 1964, 491.
21. CQ Weekly Report, 20 March 1964, 580.
22. CQ Weekly Report, 10 April 1964, 701.
23. CQ Weekly Report, 17 April 1964, 747.
24. CQ Weekly Report, 24 April 1964, 789.
25. CQ Weekly Report, 24 April 1964, 797.
26. Nicholas Katzenbach, interview, 12 November 1968, 20-22, Oral History Collection, LBJ Library.
27. Humphrey memorandum, 9.
28. For a full discussion of Humphrey's speaking strategies, see Norbert Mills, The Speaking of Hubert H. Humphrey In Favor of the 1964 Civil Rights Act (Ph.D. dissertation, Bowling Green State University, 1974). See particularly 48-69, 73-104.
29. Mills, The Speaking Of Hubert H. Humphrey, 53.
30. Mills, The Speaking Of Hubert H. Humphrey, 55, 79.
31. Mills, The Speaking of Hubert H. Humphrey, 79. Humphrey first used this phrase at the 1948 Democratic National Convention. See CQ Weekly Report, 12 June 1964, 1161.
32. Mills, The Speaking of Hubert H. Humphrey, 60-61, 87.

33. Mills, The Speaking of Hubert H. Humphrey, 61-62, 92.
34. Mills, The Speaking of Hubert H. Humphrey, 97.
35. Stewart, Independence and Control, 276.
36. CQ Weekly Report, 26 June 1964, 1274.
37. New York Times, 8 May 1964, 37.
38. Time, 17 April 1964, 36.
39. Time, 24 April 1964, 17.
40. White, The Making of the President 1964, 186-187.
41. Time, 1 May 1964, 22.
42. White, The Making Of The President 1964, 188.
43. Horn log, 90-91.
44. Stephen Horn proposed the statement. Horn log, 90.
45. CQ Weekly Report, 17 April 1964, 717. See also Time, 24 April 1964, 17.
46. CQ Weekly Report, 24 April 1964, 757.
47. Time, 24 April 1964, 18.
48. Time, 24 April 1964, 18.
49. White, The Making Of The President 1964, 189.
50. Time, 1 May 1964, 23.
51. Horn log, 43. The aide was Robert Kimball, legislative assistant to Representative John V. Lindsay of New York.
52. The speech was 10 April 1964. Quoted in the New York Times, 20 May 1964, 1.
53. Personal recollection of the author. This was a favorite phrase of anti-Goldwater Republican staff in the Senate, particularly Stephen Horn, legislative assistant to Senator Kuchel.
54. CQ Weekly Report, 13 March 1964, 500. See also Time, 20 March 1964, 20.
55. Time, 24 April 1964, 20.
56. Horn log, 74.
57. Johnson, The Vantage Point, 29.
58. CQ Weekly Report, 10 April 1964, 687.
59. CQ Weekly Report, 10 April 1964, 687.
60. Time, 17 April 1964, 37.
61. Time, 17 April 1964, 37.
62. Time, 17 April 1964, 37.
63. CQ Weekly Report, 10 April 1964, 687.
64. Humphrey, Dirksen, and Mansfield quotes from CQ Weekly Report, 10 April 1964, 688.
65. Time, 24 April 1964, 22.
66. Time, 24 April 1964, 22.
67. Time, 24 April 1964, 22.
68. Time, 15 May 1964, 37.
69. CQ Weekly Report, 8 May 1964, 905.
70. CQ Weekly Report. 8 May 1964, 905.

CHAPTER 11

1. Mike Manatos, interview, 25 August 1969, 19-20, Oral History Collection, LBJ Library.

2. Notes of the First Congressional Leadership Breakfast held by the President on 3 December 1963, 1, Appointment File (Diary Back-up), Box 2, LBJ Library.

3. Johnson, The Vantage Point, 30.

4. Johnson, The Vantage Point, 159.

5. Louis Martin, interview, 14 May 1969, 30, Oral History Collection, LBJ Library.

6. Miller, Lyndon, 368.

7. Horn log, 26.

8. Humphrey memorandum, 13.

9. Miller, Lyndon, 368-369.

10. Miller, Lyndon, 369.

11. Humphrey memorandum, 13-14.

12. Miller, Lyndon, 370.

13. Unsigned memorandum entitled Thoughts on the Civil Rights Bill dictated Wednesday April 21, 1964, 2, Senatorial Files, Civil Rights, 1964, Hubert H. Humphrey Papers, Minnesota Historical Society, St. Paul, Minnesota. The author mailed a copy of the memorandum to Humphrey's legislative assistant, John G. Stewart, who acknowledged authorship. This memorandum and others dictated by Stewart will be referred to as "Stewart notes".

14. Stewart notes, 30 April 1964, 1.

15. Rauh manuscript, 25.

16. Rauh manuscript, 25. Rauh gives an extensive account of Mitchell's proposal to arrest Southern senators and his own proposal to implement the two speech rule. He concludes with this sentence: "Neither suggestion was ever adopted -- but the talk of cloture died down."

17. This excerpted discussion was developed from Stephen Horn's notes on the pro-civil rights strategy meeting of 16 April 1964. See Horn log, 92-94.

18. Rauh manuscript, 26.

19. Rauh manuscript, 26-27.

20. Stewart notes, 21 April 1964, 3-4.

21. Neil MacNeil, Dirksen: Portrait of a Public Man (New York: World Publishing Company, 1970), 128.

22. MacNeil, Dirksen, 128.

23. MacNeil, Dirksen, 6.

24. MacNeil, Dirksen, 202.

25. MacNeil, Dirksen, 6.

26. Annette Culler Penney, Dirksen: The Golden Voice of the Senate (Washington: Acropolis Books, 1968), 62-69.

27. MacNeil, Dirksen, 176.

28. MacNeil, <u>Dirksen</u>, 166.
29. MacNeil, <u>Dirksen</u>, 219.
30. MacNeil, <u>Dirksen</u>, 222.
31. MacNeil, <u>Dirksen</u>, 226.
32. MacNeil, <u>Dirksen</u>, 226. The three "Bombers" were Clyde Flynn, Cornelius B. Kennedy, and Bernard J. Waters.
33. Personal recollection of the author.
34. Cornelius B. Kennedy, former Republican Counsel, Senate Committee on Judiciary, interview by the author, 14 August 1984, Washington.
35. Personal recollection of the author. See also Horn log, 48.
36. Stewart, <u>Independence and Control</u>, 240.
37. Stewart, <u>Independence and Control</u>, 241-242.
38. Humphrey memorandum, 14.
39. Stewart notes, 19 May 1964 to 11 June 1964, 6.
40. Clyde Flynn, Republican counsel, Subcommittee on Constitutional Amendments, Senate Committee on the Judiciary, 20 April 1966, quoted in Kane, <u>The Senate Debate</u>, 123.
41. Bernard J. Waters, former Republican counsel, Subcommittee on Anti-Trust and Monopoly, Senate Committee on the Judiciary, interview by the author, 16 August 1983, Washington.
42. Bernard J. Waters, 20 April 1966, quoted in Kane, <u>The Senate Debate</u>, 167.
43. Cornelius B. Kennedy, interview by the author, 14 August 1984.
44. Stewart, <u>Independence and Control</u>, 226.
45. Stewart, <u>Independence and Control</u>, 228.
46. <u>New York Times</u>, 24 April 1964, 1.
47. The staff member doing the dragging was John G. Stewart, legislative assistant to Senator Humphrey. The staff member pushed into the meeting was Kenneth Teasdale, assistant counsel, Senate Democratic Policy Committee. See Stewart notes, 29 April 1964, 2.
48. Stewart notes, 29 April 1964, 5.
49. Stewart notes, 29 April 1964, 5-6.
50. Stewart, <u>Independence and Control</u>, 234-235.
51. <u>Congressional Record</u> 110, Pt. 8 (6 May 1964) 10213.
52. Stewart, <u>Independence and Control</u>, 237.

CHAPTER 12

1. Stewart notes, 6 May 1964, 4-5.
2. Cornelius B. Kennedy, interview by the author, 14 August 1984.
3. Cornelius B. Kennedy, interview by the author, 14 August 1984. According to Cornelius B. Kennedy, the Mansfield staff member who had been given a "go" to write the civil rights bill was Kenneth Teasdale.
4. Memorandum, Mike Manatos to Larry O'Brien, 6 May 1964, White House Central File (LE/HU 2), LBJ Library.

5. The Dirksen assistant who made the proposal was Clyde Flynn. See Stewart, Independence and Control, 248. In his study of the Senate debate on the Civil Rights Act of 1964, Peter E. Kane gave considerable credit to Clyde Flynn, describing him as "the actual author of what was to become the Civil Rights Act of 1964." Kane, The Senate Debate, 123.

6. Winthrop Griffith, Humphrey: A Candid Biography (New York: William Morrow, 1965), 281-282. See also Stewart notes, 13 May 1964, 4-5. See also Stewart, Independence and Control, 250.

7. Stewart notes, 13 May 1964, 1-2.

8. Stewart, Independence and Control, 250. See also New York Times, 14 May 1964, 1. See also CQ Weekly Report, 19 June 1964, 1206.

9. Horn log, 179. Horn learned of the early press inspection of the amendments from another Senate aide who was informed by Andrew Glass of the New York Herald Tribune. Horn speculated that Glass was probably accompanied by Roger Mudd of CBS television news, Ned Kenworthy of the New York Times, and John Averill of the Los Angeles Times.

10. This quote and subsequent quotes are from former U.S. Senator Daniel B. Brewster (Democrat, Maryland), interview by the author, August 1982, Glyndon, Maryland.

11. Time, 22 May 1964, 24.

12. CQ Weekly Report, 15 May 1964, 948.

13. CQ Weekly Report, 22 May 1964, 1000-1001.

14. Kane, The Senate Debate, 119.

15. CQ Weekly Report, 22 May 1964, 1001.

16. William M. Bates, press secretary to Senator Richard B. Russell, 20 April 1966, quoted in Kane, The Senate Debate, 176.

17. Rauh manuscript, 27-28.

18. Joseph Rauh, Jr., interview by the author, August 15, 1983.

19. Rauh manuscript, 28.

20. Stewart notes, 19 May 1964, 2-3.

21. MacNeil, Dirksen. 235.

22. MacNeil, Dirksen, 235-236.

23. MacNeil, Dirksen, 236-237.

24. Stewart, Independence and Control, 260.

25. Papers of Representative William McCulloch, 29 June 1964, Box 43, Ohio Northern University.

26. New York Times, 28 May 1964, 14.

27. Stewart, Independence and Control, 266.

28. Congressional Record 110, Pt. 9 (2 June 1964) 12436-12437.

29. Stewart, Independence and Control, 269.

30. Humphrey memorandum, 40.

31. Stewart notes, 19 May 1964 to 11 June 1964, 7.

32. Humphrey memorandum, 17-18.

33. Griffith, Humphrey, 283.

34. Clarence Mitchell, Jr., interview, 30 April 1969, Tape 1, 27, Oral

History Collection, LBJ Library.

35. Doris Fleeson, "They're Asking: 'Where's Lyndon?', Senators Backing Rights Bill Wonder Where Old Johnson Touch Has Gone," Washington Star, 22 April 1964. It is an interesting historical note that, when Lyndon Johnson was preparing to leave office in December 1968, a copy of this newspaper article was found in his middle desk drawer. See marked newspaper article, EX LE/HU2, Box 65, LBJ Library.

36. Griffith, Humphrey, 283.

37. Griffith, Humphrey, 283.

38. Stewart notes, 19 May 1964, 3-4.

39. Stewart, Independence and Control, 251.

40. Stewart, Independence and Control, 252.

41. Personal recollection of the author.

42. Frank H. Mackaman, executive director, Everett McKinley Dirksen Congressional Leadership Research Center, interview by the author, 2 March 1984, Pekin, Illinois.

43. Congressional Record 110, Pt. 10 (10 June 1964) 13319-13320.

44. Griffith, Humphrey, 284.

45. Congressional Record 110, Pt. 10 (10 June 1964) 13327.

46. Memorandum, Stewart L. Udall to President Johnson, 7 April 1964, Executive Files, LE/HU2, LBJ Library.

47. Memorandum, Mike Manatos to Larry O'Brien, 11 April 1964, EX/HU2, LBJ Library.

48. Griffith, Humphrey, 284.

CHAPTER 13

1. Stewart notes, undated "final dictated thoughts," 7.

2. Stewart, Independence and Control, 278.

3. Stewart notes, undated "final dictated thoughts," 8.

4. Stewart, Independence and Control, 282.

5. Dodd and Oppenheimer, Congress Reconsidered, 3rd ed., 282. A postcloture filibuster on an energy bill in 1977 tied up the Senate for 14 days, required all-night sessions, and resulted in 128 roll call votes. See also Charles O. Jones, The United States Congress (Homewood, Illinois: Dorsey Press, 1982), 323-324.

6. Stewart notes, undated "final dictated thoughts," 10.

7. Stewart, Independence and Control, 283.

8. Stewart notes, undated "final dictated thoughts," 11.

9. Stewart notes, undated "final dictated thoughts," 12-13.

10. Stewart, Independence and control, 284-285. See also Stewart notes, undated "final dictated thoughts," 13.

11. Personal recollection of the author.

12. Congressional Record 110, Pt. 11 (18 June 1964) 14300-14301.

13. Donald J. Cronin, former executive secretary to Senator Lister

Hill, interview by the author, 16 August 1983, Washington.

14. "Johnson's Power and Prestige Force Cloture Vote in Senate," The New York Times, June 1964. Copy of article in Russell Papers, Series X, Box 115.

15. CQ Weekly Report, 19 June 1964, 1207.

16. Humphrey memorandum, 12.

17. Stewart notes, 19 May 1964, 13.

18. CQ Weekly Report, 19 June 1964, 1206.

19. Stewart, Independence and Control, 283.

20. Stewart notes, undated "final dictated thoughts," 11.

21. Donald J. Cronin, interview by the author, 16 August 1983.

22. Kane, The Senate Debate, 232-233. The phrase "die on the barricades" was said to Kane by Roger Mudd, then of CBS television news, in an interview on 21 April 1966.

23. New York Times, 10 June 1964, 1.

24. MacNeil, Dirksen, 238.

25. Congressional Record 110, Pt. 11 (18 June 1964) 14318-14319.

26. Congressional Record 110, Pt. 11 (19 June 1964) 14508.

27. Congressional Record 110, Pt. 11 (19 June 1964) 14443.

28. Congressional Record 110, Pt. 11 (19 June 1964) 14508.

29. Congressional Record 110, Pt. 11 (19 June 1964) 14510-14511.

30. Personal recollection of the author.

31. Congressional Record 110, Pt. 11 (19 June 1964) 14511.

32. Griffith, Humphrey, 284-285.

33. Stewart, Independence and Control, 289.

34. Stewart, Independence and Control, 287. See also Stewart notes, undated "final dictated thoughts," 15.

35. CQ Weekly Report, 3 July 1964, 1332.

36. Memorandum, Lawrence O'Brien to President Johnson, 18 June 1964, EX LE/HU2, Box 65, LBJ Library.

37. Berman, A Bill Becomes A Law, 2nd ed., 129, 134.

38. CQ Weekly Report, 11 October 1963, 1749.

39. CQ Weekly Report, 3 July 1964, 1331.

40. CQ Weekly Report, 3 July 1964, 1331.

41. Letter, President Johnson to speaker of the House of Representatives, 20 July 1964, 1, Legislative Background CR64, Box #1, LBJ Library.

42. Memorandum, Attorney General Robert F. Kennedy to President Johnson, 21 April 1964, 3-5, EX/HU2, Box 2, LBJ LIbrary.

43. Memorandum, Lee C. White to The Files, 6 July 1964, 1, EX LE/HU2, Box 65, LBJ Library.

44. Johnson, The Vantage Point, 37-38.

45. Johnson, The Vantage Point, 37.

46. Johnson, The Vantage Point, 160.

CHAPTER 14

1. Kane, The Senate Debate, 226-227.
2. In 1975 the Senate changed its rules so that only a 3/5 vote (60 votes) rather than a 2/3 vote (67 votes) was required for cloture. This rule change made it less likely that any future Senate filibuster would last as long as the filibuster of the Civil Rights Act of 1964.
3. Kane, The Senate Debate, 228-229.
4. Kane, The Senate Debate, 228, 63-67.
5. Memorandum, Nicholas Katzenbach to Robert F. Kennedy, 29 June 1963, 1, Robert F. Kennedy General Correspondence, John F. Kennedy Library.
6. Memorandum, Assistant Deputy Attorney General Joseph F. Dolan to Katzenbach, 8 July 1963, 2, Robert F. Kennedy General Correspondence, John F. Kennedy Library.
7. MacNeil, Dirksen, 224-225.
8. Joseph Rauh, Jr., interview by the author, 15 August 1983.
9. Cornelius B. Kennedy, interview by the author, 15 August 1984.
10. Miller, Lyndon, 367.
11. Miller, Lyndon. 345.
12. Clarence Mitchell, Jr., interview by the author, 17 August 1983.
13. Roy Wilkins, interview, 1 April 1969, 8-9, Oral History Collection, LBJ Library.
14. Stewart notes, 21 April 1964, 2.
15. Kane, The Senate Debate, 232-233.
16. Kane, The Senate Debate, 233-234.
17. Kane, The Senate Debate, 234-235.
18. Bernard Schwartz, Statutory History of the United States: Civil Rights, Part II (New York: McGraw-Hill, 1970), 1453-1455. See also Heart of Atlanta Motel v. United States, 379 U.S. 241 (1964).
19. Roy Wilkins, interview, 1 April 1969, 23-24, Oral History Collection, LBJ Library.
20. Whitney Young, Jr., interview, 18 June 1969, 15, Oral History Collection, LBJ Library.
21. Thurgood Marshall, interview, 10 July 1969, 19, Oral History Collection, LBJ Library.
22. Clarence Mitchell, Jr., interview, 30 April 1969, Tape 2, 30, Oral History Collection, LBJ Library.
23. Memorandum, Hobart Taylor, Jr., to President Johnson, 17 July 1964, EX/HU2, Box 3, LBJ Library.
24. Memorandum, Hobart Taylor, Jr., to George Reedy, 22 July 1964, EX/HU2, Box 3, LBJ Library.
25. Memorandum, Senator Hubert H. Humphrey to Jack Valenti, 5 August 1964, EX/HU2, Box 3, LBJ Library.
26. Memorandum, Hobart Taylor, Jr. to President Johnson, 13 October

1964, EX/HU2, Box 3, LBJ Library.

27. Berman, <u>A Bill Becomes A Law</u>, 2nd ed., 139-140.

28. James MacGregor Burns, <u>The Deadlock of Democracy</u> (Englewood Cliffs, New Jersey: Prentice Hall, 1963), 324-325.

29. <u>CQ Weekly Report</u>, 10 July 1964, 1454.

30. Memorandum, Attorney General Robert F. Kennedy to President Johnson, 21 April 1964, 5, EX/HU2, Box 2, LBJ Library.

31. Letter, President Johnson to J.W. Fulbright; Letter, President Johnson to Allen J. Ellender; Letter, President Johnson to Richard B. Russell; 23 July 1964, EX/HU2, Box 3, LBJ Library.

32. <u>CQ Weekly Report</u>, 10 July 1964, 1471.

BIBLIOGRAPHY

Berman, Daniel M. A Bill Becomes A Law: Congress Enacts Civil Rights Legislation. 2nd ed. New York: Macmillan, 1966.

Burns, James MacGregor. The Deadlock of Democracy. Englewood Cliffs, New Jersey: Prentice Hall, 1963.

Burstein, Paul. Discrimination, Jobs, and Politics. Chicago: University of Chicago Press, 1985.

Dahl, Robert A. Pluralist Democracy in the United States. Chicago: Rand McNally, 1967.

Dodd, Lawrence C., and Oppenheimer, Bruce I. Congress Reconsidered. 1st ed. New York: Praeger, 1977.

Dodd, Lawrence C., and Oppenheimer, Bruce I. Congress Reconsidered. 3rd ed. Washington: Congressional Quarterly, 1985.

Dorman, Michael. We Shall Overcome. New York: Dial Press, 1964.

Evans, Rowland, and Novak, Robert. Lyndon B. Johnson: The Exercise of Power. New York: New American Library, 1966.

Freeman, Jo. The Politics of Women's Liberation. New York: Longman, 1975.

Garrow, David. Protest at Selma: Martin Luther King, Jr., and the Voting Rights Act of 1965. New Haven: Yale University Press, 1978.

Griffith, Winthrop. Humphrey: A Candid Biography. New York: William Morrow, 1965.

Horn, Stephen. Periodic Log Maintained During the Discussions Concerning the Passage of the Civil Rights Act of 1964. Unpublished.

Humphrey, Hubert H. Memorandum on Senate Consideration of the Civil Rights Act of 1964. Hubert H. Humphrey Papers, Minnesota Historical Society, St. Paul, Minnesota, summer 1964.

Johnson, Lyndon Baines. The Vantage Point. New York: Popular Library, 1971.

Jones, Charles O. The United States Congress. Homewood, Illinois: Dorsey Press, 1982.

Kane, Peter E. The Senate Debate on the 1964 Civil Rights Act. Ph.D. dissertation, Purdue University, 1967.

Kozak, David C., and McCartney, John C. Congress and Public Policy. Homewood, Illinois: Dorsey Press, 1982.

Lachicotte, Albert. Rebel Senator. New York: Devin-Adair, 1967.

MacNeil, Neil. Dirksen: Portrait of a Public Man. New York: World Publishing Company, 1970.

Miller, Merle. Lyndon: An Oral Biography. New York: G. P. Putnam's Sons, 1980.

Mills, Norbert. The Speaking of Hubert H. Humphrey In Favor of the 1964 Civil Rights Act. Ph.D. dissertation, Bowling Green State University, 1974.

Penney, Annette Culler. Dirksen: The Golden Voice of the Senate. Washington: Acropolis Books, 1968.

Potenziani, David Daniel. Look to the Past: Richard B. Russell and the Defense of Southern White Supremacy. Ph.D. dissertation, University of Georgia, 1981.

Rauh, Joseph, Jr. Unpublished manuscript (magazine article) on the role of the Leadership Conference on Civil Rights in the civil rights struggle of 1963-1964.

Revolution in Civil Rights. Washington: Congressional Quarterly, 1968.

Schlesinger, Arthur M., Jr. A Thousand Days: John F. Kennedy in the White House. Boston: Houghton Mifflin, 1965.

Schwartz, Bernard. Statutory History of the United States: Civil Rights. Part II. New York: McGraw-Hill, 1970.

Sorensen, Theodore C. Kennedy. New York: Harper and Row, 1965.

Stewart, John G. Independence and Control. Ph.D. dissertation, University of Chicago, 1968.

Stewart, John G. Unsigned memoranda entitled Thoughts on the Civil Rights Bill. Hubert H. Humphrey Papers, Minnesota Historical Society, St. Paul, Minnesota, various dates in spring 1964.

Sundquist, James L. Politics and Policy: The Eisenhower, Kennedy, and Johnson Years. Washington: Brookings, 1968.

Whelan, Charles and Barbara. The Longest Debate. Cabin John, Maryland: Seven Locks Press, 1985.

White, Theodore H. The Making of the President 1964. New York: Atheneum, 1965.

INDEX

363

ABOUT THE AUTHOR

Robert D. Loevy was born in St. Louis, Missouri, on February 26, 1935. He received his A.B. from Williams College in 1957 and his Ph.D. from Johns Hopkins University in 1963. While at Johns Hopkins he conducted research and wrote position papers for the House of Representatives Republican Policy Committee. During the 1964-1964 academic year, he served as an American Political Science Association Congressional Fellow in the office of United States Senator Thomas H. Kuchel, of California, the Republican floor manager in the Senate for the civil rights bill that later became the Civil Rights Act of 1964. In 1968 Loevy joined the faculty at Colorado College in Colorado Springs, Colorado, where he currently serves as professor of political science. His major research interest is minority rights in the United States with an emphasis on the three major civil rights acts passed by Congress during the 1960s.